YESTERDAY'S TRAIN

ALSO BY TERRY PINDELL

Making Tracks: An American Rail Odyssey

Last Train to Toronto: A Canadian Rail Odyssey

A Good Place to Live: America's Last Migration

YESTERDAY'S TRAIN

A Rail Odyssey
Through Mexican History

T ERRY P INDELL

WITH L OURDES R AMÍREZ M ALLIS

An Owl Book
Henry Holt and Company
New York

Henry Holt and Company, Inc.
Publishers since 1866
115 West 18th Street
New York, New York 10011

Henry Holt® is a registered trademark
of Henry Holt and Company, Inc.

Published in Canada by Fitzhenry & Whiteside Ltd.,
195 Allstate Parkway, Markham, Ontario L3R 4T8.

The publisher gratefully acknowledges permission to reprint lines from
The Labyrinth of Solitude by Ocatvio Paz (Grove/Atlantic, 1985).

Library of Congress Cataloging-in-Publication Data
Pindell, Terry.
Yesterday's train: a rail odyssey through Mexican history /
Terry Pindell with Lourdes Ramírez Mallis.
p.   cm.
Includes bibliographical references and index.
1. Mexico—Description and travel.   2. Mexico—History.
3. Railroad travel—Mexico.   4. Pindell, Terry—Journeys—Mexico.
I. Ramírez Mallis, Lourdes.   II. Title.
F1216.5.P56   1997   96-31966
972—dc20   CIP

ISBN 0-8050-5598-3

Henry Holt books are available for special promotions and
premiums. For details contact: Director, Special Markets.

First published in hardcover in 1997 by
Henry Holt and Company, Inc.

First Owl Books Edition 1998

Designed by Michelle McMillian

Map by Jeffrey L. Ward

Printed in the United States of America
All first editions are printed on acid-free paper.∞

1   3   5   7   9   10   8   6   4   2

For my daughters, Molly and Katie

"Why do you come to Mexico, señor? To better learn to love?"

Yes.

ACKNOWLEDGMENTS

Lourdes Ramírez Mallis, collaborator and interpreter for the project. Dr. Mallis was involved with this work on an almost daily basis for more than a year, including traveling Mexico with me, interpreting, and gathering material; researching contemporary social, economic, and political issues; assisting with revisions, draft editing, and fact checking; and corresponding by mail and Internet with sources in Mexico. This book would have been absolutely impossible without her work and her friendship.

Nancy Ancharski-Pindell, my former wife, whose decency, goodwill, and support helped make this book a successful product of a difficult year in two lives.

Barry, Jesse, and Alex Mallis, whose support of Dr. Mallis's role in the project and tolerance of her extended absences from her home were as critical for this book as her work itself.

Señor Leonardo Rafael Aguilar, manager of Passenger Services for *Ferrocarriles Nacionales de México* (Mexican National Railways), who subdued the Mexican rail bureaucracy to smooth our journeys, often on very short "Anglo time" notice.

Pedro Miguel, editor of the Mexico City newspaper *La Jornada*, whose assistance at the beginning and the end of this project helped assure its authenticity.

Electoral Commission officials in Zacatecas who, during a very tense and trying time for them, tolerated the persistent presence and aggressive questions of two nosy *norteamericanos*.

The town fathers of San Agustín, Oaxaca, who allowed us on the inside of their pueblo's Night of the Dead festivities. May our visit leave your town living just as peacefully as we found it.

Doña Carmen, in Mármol, for inviting us into her gracious home.

All of the other Mexicans, named throughout the book, who took us into their confidence and the truth of their lives. We have changed names in a few cases to protect the privacy of our sources.

Patricia Murphy, proprietor of Casa Murphy in San Miguel, who offered us an American refuge in a garden of Mexican beauty when we needed it.

Pat Rondelli, of Sierra Madre Express, who made possible our comfortable Copper Canyon journey.

Perla Taylor, Sierra Madre Express tour guide, who provided the materials that gave us the true story of the Tarahumara.

Bill Strachan, editorial vice-president at Holt, who believed in me enough to wait five years through other projects to finally get the book he really wanted.

Darcy Tromanhauser, my editor, who once again made the publishing process a pleasure.

Joe Spieler, my agent, whose support and talents continue to keep the North American odyssey rolling.

Louise Collazo, my copyeditor, whose attention to detail and understanding of metaphor made the final phase of this project a pleasure rather than an aggravation.

Kim Christensen, "the woman from Minnesota," at whose home in Minneapolis I was able to finish writing the book without distractions and whose insights and timely companionship helped fulfill my personal quest in making this journey.

CONTENTS

Contents

The Mexican hides behind a variety of masks, but he tears them away during a fiesta or a time of grief or suffering, just as the nation has cast off all of the forms that were stifling it.

. . .

What we ask of love (which, being desire, is a hunger for communion, a will to fall and to die as well as to be reborn), is that it gives us a bit of true life, of true death.

. . .

Modern man likes to pretend his thinking is wide-awake. But this wide-awake thinking has led us into the mazes of a nightmare in which the torture chambers are endlessly repeated in the mirrors of reason. When we emerge, perhaps we will realize that we have been dreaming with our eyes open, and that the dreams of reason are intolerable. And then, perhaps, we will begin to dream once more with our eyes closed.

Octavio Paz—*The Labyrinth of Solitude*

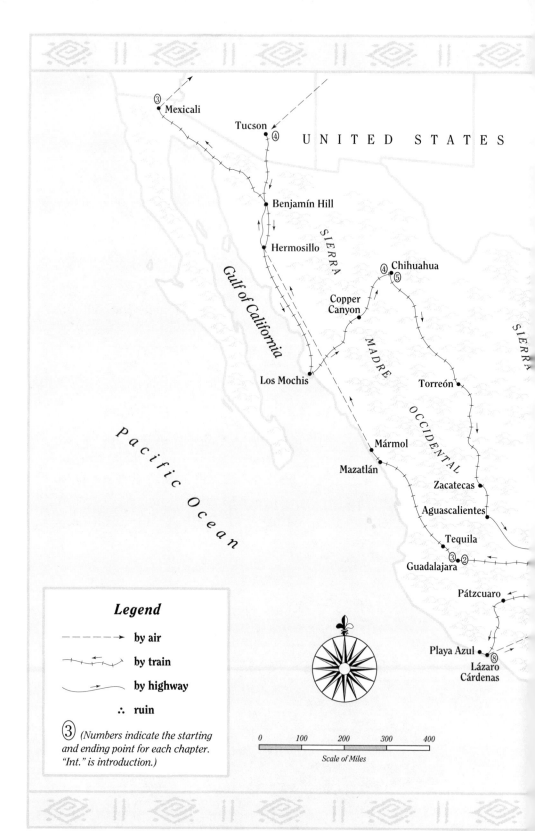

Mexicali ③

Tucson ④

UNITED STATES

Benjamín Hill

Hermosillo

SIERRA

Chihuahua ④⑤

Copper Canyon

Gulf of California

MADRE

Los Mochis

OCCIDENTAL

Torreón

Pacific Ocean

Mármol

Mazatlán

Zacatecas

Aguascalientes

Tequila

Guadalajara ③②

SIERRA

Pátzcuaro

Playa Azul ⑧
Lázaro Cárdenas

Legend

- – – – – → **by air**
- ┼┼┼┼┼ **by train**
- ──── → **by highway**
- ∴ **ruin**

③ *(Numbers indicate the starting and ending point for each chapter. "Int." is introduction.)*

0   100   200   300   400

Scale of Miles

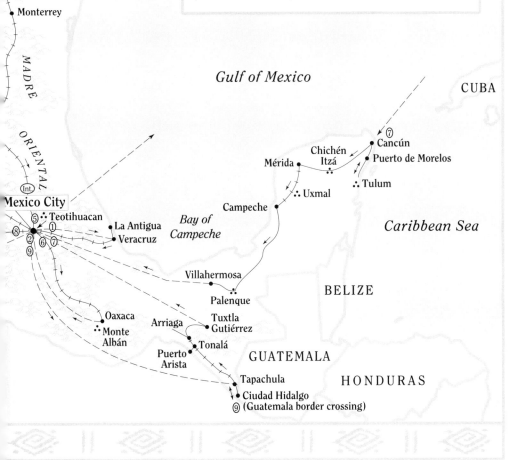

Train Routes in *Yesterday's Train*

Nuevo Laredo to Monterrey ***AZTEC EAGLE***	Copper Canyon to Chihuahua ***CHIHUAHUA PACÍFICO***
Monterrey to Mexico City ***REGIOMONTANO***	Chihuahua to Aguascalientes ***DIVISIÓN DEL NORTE***
Veracruz to Mexico City ***JAROCHO***	Mexico City to Oaxaca ***OAXAQUEÑO***
Mexico City to Guadalajara ***TAPATÍO***	Mérida to Campeche No name— **"THE DEATH TRAIN"**
Guadalajara to Mexicali ***PACÍFICO***	Mexico City to Lázaro Cárdenas ***PURÉPECHA***
Tucson to Copper Canyon ***SIERRA MADRE EXPRESS*** *(American Tour Train)*	Ciudad Hidalgo to Arriaga ***CHIAPAS***

CUBA

Gulf of Mexico

Nuevo Laredo

Monterrey

MADRE

ORIENTAL

Int.

Mexico City

⑤ ∴ Teotihuacan
① ● La Antigua
⑧ ● Veracruz
② ⑥ ⑦
⑨

Bay of Campeche

Campeche

∴ Uxmal

Mérida

Chichén Itzá
∴

⑦ ● Cancún
● Puerto de Morelos

∴ Tulum

Caribbean Sea

Villahermosa

Palenque

BELIZE

Oaxaca
∴ Monte Albán

Arriaga

Tuxtla Gutiérrez

Tonalá

Puerto Arista

GUATEMALA

HONDURAS

Tapachula

● Ciudad Hidalgo
⑨ (Guatemala border crossing)

YESTERDAY'S
TRAIN

Preface

In Mexico nothing is what it seems on the surface, and what lies beneath in layer upon layer of hidden contradiction still baffles visitors from the north. Prosperity may be founded in poverty. Cemeteries can be scenes of celebration. Apparent chaos becomes the secret of profoundest fertility. Enemies embrace one another in human fellowship while allies plot each others' assassinations. Love and hate march side by side, while time proceeds at an uneven pace no clock can measure. A murderous bandit becomes a national hero and emblem of compassion. A peaceful election can be the harbinger of revolution.

Mexico's history, politics, and culture are fundamentally alien to the North American experience known to inhabitants of the United States and Canada, even in the age of the North American Free Trade Agreement. In his book *Distant Neighbors* Alan Riding has written that mestizo Mexico is the most foreign of nations in all of the Americas—the only one that "must be understood in a pre-

1

Hispanic context; and its inhabitants alone are still more Oriental than Western."

So when professor of Spanish Lourdes Ramírez Mallis agreed to collaborate with me in searching for the soul of Mexico by train as I had in the United States and Canada, we had no certainty that the steel rails, a symbol of all that is Western, would lead us where we needed to go. The railways of Mexico do not play the same role in the country's history as they do in Canada, where the very founding of the nation was based on their construction, or in the United States, where their construction was a historical watershed securing America's identity as a great power. In Mexico the railway era denoted the outbreak of a great crisis of national identity that continues to this day. It heralded a sudden, lurching movement of a country, which already had two thousand years of identity-shaping history, toward a Western liberal capitalist model. It is this movement that now finds its culmination in the joint Mexican–foreign business enterprise that today increasingly dominates the country, NAFTA, President Clinton's bailout of the Mexican economy, and the continuing feud with its northern neighbor over drug smuggling and immigration.

Many of the American stereotypes that so bedevil Mexicans are the result of an Anglo-Saxon misapprehension of Mexican character. Mexican attitudes toward work, time, freedom, initiative, and fate are almost inverse of the Anglo-Saxon model that is so congenial to liberal capitalism. These attitudes are grounded in the Mexicans' ancient pre-Hispanic spirituality. Attitudes toward history, foreigners, power, and law, again so alien to those of Western democracy, are a legacy of conquest, economic imperialism, chaotic revolution, and corrupt government.

It isn't just the indigenous roots of the Mexican people that make them averse to their modern history. Mexico's experience of Spanish colonialism and the fanatical Catholicism of the Inquisition era tended to reinforce its non-Western character. Until the age of the railways, the European intrusion into Mexico did not have the liberalizing influence that it did elsewhere in the Americas. And by then the die had been cast so that the influences of the industrial and capitalist revolutions, when they arrived in Mexico, set up a profound conflict that has not been resolved.

Though I quickly learned that for this project I would have to trace Mexican history all the way back, centuries before the advent of the railroads, it soon turned out that the experience of exploring the country by train was just as fruitful as it had been elsewhere in North America. Even more so. Today it is largely the poor who travel by passenger train in Mexico, despite the fact that the railways were originally constructed for the regime of wealth overthrown in Mexico's revolution. And that irony is a key part of Mexico's story. Mexico's socioeconomic profile already mimics the demographers' projections for the world at large by the year 2000—a hugely increased bulge at the poverty level supporting a modest increase of people living in middle-class comfort or better. In Mexico the rail's-eye view affords a close-up look at the damnable paradigm of twentieth-century human progress—that in order for more people to be able to lead comfortable lives, even larger numbers of people seem destined to live in deprivation.

But Mexico preserves something that people in more materially wealthy societies have lost. On each homecoming to the United States during these travels, Dr. Mallis and I were overwhelmed by a sense of sterility and blandness in American life. And on each return to Mexico we were exhilarated by the colors, smells, sounds, rhythms, and richness of a world and a way of life where humanity is not stifled. There are different forms of poverty in the twentieth-century human condition. We came to hope that Mexico's push to join the modern world would not lead it to trade one form of deprivation for another.

From the train we could see that the struggle for Mexico's soul continues on many fronts. As we traveled, politicians were assassinated, we witnessed fraud in a presidential election deemed by the world to be clean, revolutionaries in Chiapas thumbed their masked noses at the government's desperate peace offers, the peso crashed, and a former president went into de facto exile. Mexico is not in chaos, but it is wrenched with changes it cannot assimilate. It is a nation marching, as a whole, into a more affluent, Westernized, and superficially democratic future. But it is a march that leaves masses of the Mexican people behind, one that departs radically from the pathways the country has walked for centuries, and one on which the Mexican spirit itself is instinctively reluctant to embark.

TERRY PINDELL
Keene, NH
June 1995

Introduction
Nuevo Laredo to Mexico City

It's 104 degrees in the shade in Laredo. Buildings here are mostly one story, hugging the cool earth against the fierce July sun. The taxi drops us off at Saint Augustín Square where we have cold iced tea in the restaurant of La Posada Hotel. Then we hike up our bags and begin to walk. The bags are heavy and I'm already sweating through my shirt.

There is the bridge and the Rio Grande—muddy green and slow—less grand than I expected. It's narrow here, an easy swim. The downtowns of American Laredo and Mexican Nuevo Laredo are both built right to the edge of the bluffs above the river. This looks less like an international border than the center of a typical river city.

Mexican kids on the bridge have their hands out offering to carry our bags. Others simply panhandle. Even at the middle of the bridge out over the river, the air is still and heavy with the smells of bodies and diesel exhaust. Trucks are backed so far up the street that we were passing them in our taxi a half hour ago. We will get to

Mexico sooner on foot than anyone on wheels, but we will sweat to get there.

In Nuevo Laredo on the Mexican side, there doesn't appear to be much of a sign code in force. Anything goes, including signs that obscure other signs, signs that obstruct pedestrian movement, signs that hang tenuously from broken chains over people passing below. In a pharmacy open to the sidewalk, drugs tightly controlled by prescription in the United States can be legally purchased if you know the generic name of what you want. Mexico has what American Republicans would call "big government"—but it is a big government that does not meddle in many areas of commerce where we Americans take government presence for granted.

In the central plaza the shoeshine men do a brisk business, even in this heat. Shoes are important in Mexico; the *zapatería* will become the ubiquitous symbol of economic life on the street wherever we go. The shoeshine men cheerfully pose for pictures and one fellow shouts in Spanish, which Lourdes translates for me, "Photograph me naked."

We take a taxi to the neglected and understaffed train station. Inside there is a line, but it's not for reservation confirmation. It's for baggage checks, for drugs or other contraband. Not everyone is checked. You push a button (the officials are very insistent that you push it yourself) and an electronic random device flashes a green light (no check) or a red light (open those bags). This is to ensure that the officials don't give the green light to criminals who have bribed them.

Our train, the Aztec Eagle, is just three beat-up blue-and-orange cars behind a freight engine and a boxcar. The safety-glass windows are pocked with spider web cracks and the air-conditioning in the first-class-special car to which we are directed works at only the front end. The cabin has a musty yet not unpleasant smell and the seats are plush, though a little threadbare. There is no toilet paper in the bathrooms. Since the air-conditioning is less than adequate, the main advantage we paid for with extra dollars is to travel in an uncrowded car. The two lower-class cars of the train are jammed with people, produce, and pets.

The train pulls out on time—actually about five minutes before its scheduled departure time of 6:55 P.M. Standing on the open back platform, I see two Mexican men in shirtsleeves sprint to catch the train, one a little ahead of the other. The first man catches up to my vantage point as the train accelerates, and he hollers something I don't understand while gesturing toward the side Dutch door against which I am leaning. I open the door for him and he hops on board with a grateful nod and then yanks the emergency brake cord. The train grinds to a halt, the second man jumps on board, and soon the train begins to move again.

The two men are engineers who work on the trains, but they do not have a legal pass or ticket to ride. The conductor appears and reminds them that they can't ride without a ticket. "Yes, we know," they say. The conductor leaves and later we see him talking congenially with them for the rest of the trip. They always ride this way, they tell us. There is no provision in their work rules for transportation to the point where the trains they work begin. Those trains simply would have no engineers if they didn't hop this train illegally.

We see this pattern again when the conductor returns to the open back platform and tells us that passengers are not allowed to ride here. "*Gracias,*" we say, but stay right where we are, sharing a beer and smoking a cigarette. When the conductor appears again, he converses with us and the other passengers on the platform and does not mention the rule again for the duration of the trip.

"*La ley se obedece, pero no se cumple,*" Lourdes explains to me. The law is obeyed, but it is not followed. It's a common Latin American saying that explains a lot of what we will see, she says.

It sounds to me like the ancient, universal code of civilized peoples ruled by alien forces. "Render unto Caesar . . ." and all of that. Despite independence, despite the revolution, that is still the reality of Mexican life today.

Mexican trains may have any combination of four classes: Pullman, first special, first regular, and second. Pullman is roughly equivalent to Amtrak's first-class sleeper service on its eastern trains—the same room and equipment configuration in refurbished forties and fifties vintage cars. During our travels there were no dining or lounge cars. Apparently these services come and go with the vicissitudes of politics and management in the *Ferrocarriles Nacionales de México (FNM)*, or Mexican National Railways. But on all Mexican trains the usual prohibition against standing in open vestibules is cheerfully unenforced, and the outside rear platform becomes a delightful substitute for the bar car with open-air advantages of its own.

First class special is intended to match Amtrak's regular coach on long-distance runs. The cars are air-conditioned, but obnoxious nonremovable dividers between seats and a lack of footrests make sleeping on these cars difficult. Concessionaires sell beer, soda, snacks, and sandwiches. In our experience the condition of cars in this class varied tremendously from train to train. On our first run on the Aztec Eagle, we had broken windows, odoriferous bathrooms without toilet paper, malfunctioning air-conditioning, and torn seats. But during a later ride on the same route, we found conditions better than on Amtrak coach.

First class regular has no air-conditioning, but the windows open, and the seats do not have the damnable dividers of first class special. If it's not crowded or hot, you can sleep on first class regular. But on a bad-luck train at a low level of maintenance, first class regular can be less than comfortable.

Second class is a third world experience. The cars smell of urine and are so packed with people that many have to stand. Garbage sometimes litters the floor, and train personnel pay little attention to passengers beyond taking tickets. The lavatory may be so odoriferous that its door is roped shut. An American riding in this section draws stares; they are not hard stares or hostile. But they are alien. The faces in the second-class cars are not Spanish-looking, or even mestizo. They are mostly Indian, descendants of those conquered by Cortés, people who have never been assimilated into the increasingly affluent "mainstream" of Mexican society.

We ride all afternoon through a thunderstorm in the desert—a rare thing, we are told. Then the sky clears, the sun sets, and a full moon rises over the tracks that stretch out behind the train. Ahead of us in the moon glow we can see the foothills of the Sierra Madre Oriental and then the lights of a great city, Monterrey, stretched out at their base. The train slows to a crawl through the Monterrey rail yards where we pass rows and rows of abandoned boxcars that are now home to poor Indians. Children wave at the train and adults watch it pass by with apparent resignation.

Ahead and to the right, the tall spires of modern downtown Monterrey light up the night sky. There's even a tower dedicated exclusively to projecting laser light shows, a symbol of the new techno-Mexico. Most of the people in our first-class-special car gather up their bags to detrain. Most of those in the lower-class cars stay put. They have a longer journey ahead.

Mexico's troubled journey began long before there were people in this part of the world, with geological violence on a scale matched in only a few other parts of the planet. Between fifty and thirty million years ago, the plates of the earth's crust shifted, clashed, and ruptured, eventually forming the familiar pattern of continents that we know today. Mexico was, at the beginning of this era, a broad shallow sea. But it was under these waters that something had to give, as Atlantic plates pushed westward by all the accumulated pressures of half of the planet met those pushed eastward by the other half and by the sinking Acapulco Trench in the Pacific.

For millennia these two titanic forces met under the Sea of

Mexico, and the ocean boiled with steam, sulfur, and churning, hardening lava. Eventually enough rock solidified so that the floor of the sea rose above the water levels. Still the cataclysm continued as two towering volcanic ranges thrust upward paralleling the coastlines of today's Mexico: the Sierra Madre Occidental and the Sierra Madre Oriental. Between the two ranges and in smaller pockets within them, molten rock flowed out to fill the depressions, forming plains at extremely high altitudes. Further upheavals disrupted even the high plains with scattered mountain ranges not part of the two main chains.

So it was that when asked by King Charles what the land of the New World looked like, Cortés took a sheet of paper and crumpled it saying, "Like this." More important, it was this geology that made Mexico a cradle for New World civilizations, with its rich volcanic and sedimentary soil and its rolling high-altitude plains in a subtropical climate.

Human beings didn't arrive in the New World until the Ice Age migration across the Bering Strait between Asia and Alaska. Those who made their way as far south as Mexico found distinct environmental advantages there, but those same advantages would eventually handicap them when they made the transition from hunting to agriculture. The ancients of Mexico, even in their highest stages of civilization, never invented the wheel. Their land was perhaps too rugged for carts to offer much of an advantage. They also lagged behind other civilizations in domesticating draft animals. Game was more plentiful for a longer period of time in the New World than elsewhere, and then when it did dwindle, species that might have been domesticated were quickly hunted to extinction. So the inhabitants of the New World took longer than most to make fully the transition to the agricultural life required to build great civilizations.

They had no significant rivers for transportation, and they were slow to develop metallurgy, perhaps because they were blessed with plentiful resources of volcanic obsidian for the making of blades. But by all other measures, the civilizations they developed rivaled those of other parts of the world, even that of the Europeans who conquered them.

Around 7000 B.C. ancestral Mexicans developed agriculture as the last of the big game became extinct. In addition to the piñon nuts, sunflower seeds, onion bulbs, and prickly pear cactus that they had gathered as supplements for their hunters' meat diets for aeons, they began to plant the triad of cultivated crops that have fed them to this day: beans, squash, and the marvelous grain, maize.

Virtually all great emerging civilizations throughout the world were based on the cultivation of one of the staple grains: wheat, rice, or maize. These are grains suitable for making a variety of nourishing foodstuffs, can be stored for long periods, and are capable of producing large surpluses to be used as a basis for trade or for insurance against a not-so-rainy day. But maize, the staple of the civilizations of the New World, had distinct advantages over wheat and rice. Wheat had a relatively low yield, since so many grains fail to sprout, and until the advent of technology, its harvesting was very labor-intensive. Rice brought higher yields but was even more labor-intensive due to the need to transplant the seedlings to flooded fields. Extensive hydraulic infrastructure was necessary to create wet rice paddies, even in rainy climates.

Maize had none of these disadvantages. It is the least labor-intensive and most productive of any of the three staple grains. It grows quickly and requires little attention. It can share the soil with beans and squash, which replenish nitrogen, and so its fields need never lie fallow. In short, maize was the perfect basis from which the civilizations of the Americas might "catch up" to those of the rest of the world.

It was almost too perfect. Much of the technological progress made by civilizations in other parts of the world was driven by the agricultural mechanics needed to ensure plentiful harvests of wheat or rice. Mass warfare spurred by famine and ensuing migrations when these staples fell short further stimulated the development of technology, metallurgy in particular. In Mexico, as long as the climate held and the land was not overcultivated, maize supported a life that was technologically easy and unchallenging. And when the climate suddenly changed or civilizations brought upon themselves ecological disaster, such cataclysm in a world so unschooled in technology simply caused those civilizations to suddenly and "mysteriously" collapse. One after another, this was the case, until a different fate befell the last of them, the Aztecs.

The volcanically fertile earth, maize, and a changing climate: These three factors are almost enough to explain the mysteries of the pre-Hispanic Mexican world. With the big game gone, control of maize and the power to feed meant the power to rule. Though requiring nothing like the waterworks of rice, even maize required irrigation as Mexico's climate became increasingly arid over the centuries. Only strong rulers could organize and command the ever more massive efforts needed to guarantee irrigation. Only strong rulers could be entrusted with the grain surpluses. Only strong rulers could divide the land so that the food supply could be assured. Early Mexican monarchs built their power on maize and enveloped themselves in religious myth associated with the natural forces governing plenty or famine. Long before the coming of the Spaniards, the great mass of Mexican people was accustomed to living under the strong bureaucratic hand of a ruling elite so far above their mortal existence that they dared not even look upon their faces in public processions.

First there were the Olmecs (People of the Rubber Country) who flourished from 1200 B.C. to 400 B.C., primarily on the Veracruz-Tabasco coast, though they left their mark as far away as the Pacific coast and in Guatemala. While they were not great city builders, the massive monolithic sculptures they left behind testify to a significant level of civilization. Materials for these works were transported from great distances by means still unknown. The Olmecs pioneered astronomy, mathematics, and glyph writing, and played a ball game portrayed in their art. But from 900 B.C. to 400 B.C. their ceremonial centers were sacked, either by invasion or rebellion, as shown by clear mutilation of monuments.

Somewhere around the first century B.C., an advanced city-state civilization began to develop at Teotihuacán, in the Valley of Mexico just north of today's Mexico City. By 500 A.D. the New World's first city was larger than Imperial Rome, its spectacular growth spurred by advances in the cultivation and distribution of maize. Teotihuacán's Pyramid of the Sun is as massive as that of Cheops in Egypt. Famine-induced infanticide, a common practice among the pre-Classic tribes of the New World, was abandoned first in Teotihuacán as its system guaranteed the feeding of even the lowliest of its highly stratified classes—but the price was despotism and ecological disaster. Slashing and burning of the surrounding hillsides and depletion of underground water supplies led to water shortages that strained the city-state's ability to feed its people when the climate began to turn more arid. Population, military power, and morale dwindled to an extent that in 750 A.D. northern barbarians, long held at bay, were able to devastate the city-state.

The Maya, who have been studied and documented so extensively, accomplished their golden age in the Yucatán, Chiapas, Belize, and Guatemala between 300 and 900 A.D. The Maya were true city builders, and some anthropologists place them on the same level as the Golden Age Greeks. They alone of New World peoples invented the corbeled arch, and they were the first to develop advanced artistic painting, which originally covered virtually all of their structures. At least six centuries before their counterparts in Asia or Europe, the Maya introduced the mathematical concept of zero; their solar calendar was more accurate than the Julian calendar in use at the same time in Europe. Mayan development suddenly declined in the 900s. Overcultivation combined with drought weakened the Maya, making them suddenly vulnerable to invasions by hostile neighbors from the outside and rebellions of oppressed peasants within.

Meanwhile, one of the northern barbarian groups that had sacked Teotihuacán, the Toltecs, followed the time-honored pattern of the conqueror emulating the conquered. At Tula, in the Valley of Mexico, they built a civilization modeled on what they had helped destroy at Teotihuacán and flourished from 900 A.D. to the 1100s. Though their primacy was relatively short, they had two lasting effects on pre-Hispanic Mexico. First, they linked up with remnants of the Mayan civilization to effect a Mayan-Toltec renaissance. It was during this period that the magnificent structures of Chichén Itzá were built in the Yucatán. And second, they were particularly articulate chroniclers of their history and mythology.

According to Toltec legend, one of the their god-kings, Quetzalcóatl ("Feathered Serpent" in Nahuatl, the language of the Toltecs, and later of the Aztecs), was exiled or exiled himself from Tula to a land in the east, promising one day to return and claim his heritage. Contemporary Mayan legends (dating from about 1000 A.D.) continue the storytelling of a Toltec warrior, Kukulcán ("Feathered Serpent" in Mayan), who came from the west to seize and rebuild Chichén Itzá. According to the chronicles of the Toltecs, ecological disaster then befell them. Following the fate of the Teotihuacanos, they endured drought, denuded hillsides, crop failures, and a weakened state before finally collapsing in the face of pressure from a new wave of northern invaders.

Simultaneous with the rise and fall of the Mayans, the Zapotecs built the great civilization centered around Monte Albán near Oaxaca. Monte Albán was nothing less than a mountain whose top was removed and flattened to create a "plaza in the clouds." The civilization of the Zapotecs collapsed around 900 A.D. for much the same reasons as those of the Maya and Teotihuacanos. They were soon replaced by the Mixtecs, who managed to hang on until successive invasions by Aztecs and then Spaniards in the fifteenth and sixteenth centuries.

Like the Toltecs, the Aztecs were great chroniclers of their history. Their legendary homeland, Aztlán, "Place of the Herons" or "Place of the Seven Caves," is described in their records with enough detail that anthropologists have spent years searching for it, but without success. It was probably a formation of caves on the shore of a rather modest lake somewhere in the northwest of Mexico, though there is a remote possibility that it actually may have been the Great Salt Lake in Utah.

What is certain is that the Aztecs spent centuries migrating slowly southward, sustained, like the people of Moses, by the legend of a promised land. Their stories are rich with regret over their lost Eden and their doubts about the journey. Approaching central Mexico, they were expelled from various locales by tribe after tribe, each of whom regarded them as particularly unsavory barbarians. Other times it was their own hummingbird god, Huitzilopochtli, who urged them onward, foretelling that they would recognize their new homeland when they found an island in a lake where an eagle perched on a cactus was devouring a serpent.

The Aztecs finally arrived in the Valley of Mexico about a hundred years after the fall of the Toltecs. By the thirteenth century, they had settled in Chapultepec near Lake Toxcoco, where they began the transition to an agricultural way of life. Still, their stock-in-trade was their skill as fierce mercenary warriors for neighboring tribes who alternately hired them and scorned them.

Their moment of history came when they were hired by the Culhuacanos, a tribe that had previously humiliated and enslaved them. After gaining victory for the Culhuacanos, the Aztecs requested that the Culhuacano king marry one of his daughters to their chieftain. When the king arrived for the ceremony, he found an Aztec priest wearing a freshly flayed bloody human skin. It was the remains of his daughter.

In the ensuing battle the Aztecs fled in their canoes to an island in Lake Toxcoco. Here their legends say they saw the vision of the eagle and the serpent promised in their lore. They named the island Tenochtitlán, settled, and began to build the city that became the master of all Mexico.

Tenochtitlán became a New World Venice, crisscrossed with canals and broad boulevards, ornamented with classic temples and monumental public works, and center of a vast trading empire. The Aztecs orchestrated an elaborate reclamation of lands from the shallow lake to enlarge their island for agricultural purposes, and their rise to greatness was largely due to their talent for organization and for this environmental hydroengineering in particular. But it was also due to their skill as warriors and their penchant for brutality. Their infamous practices of human sacrifice and cannibalism were more than religious rituals; they were calculated devices of state terror.

Despite their cruelty, however, the Aztecs aspired to civilization. Cortés himself remarked on the paradox: a people whose power rested on the most hideous practices who otherwise created a way of life full of refinement, grace, and beauty. The ruthless adventurer genuinely grieved when he finally concluded that he had to destroy Tenochtitlán in order to conquer it. He believed the Aztecs had created a place for human existence finer than any he had seen in the European world. And then there is the issue of cultural relativism. When Cortés ordered one malefactor summarily burned at the stake, Aztec nobles were appalled. What kind of people were these who could roast a man alive but then not deign to eat him when fully cooked?

Like barbarian conquerors everywhere, the Aztecs adopted as their mythical forefathers a previous civilization, the Toltecs. As part of that myth they incorporated the legend of Quetzalcóatl, the god-king who had sailed off to the east promising someday to return and reclaim his lands. It was a fateful inheritance, this legend, for when Cortés's sails appeared off the coast in 1519, the image helped ensure an end for the Aztecs worse than anything they had inflicted on their conquered subjects.

During our two-day layover in Monterrey, the NAFTA-primed city offers teasing first pieces of the puzzle that is Mexico today. Monstrous construction cranes tilt against new high-rise frames, and scaffolding with scurrying workmen creeps over the sides of older buildings undergoing renovation. In the fumy, congested streets the ubiquitous din of jackhammers rises above the grumble of trucks, bumper to bumper with their heavy cargoes.

The central market teems with people and smells of spicy food and leather. Like those throughout Mexico, it occupies an entire central city block with its warrens and stalls—it's an easy place in which to get lost. There may be some plan to it, but not one that's readily apparent. At first there appears to be some rough zoning of foodstuffs and pottery into one quadrant, live animals and animal products in another, electronic gear in a third, and clothing in a fourth, but then we find hardware next to live rabbits and cheap video games hard by a region of indigenous ceramic dishware. The market is an organic entity, growing and changing its anatomy under the driving forces of supply and demand, opportunity and need, initiative and adaptation.

And here, perhaps, is a first Mexican lesson for us Americans. For some thirty years now we have been trying to replace our Main Street merchandizing and its discrete storefront properties with exurban shopping malls, whose advantage besides auto convenience is the centralization and communalization of the marketplace. But we have too often got it terribly wrong and instead have created monuments to a slick but bland way of life.

The Mexican market is always, first of all, located in the heart of town. It brings people together in a setting that is a web of civilized life, not an expanse of pavement out by the interstate interchange. Second, the Mexican market is 90 percent market and 10 percent passageways instead of the other way around. You rub shoulders with people in the Mexican market and have no chance to experience that feeling of spacious emptiness so common in the vast corridors of American malls.

And finally, the Mexican market is not antiseptically sterile. Neither is it dirty, as some Americans think. It's just fecund, full and rich with the froth of commerce and the variety of human instincts toward enterprise. It seems as though you can get anything here, from Indian dresses to dinner dishes, guinea pigs to parakeets, silver to cilantro, guava to guacamole. There is even fast food. At one of the hot food stalls, we find a woman working at a bench of exquisite blue tiles trimming the spines off pieces of prickly pear cactus (nopal). "It's for *platillo de nopalito,*" she says, and then gives us a free taste and the recipe. The nopal is cut into strips and sautéed with tomatoes, onions, cilantro, and garlic and served with slices of hard-boiled egg. She can put together a freshly cooked plate in about the same time it takes McDonald's to deliver a burger. Real food from warm hands. Because of the setting's humanity, what you eat in the Mexican market seems worth eating; what you purchase in the Mexican market seems worth purchasing and has some weight and substance as you carry it out to the street.

In one of the historic barrios, we find an avenue blocked off to traffic and a team of workmen bending over their task. There is no power machinery here, just men laying a cobblestone street by hand. "The streets with the big, flat stones are not the real thing," the sweaty foreman tells us. Those were laid during the nineteenth century. The authentic colonial street is paved with millions of small round stones, less than two inches in diameter. Through a national trust to restore historic neighborhoods, the government is sponsoring this project.

Antonio Espinoza is proud to explain the modern version of the ancient process to us. First the old pavement underneath is chipped to make it adhere better to the new cement and then scrubbed and sealed. In a concession to modern engineering, a net of reinforcement steel is laid on and bounded by wooden frames of one-by-fours that form the gutters. Meanwhile, the stones will have been gathered from the river, selected, cleaned, and stacked in piles at intervals all down the street. The frantic work begins when the cement truck arrives. As cement is poured from the truck onto the old pavement, it is troweled and then the stone setters plant the stones in the wet cement, one by one by one. They have to work fast to get the stones in place before the cement begins to set. As each section is fully stoned, a two-by-four is used to pack the stones down tightly. Then, just as the cement begins to set, the surface is brushed with rakes and sponges. As it sets further, the surface is hosed and brushed again and again till the cobblestone tops are clean and free of residual cement.

A beginner gets paid 200 pesos a week for this work, a master like Antonio, 400 pesos (between U.S.$80 and U.S.$100 before the 1995 devaluation). He learned the trade when he was fifteen years old. Friends taught him and now he teaches others; there are no schools. It is good work, he believes, leaving something behind for all to see of which he can be proud. "The old streets without the rebars lasted hundreds of years, señor; mine will last a thousand," he boasts.

As Antonio has been talking to us, his crew has continued to work hard, albeit casting curious glances toward us from time to time. It's one of many vignettes we see throughout Monterrey that put the lie to the old gringo prejudice about Mexicans and work. Especially in the cities, any first-time visitor unburdened with preconceptions is likely to come away saying, "What a hard-working people!" Mexican workers may take a siesta, but they begin their labors while Americans are still sleeping and quit after we have had our supper.

"I do it like the devil tells me to," says young sculptress Rosa María Robles when we meet her at her show at the Cuauhtémoc Brewery. Rosa María is a volcanically energetic woman with heavy long dark hair and fire in her eyes. Her sculptures are massively abstract suggestions of agonized human torsos made from the trunks of poplar trees, steel construction bars, and hunks of basalt. The show is called simply *Rage*. In a Catholic land where revolution is institutionalized and a surprising tradition of anticlericalism runs deep, the aesthetic of a liberated woman gets her national praise from the avant garde.

The trees she uses are poplars, uprooted from the river by the government. "Phantoms of the river" she calls them, referring to the anthropomorphic qualities they take on when she reclaims them and introduces them to steel and stone. "They stop being trees. They become something that neither nature nor I intended," she says. She shows us some new works that reflect her most recent fascination, putting big phallic stones inside the trees. She finds the basalt columns crystallized out of volcanoes in the mountains of Sinaloa.

Eight years ago she started studying at the Academy of Beaux Arts. She had a passion for sculpture from the beginning. "It gives me strength to see stone and wood together. Nothing I ever finish is what I started to do," she explains. "It just comes out of me. And it's very different in Mexico, so it gets acclaim."

Some of her most outrageously violent and phallic sculptures couldn't be shown here at the brewery museum. There are limits, even today. "I am expressing a woman's anger and passion that is untouchable, prohibited in a society that is still very closed, highly religious, and prejudiced. But we can still show people as far as the museum will let us go."

Before we part, I notice that the buttons from the ankle to the waist of her denim pants are labeled "Do not enter." I comment on it and Lourdes wrestles with the awkward translation. "What did she say?" I ask as we walk to our taxi.

"She said, 'Oh, but I wish they would.' "

We find other quirky stories of unlikely juxtaposition during our two days in Monterrey. Doña Cavazos, an elderly woman running a traditional clothing shop, once relied heavily on American tourist traffic. But since NAFTA, the Americans who come to Monterrey are all businesspeople who don't spend money in the markets. Her livelihood has been saved by the resurgence of national pride in the pre-Hispanic past. Her customers are now almost entirely schools and families needing historic clothing for festival occasions. As the economic world has changed around her, she has survived thanks to the demands of tradition.

We have lunch at La Taquería las Monjitas (the Little Nuns' Restaurant) where owner-entrepreneur Vicki Juárez wanted to claim her own little piece of Monterrey's economic boom. She had the place remodeled to resemble a convent and dressed her rough waitresses in nun's habits. "I just wanted to draw some attention," she says. She succeeded so well that one woman sent her niece, who aspired to the convent, to work there with "the nuns." The girl quit, reporting to her mother that these nuns didn't make quite the kind of talk she thought she'd hear in the convent.

Tradition and innovation, bondage and liberation—Monterrey presents some of the contradictions of Mexico. But Monterrey is too close to the United States—it is not Mexico. And too many *norteamericanos* see only this modernized edge of a nation under siege by its history.

The Aztecs founded their state on an island in the middle of a lake. The site offered safety from the other Valley of Mexico tribes whose enmity they had earned during their years as barbarian mercenaries, and it also offered a cornucopia of fowl and fish to a people forced by circumstance to make a quick transition from hunting and gathering to sedentary farming. They began by molding their environment to fit their needs. Like the Dutch reclaiming the polder lands, the Aztecs learned from their old enemies, the Culhuacanos, the trick of building artificial islands (*chinampas*) in the shallows of the lake near their big island and then connecting all of them to expand their available arable land. Like the Venetians, they had more water than they needed, so they were able to maintain a network of canals for transportation as they expanded their island. But more significant than all of this for the subsequent history of the nation, they had to radically rearrange their social structure because of their new geographical circumstances, and they had to aspire to empire; there was just no way to reclaim enough land with the *chinampas* to make their island world big enough to sustain a thriving society.

During the years of the exodus, Aztec society was structured around numerous family clans, the *calpilli,* whose elders formed a relatively broad and egalitarian leadership. There was little social distance between the multiple chieftains at the top and the lowliest hunter or tender of cooking fires. But in the dense urban-agricultural setting of Tenochtitlán, the chaotic *calpilli* system proved inadequate to the monumental tasks of building *chinampas* and canals. When the ascendant chieftains assigned real authority over the *calpilli* to the city's leadership, a revolt broke out and some of the clans moved to the nearby island of Tlatelolco to set up their own society. *Chinampas* eventually connected Tlatelolco to Tenochtitlán, and the schism was bridged by geography, but the episode bulled the momentum of Aztec history toward centralized control and a radical experiment in restructuring of society.

For the first time the collective Aztec leadership conceived of a need for an actual king—a person in whom to invest all centralized power. Because effective power was more important than tribal identity, and particularly to prevent further episodes like Tlatelolco, they decided the new king should come from outside the Aztec family. So the Aztecs turned to their old enemies, the Culhuacanos, and invited one of their noblemen, whose mother was conveniently Aztec, to become the first Aztec king. The choice was also driven by the supposed connection between the Culhuacanos and the Toltecs, the mythical link of all the new peoples in the Valley of Mexico with the glorious Teotihuacano past.

Acamapichtli's reign began in 1375 and marked the creation of a new class, the noble *pipiltin*, largely because Acamapichtli's wife was barren and so he was allowed to have a "harem" of women from the old *pilpilli* chieftain class. The harem concept caught on among the subordinate chieftains and among the new male *pipiltin*, so that within a generation, a new stratum had been created between the old chieftains and the king at the top. The pyramidal structure of Mexican society had begun.

The most serious threat to the emerging Aztec state was the mainland tribe known as the Tepanecas. For years the Aztecs had to offer them tribute and even allowed the offspring of an Aztec-Tepaneca marriage to ascend the Aztec throne. But by 1428 the Tepanecas made a major miscalculation in attempting to establish a formalized empire throughout the valley. In response, the Aztecs formed the Triple Alliance with the cities of Texcoco and Tlacopán, two other disgruntled vassals of the Tepanecas. The allies attacked the once-feared Tepanecas and devastated their city. Through this victory, the foundations of the Aztec empire were laid.

With military dominance of the valley established and imperial expansion beyond it now a reality, another layer of Aztec society was created: the warrior-noblemen. As in other warlike societies, distinguished service in battle offered the one avenue for men of humble origins to aspire to elevated status.

Like the Spanish who would later conquer them, the Aztecs themselves used religion to cement the bonds of empire. The expansive role of the priesthood in Aztec imperial society promoted another layer of power near the top of the pyramid linked directly to the superstructure of Aztec ascendancy. While allowing established rulers to retain their seats in conquered lands, the Aztecs demanded adherence to the cult of Huitzilopochtli. This meant that the tribute owed by vassals included a steady supply of victims for sacrifice. Human sacrifice had long been a feature of Mesoamerican societies everywhere in the belief that death, and the spilling of human blood, was the engine that helped the gods drive the universe. But the Aztecs exploited this religious belief for political expediency with the sheer numbers and scope of the bloody rituals performed on the platforms at the tops of the pyramids. The practice finally became both the hallmark and the Achilles' heel of the Aztec state.

Some historians set a date and a circumstance for the orgy of human sacrifice that marked and marred the Aztec civilization. They identify the drought of 1450 as a critical moment. Aztec priests, seeking to appease both Huitzilopochtli and Tlaloc (the rain god), performed an unusual number of human sacrifices that year. The drought immediately lifted, and the Aztec priests made further human sacrifices as offers of thanks to the gods. It was at this same time that the Aztec leadership was pondering the question of how to avert the fate that had befallen the Tepanecas and the Toltecs before them. Skillful diplomacy, military supremacy, and judicious alliances were certainly to be part of the equation. But a key formula would be what today we would call state terror.

Human sacrifice soon became something other than religious practice. Defeated enemies were ritually sacrificed, their chests ripped open and their hearts yanked out as they screamed. Sliced free, their organs were held high still throbbing and spurting blood before audiences of noblemen from the conquered as well as the soon-to-be conquered. Long parades of defeated warriors marched up the temple stairs to meet the same end, over and over again, always with key leaders of neighboring tribes as guests and witnesses—feted and lavishly honored but unable to miss the point of the proceedings.

When their neighbors had been subdued to the point where real wars were rarely necessary, the Aztecs initiated the practice of the Flower Wars, fake conflicts with real bloodshed to demonstrate their dominance and provide a steady supply of victims for sacrifice. When the last surviving leader of the early Aztec empire, Tlacaelel, was nearing the end of his life, he organized a four-day ceremony to celebrate his and his people's accomplishments.

Nobles of all the surrounding tribes were invited to feast and then to witness the sacrifice. Anywhere from twenty to eighty thousand victims marched up the steps of Huitzilopochtli's temple during those four days to the beat of great drums and the chants of priests. Amid the mists of incense at the top of the pyramid, their hearts were sacrificed one by one, and a cascade of blood flowed down the temple steps to the base, where butchers waited to cart off the bodies for dismemberment and cooking. When the guests returned to their peoples, they remembered what they had seen.

These performances chilled the living blood of potential challengers and rival tribes at least as much as the proficiency of Aztec warriors on the battlefield. Besides administrative efficiency, this is what the Aztecs brought to the field of conquest that made them masters of Mexico. There were at least two tribes, the Tarascans and the Tlaxcalans, whose military prowess matched the Aztecs'. But though they were never conquered, neither did they build empires. Huge quantities of sacrificial blood and terror may very well have been the difference.

They probably also played a role in the Aztecs' ultimate demise. On his arrival, Cortés found tribes chafing under the yoke of tribute, the demands for so many sacrificial victims being particularly repugant. Our modern, politically correct sensibilitity may reject the missionary, Christianizing impulse of Cortés and his followers, but their revulsion at the sacrificial blood lust of the Aztecs was historically correct. The Aztecs' neighbors had already had enough.

One cannot read the histories of the conquest and remain skeptical about the power of destiny. Aztec prophecies foretold over and over again exactly what was to happen, so that when the apocalypse finally came, it seems almost as if Aztec leadership, Moctezuma II in particular, stood frozen, transfixed before the unfolding of a history they already knew.

As far back as the 1440s, the first Moctezuma sent an expedition of priests on a quest northward in search of the site of Aztlán, the mythic place of Aztec origin, and the birthplace of Huitzilopochtli. When the priests returned, they told a tale of a horrific and dangerous journey leading to a magical flight on wings to Aztlan. There they encountered an old man who, after chastising them for the life of luxury they had built in Tenochtitlán, took them to meet with Huitzilopohtli's mother herself. The priests entertained her with stories of the glorious rise of the Aztec empire, but she was unimpressed and foretold that they themselves would be conquered by an even greater empire and all their mighty works would be broken to rubble.

In 1509, when the second Moctezuma was facing a string of rebellions from vassal states groaning under Aztec demands for sacrificial victims, priests of the ancient cult of Quetzalcóatl in Cholula invoked his name in opposition to the Aztec cult of the bloodthirsty Huitzilopochtli. Over the years Quetzalcóatl had come to represent the "higher" civilization of the classic Toltecs and was held, in the eyes of some, to be offended by the Aztecs' sacrificial practices.

During these years the city-state of Texcoco, Tenochtitlán's closest and most powerful ally, was ruled by Nezahualpilli, son of one of the founders of the Triple Alliance and the Aztec empire. Now an old man, greatly respected throughout the Aztec world, he could speak directly to Moctezuma in words for which others would be put to death. He came to him and foretold a "wondrous event, that by the will of the lords of the skies, the night, the day, and the air, will occur within your lifetime." He went on to predict that the cities of the Triple Alliance would be laid to waste and that the allies would be annihilated. Nothing could be done to avert this end of ages, and signs would soon appear in the skies confirming what was foretold. As further proof of what must come to pass, Nezahualpilli told Moctezuma, the Triple Alliance would never again win a Flower War.

Immediately Moctezuma rushed into a poorly planned Flower War with the hated Tlaxcalans, who routed the Aztecs, taking prisoner and sacrificing all of their generals. In a rage, Moctezuma launched a second Flower War with the Tlaxcalans and this time fared better—the event ended a draw. Moctezuma could console himself that he had not lost, but when shortly thereafter a great comet suddenly appeared in the skies, he trembled at the thought that neither had he won. Now every night seemed to bring another harbinger of catastrophe: A mysterious fire damaged Huitzilopochtli's temple, Tlaloc's temple was struck by lightning, a waterspout appeared over Lake Texcoco out of a cloudless sky, a strange glow rose each night from the east, and women roamed the midnight streets wailing for their children.

Terrified, Moctezuma appealed to Nezahualpilli and the Texcocans to join him in another Flower War with the Tlaxcalans to prove the prophecy wrong. But secretly he schemed revenge against Nezahualpilli, informing the enemy Tlaxcalans that his troops would hold back while they mauled the Texcocans. In the ensuing massacre, the Texcocans cried out for help, but Moctezuma's troops watched passively—as a member of the once-united Triple Alliance lost another Flower War.

In the meantime, to appease and strengthen Huitzilopochtli, Moctezuma had been ordering up nightly banquets of human flesh and had sent his engineers in search of a massive boulder to enlarge the temple. After being sculpted and carved with the appropriate religious markings, the boulder was being transported on rafts across the lake when it suddenly fell into the waters. Divers searched for days in the shallows, but the boulder was never found. Now Moctezuma ordered old men brought before him to describe to him their dreams, promising them no harm. When the old men all told of seeing the city in flames, of seeing people screaming as they were cut down by supernatural forces, of seeing the mighty temples toppled, Moctezuma broke his word and ordered them starved to death.

All this had passed when sentinels on the coast of the Gulf of Mexico reported seeing moving white mountains out at sea to the east. Moctezuma collapsed, his passion spent in terror. It was the 1517 sortie of Francisco Hernández de Córdoba, first forerunner to the expedition of Cortés. A year later there were further sightings of men with beards and white faces moving on the water beneath white wings. This was the second expedition, led by Juan de Grijalva. Fearful that the apparition might be Quetzalcóatl returned to claim his lost throne, Moctezuma sent a delegation to meet these strangers bearing gifts of gold, silver, and jewelry. If the gifts were accepted, it would be proof that Quetzalcóatl had returned, for the ancient legends foretold that the thing he prized most of all that he had lost was the "gold and silver and precious stones he had left hidden in the mountains." The year in the cyclical Aztec calendar was I Reed, the same as the year of Quetzalcóatl's departure.

The strangers' enthusiastic response to the gifts convinced Moctezuma that Quetzalcóatl or his descendants had come home, but he still harbored hope when they sailed away and did not return for months. Perhaps the god had visited merely to retrieve his precious rocks. But in 1519 the white wings and pale-faced aliens were sighted again. This time they did not sail away. Never again would

Moctezuma be moved to such decisive actions as had characterized his behavior in the years leading up to the encounter. History had come round. It was already all over, even before it started.

Politics is on the mind of the driver of the cab that takes us from our Monterrey hotel to the train station in the evening. In just a few months Mexico will elect a new president, and though many do not really believe in the process, it is the conversation topic of the time.

"We've lived in a dictatorship for sixty-five years," he says. "People are tired and ready for a change." And then, referring to the recent assassination of the original candidate for president from the ruling party (the Partido Revolucionario Institucional or PRI), he confides, "Salinas and Colosio were really good friends, you know. But Colosio started talking about a truly democratic Mexico, and the six families who control the PRI decided to get rid of him." It is a shocking statement that we will hear more than once during the next few months. News coverage of political upheavals in Mexico tends to be very partisan—either government or opposition propaganda. No one believes anything in the media. Instead people talk and speculate and trade in rumor. But the rumors one hears have a striking consistency and are often borne out by later revelations of fact.

The Regiomontano has long had the reputation of being Mexico's finest overnight train. Departing Monterrey at 7:30 P.M., it climbs through the Sierre Madre Oriental to Saltillo, the capital of the state of Coahuila, before turning south and running all night along the interior highland plateau to Mexico City in the morning. Tonight as the train winds up through the canyons to Saltillo, the air is warm, the sky is clear, and a full moon casts a blue glow across the towering peaks of the Sierra Madre. The country we are passing through here seems virtually uninhabited. Fellow passengers who come out to the platform to catch a smoke and see the world are quiet and contemplative. It is one of the singular impressions of Mexico, that such a crowded and overpopulated country can have such great spaces of solitude. I once wrote that Canada is a collection of little crowds separated by vast tracts of howling wilderness. In Mexico the crowds are bigger and the spaces are smaller, but the intensity of isolation in the wide lonely places is just as great, if a lot warmer. It's a persistent truth of this mighty North American continent. Much of it has always been, and still is, just too promethean to succumb to the numbers of humanity.

After the stop at Saltillo, the train makes a stately fifty-mile-per-hour progress southward up the high central plain between the mountain ranges. The night air is cool, altitude more than compensating for the summer season in which we are traveling.

When we are joined by our conductor, we ask him why Mexico has cut back so drastically on its once proud passenger train service. We get an earful for an answer. "People don't know the security of the train anymore," he says. "So they don't use it. People now want to live too fast—they want everything to go fast. It is sad, but Mexicans are ready to let this piece of our heritage slip away." He finds it disturbing, rather than heartening, that Japanese, American, Canadian, and French investors are rumored to be looking to take over the Mexican passenger rail service through privatization. "It's a struggle for something nobody in our country seems to want. But you can't buy the railroads. You can rent them, but you can't buy them. That's why our revolution happened—because private interests and foreigners thought they could own pieces of Mexico. Our ancestors fought for this ownership; that's why we can't sell it. If they sold the trains, there would have to be another revolution." He reminds us that Pancho Villa and other celebrated revolutionaries used the rails as routes of revolution. The dictatorship of Porfirio Díaz built the railroads to connect its domain but ended up providing the revolutionaries with the mobility to overthrow it. It could happen that way again.

It's all going to explode in August after the elections, he thinks. "The elections will be dishonest and people won't tolerate that this time. There will be little wars, like what is starting in Chiapas. There are groups everywhere; things are brewing. It already started way back when Salinas took power after everyone knew he really lost the election in 1988. A potentially powerful competitor was killed in a mysterious car accident that time. Colosio was shot this time. People won't stand for it much longer."

I hardly expected this kind of response from a simple question about the trains. But it will not be the only time this will occur. The conductor nervously gives his name, but we decide to keep him anonymous for his own security after we learn more about Mexican fears over the peril of talking too freely.

In the morning—coffee in hand—my view from the back platform is of green sharply rolling corn and cactus country framed by ragged purple mountains in the distance. No scene of conflict and struggle here. This is the high fertile interior plain of Mexico where the gap between the Oriental and Occidental Sierra Madre begins to narrow into the Valley of Mexico. The soil is volcanic and its profusion of rocks has been turned by human hands into networks of stone walls, the lines of which are particularly striking in this open, treeless country. Peasant homes of stone and brick and corrugated tin pass every few miles between the cornfields, and children and dogs gambol at the passing of the train. Crosses and little flowered shrines at trackside mark the death sites of rail workers remembered by their loved ones. Occasionally a larger cemetery filled with flowers indicates the presence of a nearby Indian pueblo.

A series of tunnels in late morning announces that the train is breaking through the mountainous northern barrier of the Valley of Mexico and into the ancient Aztec capital, Tenochtitlán—today's Mexico City. If the weather is clear (which isn't often because of Mexico City's world-class smog) you can see the valley spread out before you as the train winds down from the northern rim. We only get glimpses today. On the outskirts of the city we see the descendants of the proud Aztecs living in abandoned boxcars and cabooses at the edge of the rail yard.

Our stop at Mexico City is quick; we will explore this place more thoroughly during later trips. For now, we are content to discover our crash site for future trips and then get on to Veracruz, where we will begin following Mexico's history from the site where Cortés began his conquest.

The María Cristina Hotel, located just off the Zona Rosa section of the city, is a classic old-world hotel catering primarily to foreign guests. No one would ever mistake this livable place for the dull uniformity of Americanized chains. The desk people don't speak English particularly well, and most of the Americans here do speak Spanish. In the lobby, with its dark hardwood and red plush sofas, its big-screen TV tuned constantly to CNN, a handsome international clientele meet one another, and a spiral staircase to the upper rooms frames entrances grand or surreptitious. You could make a movie here about international romance or intrigue. We will be back.

If the story of America's northern neighbor is a crisis of national identity and material success, the story of its southern neighbor is a crisis of national identity and social tragedy. Mexico has made tremendous economic progress as a nation; it has stepped out of the third world to become a partner with nations it once feared and envied. But the stubborn fact is that nothing in five hundred years of the country's history has ever lifted its huge poverty-stricken masses to anything like the prosperity they enjoyed before the coming of the Europeans.

There are benighted places in the world that the cynical Westerner might be tempted to write off. Their problems are too great; their potential contribution too slight. Not Mexico. That same clash of cultures that engendered Mexico's horrific problems also germinated the flowering of humanity at its best. There were times during our travels in Mexico when we felt as though we were sojourning through Eden. Mexico is what happens when you put a mix of particularly creative people on a fertile piece of the planet. Mexico is a garden that has not yet been paved over or chartered into modern commercial wrack and ruin. It is a place where, as I found for myself, one can learn again how to live and love, each bell-toned morning can be a reminder to us soulless Americans: This is what it is to be human.

1

Apocalypse

Veracruz to Mexico City

The roots of the old tree are twisted; the trunk bends and leans parallel to the ground, just a few feet above, and its branches writhe outward and upward like the arms of a tortured torso. There are leaves. It is alive, but grotesquely so, as if cancered, not to death but to mutation. Trees have always been the scenes of great human tragedy, great human sin: the cross, the gallows, the guillotine, the burning stake, the Inquisition rack, and the mast of the *Santa María*. So is this tree, surrounded by an ancient sea chain a few hundred yards inland from the river shore in La Antigua, a few kilometers north of Veracruz. This is the tree, according to local tradition, to which Cortés chained his ships when he entered this river in 1519. It has survived hurricanes, fire, the receding of the river shore, and five centuries of human turmoil. Nourished by the Mexican earth, which nonetheless seems to poison it with protest, it is a tree like no other on this continent.

At the ruins of Cortés's house, a little farther up the dusty road, there is a similar tableau. Fig trees and ceibas twist and wend their way up the broken walls of the old hacienda, their extended roots like long, hoary fingers that seem to be all that holds many of the stones in place. They grow deformed and contorted until their tops break free of the shade around the house into the sunlight high above. Lourdes sees nature reclaiming what has been taken. Some might see a motif of heroic enchantment. Again I see the earth itself in protest.

Next to the house of Cortés lives an ancient man who putters with his fishing nets on the dirt floor of his stone-walled back porch. "I am the inheritor," he says. He has been the house's only caretaker for forty years. The property was once owned by some Spanish families who never knew quite what to do with it, and when the government took it over as part of a program for nationalizing historical assets, it promised to retain don Juan on the recommendation of the previous owners. "But they have never paid me, and as you can see, they have done nothing with it. And then they said I was too old," he shrugs. He supports himself as a fisherman and as a member of a productive *ejido* (community farm). Meanwhile he has continued to clean up the site and to replace the fallen stones without pay. "Someone has to take care of it," he says. "It is the past."

Don Juan wants us to sample a drink he makes from the figs of the trees and another plant, the *zapote*. "I peel the *zapote* and cut the centers with the resin into little pieces," he says. "I mix these with the figs from up high where they feed the little birds and add some mescal. Then I let it ferment for over a year."

He pours me a glass of the yellow fluid. I drink. It is strong, sweet, and heady—a communion with the spirits of these trees and this earth. Now the words of a poem carved into a sign in front of the house seem more laden with meaning.

> *Antigua—sleeping beauty,*
> *Without laurels of victory,*

Apocalypse

Only the pitiless tyrant
Will erase you from his mind—
But never from history.

And that's all there is to mark the site. In all of Mexico there are only two monuments to Cortés, one in a hospital he founded and capitalized in Mexico City and another in his old fiefdom at Cuernavaca. There is little ambivalence in Mexico about this man who conquered and changed forever the civilization that once existed here. He cannot be honored; he cannot be memorialized. The negative revisionist history that is currently politically correct in the United States regarding the Columbian and Cortesian escapades is here a matter of long-established feeling. What began in La Antigua is widely regarded as a great historical rape.

La Antigua is a quiet town despite the occasional busloads of tourists who come through. The bell still tolls for mass at the continent's oldest chapel, a tiny stucco structure whose only adornments are the stations of the cross, pictured on blue tiles embedded in the interior walls. Burros nod in the shade of the stony avenues, good cooks serve spicy fresh shrimp and mussels at open-air cafés like Doña Carmona's, and fishermen mending their nets by the river will argue among themselves, when asked, about the exact location where Cortés burned his ships in a spectacular gesture of commitment to success or death. Children too young for school climb on the old tree as if it were a jungle gym. Today La Antigua sleeps, but here began a story like no other in human history.

When the English-speaking colonists came to the northern part of the continent, they sought land. The Indians were on it, so they had to be removed or killed, pure and simple. Cortés and the Spaniards came with radically different motivations. Materially they wanted precious metal, and far from being an obstacle, the Indians they encountered could help them get it. Spiritually they wanted to expand the Catholic realm of saved souls. This colonization of the newly discovered world was to be the last Crusade at a time when Spaniards everywhere celebrated the lesson of their recent victory over the infidel Moors at Granada. Through strength of arms and Catholic faith, they had become at last the masters of their own house with designs for mastery of the world. It was the era of the militant Inquisition, when Spaniards felt their hearts charged by God to expand His spiritual domain while their hands gathered the material rewards in gold and silver.

The men who came to seek fame, fortune, and vindication of their faith in the Caribbean were daring, vainglorious, and so religious that they would not fornicate with native women until their partners had been baptized. They brought to the New World a mind for legal process and order that many of the Indian tribes, so used to arbitrary despotism under the Aztecs, found very attractive. They had no instinct for racial annihilation of their enemies—even the Moors and Jews had been encouraged to convert and live on in Spain. The Spaniards conquered not to eradicate but to win hearts and minds—and treasure.

But make no mistake, the conquistadores were absolutely ruthless in their pursuit of conquest and wealth. After seven centuries of struggle against the Moors, they were masters of land battlefield tactics and not squeamish about slaughter or devastation. Despite the royal prohibition against slavery, they quickly exhausted the labor supply among the weak Indian tribes of the Caribbean islands, through their *encomienda* system, whereby Indians were cared for and educated in the ways of Christianity in return for their labor. The Spaniards of the colonizing era were also obstreperously individualistic. Unlike the English, who could assert the primacy of individual rights while remaining subservient to class structure and the rules of politics, the Spaniard typically resented subservience to anyone. He passionately needed to assert himself. Latin Americans will contend today that this heritage is one reason for the often chaotic conduct of entrepreneurial and governmental affairs in their part of the world.

It was these two factors, the declining labor force of the colonized Caribbean islands and the cantankerous instinct to make one's own mark, that set Hernán Cortés on his journey of conquest in February 1519. Two expeditions had sailed westward from Cuba in the previous two years with the express purpose of finding new sources of labor and souls to convert. Instead they brought back Moctezuma's gold and silver. Spanish adventurers jockeyed for position to lead the third and perhaps decisive expedition to the newly discovered western land mass. Even after Cortés had been assigned the task, the governor of Cuba, Diego de Velázquez de Cuéllar, revoked his decision and sent troops to stop Cortés as he and his little squadron of eleven ships set sail. Throughout his campaign in Mexico, Cortés endured the fierce enmity of key factions in the islands and back in Spain.

With five hundred soldiers (swordsmen, lancers, and harquebusiers), seventeen horses, and ten small cannons, Cortés landed first on the island of Cozumel, where he encountered mild, timid Indians, like those in the Caribbean islands. To his troops he laid down three commandments that he enforced throughout the campaign: no wanton killing beyond the requirements of his strategy of conquest, no pillage, no rapes. If such a small force was to succeed in conquering a large land mass of who knew how many millions of Indians, the inhabitants must be pacified, Christianized, and induced to willingly accept Spanish rule.

It was on Cozumel that the first of a series of strangely fortuitous incidents occurred. If he was to win over these Indians with means other than massive force, he would have to be able to talk to them, but he had only one Mayan boy—originally brought back to Cuba by one of his predecessors—to act as translator. And this boy had learned only rudimentary Spanish. Cortés made inquiries through him about white men who had been lost here during the previous expeditions, but to no avail. However, after leaving Cozumel to sail farther up the Yucatán coast, one of Cortés's ships sprang a leak and he had to return briefly to Cozumel to repair it. Just as the squadron was about to depart Cozumel the second time, a canoe was seen heading out from the shore. The man paddling it was Jerónimo de Aguilar, a Spanish priest who had survived a Caribbean shipwreck and washed up on this coast, where he lived as a slave with the Yucatán Indians. He was fluent in Chontal Mayan.

In March, Cortés sailed around the Yucatán Peninsula to Tabasco, where he landed and encountered fierce warriors who had harassed one of the earlier expeditions. The Tabascans were again spoiling for a fight, and so Cortés dutifully observed one of the legal niceties of Spanish conquest, the *requerimiento*. Through Aguilar, who had to shout above the din of the excited warriors, Cortés delivered a legalistic message advising his adversaries that the pope had granted these lands to the Spanish crown, that they must now submit themselves to Christ and king, and that, failing to do so, they would be responsible for any hostilities and calamities that would befall them. Then the battle began and lasted several days.

Quickly the superiority of Spanish weaponry and tactics proved itself. Besides their disadvantage in armaments, the Indians fought as a disorganized crowd, and the disciplined Spaniards mowed them down with a kill ratio of four hundred Tabascans to each dead Spaniard. The Tabascans brought gifts to sue for peace. Among these gifts were young, attractive slave girls, one of whom particularly caught Cortés's eye. Her name was Malinche, and she came to be known, depending on one's viewpoint, as either the mother of Mexico—or the devil's very mistress.

As Cortés sailed farther west along the coast, he encountered Indians of different tribes whose language Aguilar could not comprehend. Anchored near the island of San Juan de Ulúa, at the mouth of today's Veracruz harbor, Cortés entertained a delegation of Indians who appeared eager to communicate but whose language no one could understand—until Cortés noticed Malinche conversing casually with some of them. Having once lived in these lands, Malinche spoke Nahuatl, the language of the entire Aztec empire, as well as the Mayan Aguilar knew. It was Cortés's second stroke of divine luck. For the remainder of the conquest, Cortés communicated with the Aztecs through the language chain of Aguilar-Malinche. Malinche eventually was Christianized, became Cortés's lover, accompanied him throughout the campaign, and bore him a son. In a sense, she became the womb of the eventual mestizo Mexican nation, and if that nation is to be seen as the product of a historical rape, then she is also the traitor aiding those who would ravish them.

It was during this stop at San Juan de Ulúa (near today's Veracruz) that a local chieftain spoke of a great emperor in the mountains named Moctezuma. Cortés cannily responded that his king knew all about the great king of Mexico and expected Cortés to present himself before him. He impressed his visitors with a display of horses and cannon firepower and then posed for drawings to be made by Indian artists. When reports of this foreigner reached Moctezuma, he responded with a shipment of gifts, including, of course, gold. Attached to the giving of these treasures, in time-honored Indian custom, was a wish—that the strangers relinquish their desire to meet with him and go away in peace.

Writers of the history are at odds over the question of to what extent Moctezuma was moved by fear that Cortés was Quetzalcóatl or his descendants returned. For centuries after the conquest it was Spanish dogma that a prophecy about Quetzalcóatl's return was paramount in explaining Moctezuma's timidity toward this tiny force he could so easily have snuffed out with his vastly superior numbers. The theory has been challenged by recent historians. They argue that the gifts-cum-wish are evidence that Moctezuma thought he was dealing with a typical embassy of a foreign tribe far below the status of deity and that the legend of Cortés as Quetzalcóatl was merely the propaganda of the colonial world, since native versions of the Quetzalcóatl story do not always include a prophetic return.

What appears to have happened during Spanish revisions of Aztec history was a confusion of a prophecy, a myth, and a fantasy imagined by Moctezuma himself. There was a well-established prophecy of an apocalypse. There was an unrelated myth of the departed god-king Quetzalcóatl, though not necessarily any foretelling of his return. Moctezuma was well aware of both stories and was particularly disturbed by the prophecy of doom. A troublesome cult of Quetzalcóatl in Cholula had been agitating against the demands for human sacrifice as part of the state worship of Huitzilopochtli at the time of Cortés's arrival. Cortés came from the direction toward which Quetzalcóatl had sailed. Thus Moctezuma didn't need a specific prophecy about the reappearance of Quetzalcóatl to arrive at the fearful conclusion that Quetzalcóatl, or his descendants, had returned to reclaim their lands. The myth the colonial Spanish perpetuated was probably a product of Moctezuma's own mind.

Regardless, it is difficult to see Moctezuma acting out of anything but fear and trepidation of the fulfillment of an apocalyptic prophecy and his own nightmare that Quetzalcóatl would be its agent. Though they were passed to us through scribes of Spanish conquest, the only records we have of Moctezuma's own words would seem to put the argument to rest.

With treasure in hand now, some of Cortés's troops wanted to leave the sultry, mosquito-ridden coast and return to Cuba. Cortés would have none of this and sailed on a few miles farther up the barren beach where a small but deep river offered a semblance of a harbor. Here he unloaded all of his supplies and chartered a town and a colony in the king's name. He built a church and a house and a fort in the town and hunkered down to devise strategy for conquest. The town was named la Villa Rica de la Vera Cruz. But as the burgeoning city named Veracruz grew up adjacent to San Juan de Ulúa, little Villa Rica has come to be known simply as La Antigua—the old one.

It's a hot Sunday night in Veracruz, a notoriously slow evening in most Mexican cities, but the *zócalo* is thronged with people dressed for a night out. Every Mexican town, big city, or small village has its *zócalo*. This is the central plaza or park, usually located in front of the regional cathedral or the largest local church, and it is the focal point of social, civil life for all Mexican places. A hugely amplified version of the traditional, imperiled, and now reviving Main Street, USA, it is, in a Western context, what Ray Oldenburg would call "the third place," after the first—home—and the second—work. In a Mexican context it may be the first place. Mexicans certainly have a stronger connection to their *zócalo* than they do to their place of work. And the *zócalo* may not be an alternative to but rather an extension of the home.

It is the place to which people gravitate for public, outdoor living, such an essential part of the Mexican lifestyle. People gather here at all hours; this is where you go when you have time on your hands and when you want to exercise the natural instinct of a social animal. The restaurants, cafés, and shops bordering the *zócalo* occupy the most important real estate in the whole municipal area. There is life on the *zócalo* most nights until well after eleven, and on Fridays and Saturdays, the place bubbles with congenial ferment till the wee hours. Only on Sunday evenings does the *zócalo* in most places empty out, as people retreat to their homes for dinner with their families.

But not tonight in Veracruz. We watch from the sidewalk café of the Hotel Imperial, where particularly aggressive child vendors bother us with everything from Chiclets to cheap watches, as couples out in the plaza dance traditional Spanish steps before a live band. To my un-Latin eye, they seem at first to lack spirit, they move so formally and stiffly. But further watching convinces me that the dance is an expression of grace and dignity. Though the scene contains several generations, it is dominated by the oldest, at least one member of most of the couples appearing to be over sixty years of age.

As we travel further in Mexico, we will learn that Veracruz is different from most Mexican cities; it is more Spanish. You see more people here with light-colored skin (though paradoxically, Veracruz is home to one of Mexico's largest concentrations of African blacks), and the Spanish influence is more evident in people's clothing than is the indigenous aesthetic seen elsewhere. The port city's centuries-old role as the nation's link to Spain has left its mark, even after independence and revolution.

In the morning we visit the island of San Juan de Ulúa, where Cortés first landed just outside Veracruz harbor. There is not a tree in sight today. Besides acres and acres of gritty port facilities and trucking depots, there is nothing on this island but the Spanish fortress that guarded the gateway to Mexico for four centuries.

The fortress is built of coral and stone block with none of the whimsically creative adornments characteristic of Mexico's pre-Cortesian ruins. Except for their churches, what the Spanish built in Mexico was no-nonsense, utilitarian. Still, internal moats, arched passageways, and sequestered courtyards do lend the place a romantic quality, enough that the producers of the film *Romancing the Stone* chose this as a site for their work. Our very articulate guide hastens to disabuse us of any such notions. "It is a monument to human misery," he says. "Through these portals passed six hundred thousand slaves who were eventually worked to death. The Spanish thought the local people here didn't work hard enough, so they imported Africans."

He shows us three dungeons, traditionally called "Purgatory," "Heaven," and "Hell," that were reserved for political prisoners. But for a tiny slit in the back stone wall of each, there is no light.

Stalactites hang from the ceilings. Prisoners who would otherwise have been killed but whose live bodies somebody thought might come in handy someday, lived here in their own excrement on a rough stone floor. They were fed on garbage thrown in daily, and guards came in to remove the dead once a month. The horrors of the place were so legendary that one of Venustiano Carranza's first acts on assuming power during the revolution in 1915 was to declare that no prisoners would be held here again for one hundred years. "That means we're safe from this place until 2015," says our guide.

Just a few feet away from the dungeons is a prayer house where knelt the men who came to this land to claim it in the name of God. Emperor Maximilian and Empress Carlota lived nearby in the royal splendor of the main palace. The rest of the fort is devoted, aside from defense, to storage chambers for the riches taken from Mexico for shipment back to Spain.

Afterward, we pause to chat with our guide. I ask him about the good and evil brought to Mexico by the Spaniards. "The good was horses, the wheel, the Spanish language, and, I suppose, since I have to agree with the majority of Mexicans, the Catholic church," he says. "Also our names," he adds as an afterthought. "The bad was smallpox, rats, syphilis [actually syphilis might have been a gift transmitted the other way], slavery that still exists in certain forms, and racism. We are all colored darker or lighter and it matters too much."

When I mention that there are only two monuments to Cortés in all of Mexico, he says quickly, "We have to destroy them. He destroyed our culture. Except for the very wealthy whites, we all trace our lineage to the Indian, not to Spain. Maybe Cortés wasn't really such a villain as some would say, but he is certainly no hero worthy of a monument."

There are other parts of the world that benefited greatly from the campaigns of Cortés, he believes. "Twenty billion pesos of treasure were taken out of this country. The strength of the British pound traces directly to the riches that country received through piracy of Spanish galleons, our Mexican treasure twice stolen."

I suggest that the original Mexicans were fortunate to have gotten the Spanish rather than the British. Here the newcomers married and mingled with the native people; in my country the natives became victims of genocide, and those who survived were put on reservations.

He demurs, "Who knows? Is it sadder to die as a pure indigenous person or to live all mixed up? Imagine what it is to know that all the Spaniard had to do was to arrive here and he was given a chunk of our land and two hundred of our people to work in a disguised form of slave labor, and to know that what you are is the product of that crime. The Mexican today doesn't really think well of the true indigenous or the Spaniard. He is still searching for his true self, and he knows he is neither of them. What happened five hundred years ago shouldn't affect us but it does. Maybe rape is worse than genocide."

Perhaps the Spanish conquest eventually came to resemble a rape, but at the time of Cortés's arrival, many of the tribes under Aztec domination were more concerned about the cruel tribute demanded of them by the Aztecs, in particular the unrelenting call for young men and women to be sacrificed to Huitzilopochtli. Cortés encountered one such tribe, the Totonacs, a few miles north of Villa Rica at Zempoala. When the chief invited him to enter their town, Cortés responded with caution and military preparedness, recalling his experience with the Tabascans. But he was greeted courteously and told the story of how the Totonacs had only recently succumbed to the Aztec armies after generations of resistance. They wondered, having heard of Cortés's success against the fierce Tabascans, if he might not be able to help relieve them of the tyranny. It was Cortés's first intimation that there were intertribal animosities in the Indian world. These he could exploit, and now he would have allies.

While Cortés was staying with the Totonacs, a tax-collecting delegation arrived from Moctezuma announcing that the Totonacs owed twenty additional victims for sacrifice as punishment for their dalliance with the Spaniards. The Totonacs turned to Cortés, who advised them to imprison the Aztec nobles and inform them that there would be no further tribute paid. The Totonacs were aghast, but under Cortés's firm prodding did as he asked, and by their insult to Moctezuma's embassy, guaranteed their allegiance to Cortés's cause.

Maneuvering further that night, Cortés went secretly to the Aztec nobles and told them his actions had been taken to spare them certain death at the hands of the angry Totonacs. Repeating his pledge that he wanted only friendship with Moctezuma and looked forward to the day when they might meet, he released the nobles and provided Spanish guards to escort them safely out of Totonac country.

When the tax collectors reported back to Tenochtitlán, Moctezuma's priests were agitated over the possibility that these haughty, seemingly invincible strangers might indeed be Quetzalcóatl or his minions. In response, Moctezuma sent a new delegation to Cortés with more treasure and the most unequivocal of peace messages yet. For the first time the messengers broached to Cortés the possibility that he might be a descendant of Quetzalcóatl, saying that since Moctezuma himself traced his lineage to Quetzalcóatl through the mythical ancestry of the Toltecs, he and Cortés could be kin. Blinded by his Christian insensitivity to the religious mythology of other peoples, Cortés missed the point entirely but still was able to benefit from it. He reciprocated with gifts from Spain and restated his intention to come to Tenochtitlán to meet with Moctezuma. The Totonacs were impressed by this gesture of mild diplomacy from Moctezuma. Never had anyone who had misused his agents been spared from quick and devastating punishment. The Aztecs, for their part, took Cortés's dismissal of the Quetzalcóatl peace feeler as a sign of divine inscrutability. What the Aztecs could not comprehend was assumed to be something from beyond the mortal.

Throughout these first months in Mexico, Cortés and his conquistadores were appalled by the Indian ritual of human sacrifice. It wasn't just the Aztecs who did it. Again and again, Cortés would stumble into a smoky temple whose walls and floors stank with the congealed mess of human blood. While certainly not squeamish about bloodshed on the battlefield, Cortés was so sickened by these displays that he ignored the coolheaded go-slow advice of his priests and attempted to force instant conversions of whole tribes to Christianity. His efforts met with mixed results; the Indians were befuddled by the images of cross and mother with child that these strangers so revered. But Cortés was also moved by the Spanish belief, forged in the wars with the Moors, that conversion was the surest way to the success of conquest. And without knowing it, he was enlisting the aid of myth. The Indians all knew that Quetzalcóatl was thought to be an adversary of human sacrifice.

In Cortés's own camp there was dissension at this point, many of his men urging him to take the treasure gained thus far and return to Cuba. Some were outright supporters of Cortés's nemesis, Governor Velázquez. Retreating to Cuba might have seemed sensible, clear as it was that despite Moctezuma's mild handling of the conquistadores so far, the small force of Spaniards, even with the alliance of the Totonacs, would be overwhelmingly outnumbered in any attempt to conquer Tenochtitlán by military force. A larger force could be mounted from Cuba for the next offensive.

But Cortés knew the intrigues that awaited him in Cuba and he was rabid to enter Tenochtitlán as the sole conqueror of all of Mexico. He believed the alliance with the Totonacs was just the beginning. So he hit upon a desperate strategy to marry his men's fortunes to his own. After stripping the ships of their hardware, he sent his most loyal men to scuttle them in the river at Villa Rica. Now, cut off from the world they knew and marooned on this alien shore, it could be only total success or death for all of the conquistadores.

In August of 1519 Cortés began to move. Word of Cortés's open challenge to the Aztec nobles had spread throughout the eastern tribes, and the Totonacs informed him of another tribe, the Tlaxcalans, who had so far held off the Aztec armies for generations and surely could be counted on as valuable allies. Spurred by this advice, Cortés marched inland toward the Tlaxcalan kingdom. The spirits of his men revived with the activity and with the higher, drier inland altitude. But the fiercely independent Tlaxcalans distrusted the Totonacs, still considering them to be allies of the Aztecs. Aware of the gifts Moctezuma had sent Cortés, they refused him entrance into their kingdom and would not talk of forging an alliance.

Thus ensued the nastiest fight Cortés had yet encountered. The Tlaxcalans seemed unfazed by the conquistadores' strange weapons and cavalry. They fought with a frenzy and were the first Indians to succeed in killing some of Cortés's horses. For nearly a week the battles raged, some of which were clearly won by the Tlaxcalans and severely mauled Cortés's troops. But they were taking an even greater toll on the Tlaxcalans, who, in one last desperate attempt to dislodge the Spaniards, attempted something the Indians had never done in all their years of warfare—a night attack. If the Spaniards were a little more than mortal, they reasoned, they would not have the same strength without the presence of the sun. Unlike the Indians, the Spaniards were accustomed to night fighting, and the final battle became a chaotic melee that convinced the Tlaxcalans finally that they could not defeat these strangers. In the morning their envoys brought food to sue for peace.

Now an embassy arrived in Cortés's camp with more gifts and a new proposal from Moctezuma. If Cortés and his men would leave Mexico, Moctezuma would agree to become a vassal of the king of Spain and regularly deliver such tribute to the coast as Cortés determined. Modern historians debate what was on Moctezuma's mind now that the conquistadores had penetrated inland and defeated the great Tlaxcalan army. Some argue that he was just as devious as Cortés, escalating his offers of accommodation while luring Cortés deeper into the hinterlands, where superior numbers could overwhelm him. No doubt this was a part of his strategy, but the further conclusion that Moctezuma sat through all of this with unshaken confidence is simply not borne out by his subsequent behavior.

Though still wary of the Tlaxcalans after his hard handling by them, Cortés declined the Aztecs' offer of alliance and accepted the Tlaxcalans' proposal to meld forces with the Totonacs to break the grip of the Aztec empire. Now Cortés had the beginnings of a force to be reckoned with, if only he could trust the tribe that had come close to snuffing out his expedition.

When Moctezuma heard of Cortés's alliance with his longtime enemy, he was stirred to action. He sent an embassy inviting Cortés with elaborate courtesies and promises of good treatment to come farther inland to the city of Cholula, one of his vassals. The Tlaxcalans warned Cortés of Aztec and Cholulan duplicity, and no chief from Cholula would come to Cortés to confirm the invitation. But Cortés could not show fear to the Aztecs now; the time had come to advance the conquest, so he advanced cautiously on the city with a huge contingent of armed Tlaxcalans along with the loyal Totonacs.

As promised, the conquistadores were at first well received—until it became apparent that the city was being evacuated. One of the Cholulan women who had befriended Malinche warned her that the Aztecs had set a trap with thirty thousand soldiers encamped in hiding just outside the city. Moctezuma, however, had his own problems with his Cholulan allies, who feared that if the

Aztec army was allowed to enter Cholula to attack the Spaniards, they would never leave and Cholula would lose what little independence it had left. Instead the Cholulans informed Moctezuma that they would starve the Spaniards out of the city, and then the Aztecs could attend to them and their allies as they saw fit.

When Tlaxcalan spies informed him of this plan, Cortés chose to respond to the duplicity with calculated barbarity. Announcing to the Cholulan nobles that he was planning to leave the city, he mounted his troops and prepared as if to leave. But then, just as the Cholulans were crowding around, Cortés gave the order and his troops massacred them without warning. Hoping to instill in the Indian tribes a fear of the Spaniards equal to that they already felt toward the Aztecs, Cortés departed from his usual policy of holding back the fury of his Indian allies and allowed the Tlaxcalans to sack the city. In the aftermath he called for the Aztec nobles to come to him in secret and confided to them that he doubted the stories of the Tlaxcalans and the defeated Cholulans that Moctezuma had ordered the deceit. This time when the confused nobles reported to Moctezuma all that had transpired, he sent messengers back saying that he would be happy to personally meet Cortés whenever he chose to come to him. The way was now clear to Tenochtitlán, and Cortés had not had to fight a single battle against the masses of the Aztec army.

It's hot and humid in Veracruz. No breeze wafts from the doldrum waters of the Gulf out beyond San Juan de Ulúa; the air hangs still in the long listless afternoon. Siesta time runs a good three hours here, and the few people who are out in the streets show no sign of the stately energy we saw on the *zócalo* last night. Those vendors you can find at the market by the inner harbor don't even haggle—name your price and it's just *"sí"* or *"no."* Despite the growth of the city, its modern hotels, and its waterfront location, Veracruz is not much of a tourist destination. Malaria-bearing mosquitoes are still said to be a problem, and the usual precautions about drinking public water in Mexico are taken very seriously here. Veracruzanos encountering visiting Americans assume that you are either on business or lost. "Shouldn't you be out at Cancún?" they seem to say.

Small wonder that the Spaniards gave little thought to establishing their permanent capital at the coast and that a posting to Veracruz during the colonial era was regarded as an inconvenience to be renegotiated as soon as possible. Yet the port remains Mexico's shipping gateway to the world. During the daylight hours, the energy of the city is sweatily focused on getting the stuff of commerce to and from the ships. Slow-moving lines of trucks crawl out to the dusty docks at San Juan de Ulúa and back. Those who work in air-conditioned offices tally ledgers of goods and shipping insurance premiums.

The *zócalo* and the sidewalk cafés are sparsely peopled during the daylight hours. Not until the long evening shadows shade the streets do people begin to come out in the usual Mexican gregarious mode. And when they do, they love to just sit and talk.

El Café de la Parroquia is a social institution in Veracruz. Not much of interest is served from the menu; people come here to drink coffee and to talk. Agile waiters scurry about carrying two pots: one of high-test espresso and the other of hot milk. Clink your spoon against your glass and shortly an inch of the coffee is poured into the glass followed by a sloshing with the hot milk.

After an uninspiring dinner of turkey and gravy, we are intrigued by the intellectual talk of three men and a woman at the table next to us. Lourdes strikes up a conversation and we join them. One speaks clear English and it's a treat for me to talk in my own language with an articulate Mexican.

They have been discussing a book, *México profundo,* by Guillermo Bonfil Batalla, whose thesis is that there are two Mexicos in conflict, the formal Mexico and the deep Mexico. "That's why nothing in Mexico makes sense," says the English speaker, a journalist and visiting lecturer at the university named Pedro Miguel. "We've had presidents, Salinas was one, who would have made fine presidents of a country like Denmark, where there is a unity between the deep and the formal nation. Here, Salinas's formal math said that two plus two should equal four. But when he looks, there are seven. The other three are Indians and they don't count—they exist only in the deep Mexico."

For the remainder of the conversation, Pedro is the spokesman for the whole table, with nods all around to points he makes. He warns us to be skeptical toward some of the most vaunted writers about Mexico. "Fuentes is as overvalued as the peso," he says. "And Octavio Paz is a genius, but he hangs too much on analysis of Mexican language. Who says that if you are a genius with words that you should be an authority on a culture?"

I press him on what he means by "the formal Mexico." He explains that it is an artificial construct for dealing with a reality that you don't understand. It's what the Spanish and their like have had to do here since their arrival. While they themselves were individualistic, vainglorious, and personal; the Indians here were collective, intuitive, and universal. The Spanish couldn't deal with that, so they imposed this formal construct.

"Today the formal Mexico shows itself in things like our newspapers," Pedro, the journalist, goes on. "Nobody reads them and those who do don't believe them. They are all partisan, one way or another. We have elections. How many people have you met who will vote for the PRI?"

I surprise myself; none is the answer.

"Of course, but the PRI will win."

Religion is another example. "Catholicism looks like a big success here, but, and now I'm saying an atrocity, Mexico is not a Catholic country. What is our greatest Catholic shrine?"

"The Básilica de Guadalupe," I answer, referring to the shrine built on the site where a Mexican peasant witnessed an appearance of the Virgin Mary, confirmed and authenticated by Rome as Mexico's national Catholic miracle.

"The location was already the pre-Cortesian holy site of Tonatzín, where people went to have visions," Pedro says. "That's the way it is throughout Mexico. Underneath almost every Catholic church lies an Indian holy place. What is a holy place? A place where one speaks to the gods, whoever they may be."

Thus religion looks like one area where there is at least a superficial success in laying the formal Mexico over the spiritual infrastructure of the deep Mexico. But there are ways the two conflict.

"Despite Catholicism, we do not have the moral bigot here in Mexico," he says. "The Spanish knight was ruled by a strong moral imperative. Castro is perhaps the last example of the great Spanish moral bigots. Franco was one too, and despite the superficial differences in ideology, they had much in common. Their moral code was more important than other human needs and realities."

The Indians of Mexico, on the other hand, were ruled by their need for harmony with the natural elements. So concerning human relations, they were much more tolerant. "It's not that we are immoral," Pedro argues. "We are simply flexible where invisible human moral imperatives are concerned. Have you ever seen a case anywhere else in the world where a revolutionary group declares all-out war on the government, and the government responds with offers to meet to find peace?"

Mexican wars have never been like those in other parts of the world, he argues, pointing out that during the twenty years of the sometimes horrific Mexican Revolution, daily life in Mexico City was disturbed for only twelve days. "Compared to the total wars of Europe, our wars have never been serious. The deep Mexico knows that life goes on. We have had an apocalypse, but never a holocaust.

"And there has been only one Mexican war with true historical significance," he concludes. "Never mind the revolution, the American and French invasions, the war for independence. The only war here that ever mattered was the war with Cortés. And that one still goes on."

After Cholula, Cortés at last set out for Tenochtitlán. Accompanied by his Tlaxcalan allies and a delegation of Aztec nobles (the loyal Totonacs felt they had strayed too far from their home territory, and Cortés allowed them to return to the coast), his forces climbed into the mountains surrounding the Valley of Mexico. Passing over the shoulder of the seventeen-thousand-foot volcano, Popocatépetl, they marveled to see a plume of smoke from its top. It had just begun to erupt, thus fulfilling another of the ancient Aztec prophecies auguring the apocalypse.

The conquistadores had now traveled from the steamy tropical coast through the temperate seven-thousand-foot plateau of Tlaxcala and into high altitudes of snow and ice. For this they were unprepared and suffered terribly in their tropical clothing and metal armor. They crossed the high pass in a snowstorm, fearing an Aztec attack while they were frostbitten and vulnerable, but descended unmolested down the northern slope of the volcano. Now the snow ceased, the sky cleared, and the air warmed. Before them sprawled the sparkling waters of the lake system in the Valley of Mexico. The land surrounding the lakes was cultivated in geometric patterns and marked by glittering cities of painted stone, canals, and roadways. In the center of the tableau rose Tenochtitlán, an island of towering pyramids, ritual plazas, and vast marketplaces in the waters of Lake Texcoco. Awestruck by the scene, some of the Spaniards wavered and asked Cortés to turn back; they quaked at the thought of participating in an assault on what looked like heaven itself.

Again Cortés's instincts had foiled one of Moctezuma's timid stratagems to defeat him. The Aztecs had laid another trap for the Spaniards in the easier route around the mountain that Cortés had chosen not to take. Now the strangers had arrived on the very shore of the lake system, so Moctezuma reverted to accommodation, putting a magnificent country house surrounded by gardens at Cortés's disposal. Here the invaders would relax, perhaps lowering their guard, while Moctezuma sent another delegation with an even more specific proposal of wealth for Cortés personally, and tribute to the king of Spain if the strangers would only go away. When Cortés made his usual response, Moctezuma sent his brother and nephew to escort the Spaniards right into Tenochtitlán.

By now Moctezuma had abandoned all thought of opposing Cortés's entry into his capital. Perhaps he reasoned that here the conquistadores would be most at his mercy. Perhaps he had no choice, feeling that all opportunity to challenge Cortés on a battlefield beyond the city had passed. Or maybe he was paralyzed with fascination and awe at the historical events unfolding before him.

Cortés, for his part, was suddenly swept up by developments beyond his control as well. With a deliriously welcoming Aztec public watching, he had to enter the city over one of the narrow causeways that connected it to the mainland. No fear could be shown now, and so his 750 Spaniards, followed by a few thousand Tlaxcalans, advanced, in dangerous single file over the causeway into the city of a quarter million. It was November 8, 1519.

A fabulously dressed entourage lined the boulevard for Cortés's arrival in Tenochtitlán. And then, after an interminable ritual of greetings from Aztec nobles, suddenly there was Moctezuma himself. As he approached wearing sandals of gold, his subjects all averted their glance. It was sacrilege to look the monarch in the face. When Moctezuma identified himself, Cortés attempted to enfold him in the traditional Spanish *ambrazo* but was firmly restrained by the monarch's brother and nephew. After an exchange of necklaces, Moctezuma welcomed Cortés as his "returning lord," citing the lineage of kings linking him to the era of the Toltecs and Quetzalcóatl. He confessed that he had been "troubled for a long time" and had "gazed into the unknown from whence you came—the place of mystery." Now, he said, "it is fulfilled, you have returned, suffered fatigue, and spent yourself." He ended by inviting Cortés and his men to rest in the palace of his father before joining him in a banquet.

As Cortés rested, the Tlaxcalans, now well trained in setting up Spanish defensive positions, turned the palace of Moctezuma's father into a fortress. When Moctezuma returned, he made a more detailed speech in which he excused his initial opposition to the Spaniards' approach on the grounds that it disturbed his people. After relating the Aztec mythology of his people's origin and how they came to dominate Mexico, he went on to explain his belief that Cortés was indeed Quetzalcóatl's descendant returned to take the Aztecs as his vassal. He promised fealty to the lord he had so long expected but ended with a gesture that has set the historians buzzing with controversy ever since. Moctezuma lifted his robes and declared that he was not a god himself but mere flesh and blood *as, he knew, was Cortés.* Further, he added, he understood that the horses and cannons were only mortal animals and advanced extensions of devices with which he was familiar.

On this declaration some historians rest their case that Moctezuma's allusions to Quetzalcóatl were merely part of his campaign of guile against Cortés. It seems more likely that Moctezuma was pursuing a dual strategy, one defensive, offering appeasement to cover his personal fear that Cortés was Quetzalcóatl's descendant, and the other a disguised offense in case Cortés turned out to be a mere mortal, and thus defeatable, enemy. Whatever the case, it was an aggressive move by Moctezuma that provided Cortés with the key to the next doorway to conquest.

Back on the coast, chieftains acting under Moctezuma's orders incited an uprising against the Spaniards at Villa Rica and succeeded in killing nine of them. Moctezuma denied responsibility. Under this pretext, Cortés demanded that Moctezuma reside with the Spaniards in his father's palace, in effect holding him hostage until the matter could be resolved. Moctezuma would continue to administer his empire and conduct his royal affairs but under the watchful eye of the Spaniards. It was Cortés's boldest and most desperate act yet. Amazingly, Moctezuma complied.

For five months, Cortés remained in Tenochtitlán under this arrangement, during which time Moctezuma became quite friendly with the Spaniards. Meanwhile his noblemen came and went, their smiles slowly turning to grim frowns. Cortés sent for the chieftain who had conducted the raid against the Spaniards on the coast and ordered him burned at the stake. The disruption of Aztec order soon became intolerable to the Aztec leadership outside of Cortés's compound. Finally Moctezuma had to inform Cortés that the Spaniards must leave. If Moctezuma were now to return to his people, they would demand that he lead them to kill the intruders. If he stayed where he was, other leaders would emerge charged to do the same thing.

To make matters worse, it was at this key moment that Cortés received messages from the coast announcing that a force dispatched by his enemy, Governor Velázquez, had arrived at Veracruz to take the expedition out of Cortés's hands. In this critical situation, Cortés left a small contingent to hold the palace and Moctezuma at Tenochtitlán while he departed with his main force for the coast. He sent ahead secret emissaries bearing gifts of gold with which to bribe the soldiers in Velázquez's force. Arriving during a murky, rainy night, he surprised the new Spaniards and after a sharp fight took control of the situation. Most of the newcomers joined Cortés for his return to Tenochtitlán. Now he had more than a thousand disciplined Spaniards with which to continue the conquest.

But back at Tenochtitlán things were going badly. With Cortés gone, Moctezuma retired to his chambers and refused to speak to the officers Cortés left in charge. The Aztecs knew of the infighting that Cortés faced on the coast and determined to use this opportunity to rid themselves of the strangers in their midst. Conveniently, a major festival was imminent, and they decided to celebrate it by sacrificing all of the Spaniards Cortés had left behind. But the ever trusty Tlaxcalan spies informed the garrison of the Aztecs' intent and so Pedro Alvarado, the officer Cortés had left in charge, mimicked the tactics of his commander back at Cholula. On the day of the festival, nearly all of the Aztec nobility were invited to celebrate within the Spaniards' compound. Expecting this to be a big dance in anticipation of their hosts' sacrifice, they complied, whereupon Alvarado had the gates closed, and his troops massacred them. Then all hell broke loose.

The people of the city rose up and stormed the compound, setting fire to its ramparts and assaulting the Spanish formations in the face of cannonry and musketry. Alvarado and his small contingent hung on fiercely, and it was only the arriving news of Cortés's success on the coast that finally quieted the situation into a sullen standoff. During this pause Cortés returned to Tenochtitlán with his newly expanded force. But once he was back in the Spaniards' compound, the Aztecs resumed their attack, now led by Moctezuma's brother Cuitlahuac. This time the offensive was coordinated with Aztec troops from throughout the empire. Hordes of warriors, advancing in rank upon rank, assaulted the gates and walls of the compound from all directions. The Spaniards mowed them down with their cannons and harquebusiers, and periodically the cavalry would move out through a breached gate and annihilate an Aztec formation in a frenzy of spearing and sword thrusts. But still the Aztecs came on. In desperation, Cortés led Moctezuma up to the rooftop, protected by Spanish shields so that when suddenly revealed, he might command his people to cease their attack. But when the shields were removed, the enraged Aztecs stoned their own emperor and he fell, mortally wounded.

Refusing attention to his wounds, Moctezuma languished for

several days while the fight raged on outside the compound. He died, broken and pitiful. Respectful Spaniards returned his body to his people, and the fight continued.

Cortés could not take long to mourn the death of his companion in history. Short on food and water, he decided to attempt to escape from Tenochtitlán and return to Tlaxcala. In the fog of a July night, his treasure-laden troops filed out through the streets and headed for the causeway. It was not long before the Aztecs discovered their movements, and before the Spaniards had crossed the first of eight gaps where the bridges had been taken away, the massacre began. This time it was the Spaniards who fought at a disadvantage, strung out over the narrow defile and foolishly clinging to their chests of treasure while the Aztecs attacked in their canoes and on foot from both ends of the causeway, killing the horses and taking Spaniards who survived the onslaught as prisoners for sacrifice. When the mauled remnants of Cortés's once invincible force stumbled into the square of a mainland town in the morning, nine hundred of his soldiers had been lost along with most of the horses, cannons, and the damnable treasure. Only four hundred men, mostly wounded, and two dozen horses remained. This was the *Noche Triste*, the Sorrowful Night, remembered still today by those in Mexico who are proud of their light skin and their predominantly Spanish blood.

Aztec armies continued to ravage Cortés's remaining troops and his Indian allies as they got lost in the mountains and groped their way back to Tlaxcala. His skull fractured, two of his fingers crushed, and his body covered with lacerations, Cortés had no choice but to hope that somehow the alliance with Tlaxcala would hold and his survivors could rest and heal in their care. As his mangled force entered the Tlaxcalan kingdom, the Aztec attacks ceased. But crowds of Tlaxcalans came out of their dwellings to stare, stony faced, at the limping vestiges of the force they had counted on to liberate them from Aztec tyranny.

• • •

The train station in Veracruz is a magnificent vaulted stucco building built like a great portal between the streets of this port city and the tracks that connect to the rich Mexican interior. It is a place where the traveler passes from one reality to another; and when we arrive close to midnight and see several trains in position by the platforms with agents and signs directing us to the train to Mexico City, my hopes rise that this train might be different, with lounge and dining cars. Following the route of Cortés to Tenochtitlán eating and drinking with the people who are the product of his adventure—that's what I came here for.

We find our train and there are no dining or lounge cars. And the back platform of our sleeper car is webbed with jury-rigged wiring; someone forgot to bring the kerosene for the running lights. "Be careful what you touch back here," advises the porter as we clamber on board. Our rooms are clean and the beds properly made, but when I flush my toilet, it floods all over the floor. "Your wish is our command," says the porter as he bends down to clean up the mess while I sip tequila in Lourdes's room. Soon the train pulls out and when I explore it seems everybody on the train has gone to sleep—no one to talk to. Lourdes admonishes me, "How many times have I told not to enter into situations with preconceptions when you're in Latin America?" And then she too is gone off to bed.

Something is wrong with either the engineer or the brakes on this train. It makes a repetitive halting motion, like a bad driver alternately pressing on the accelerator and the brake. I can't sleep, so I wander back to the wire-tangled rear platform where a three-quarter moon lights mountains I imagine Cortés passing five centuries ago. But quickly the natural scenery gives way to more prosaic surroundings.

At 12:15 we pass a series of factories lit with winking electric blue lights and pull in to Potrero. The air is heavy with a pungent industrial smell, like that produced by a pulp mill. After the stop we pass through a grubby little rail yard with piles of garbage and rail cars reeking of something agriculturally odoriferous, perhaps fertilizer or silage. The railroad right-of-way along the tracks beyond the yard is crammed with the squalid shacks of squatters.

At Pazuela, 12:45, instead of visions of Cortés's train and its packhorses, I see rows and rows of trailer trucks lined up for transshipment of goods from the railroad to the highways. Again my fantasy of somehow revisiting Cortés's trek over this route gets dashed.

But then there is something. As I lean out the rear vestibule window, we roll slowly through a neighborhood of ramshackle houses where a number of people are still awake and standing in their doorways watching the train pass. Several times, as a dark face sees my white face on the train, there is a clear startle, a reaction— sometimes followed by a big smile or wave and sometimes by an intense, inscrutable stare. I don't feel quite like one of Cortés's soldiers, but the sense of alien encounter is palpable.

At the city of Córdoba a little later, a large number of passengers board, including half a dozen who come on to our sleeping car. Again I meet shocks of surprised recognition and then big smiles and greetings as these fellow travelers climb past my station at the back platform. One of them, a middle-aged man, asks me in clear English, "Are you from the United States?"

"Yes," I say.

"Do you see how people react to you?"

Delighted that he has noticed the phenomenon, I ask him why. "The people who ride this train depend on its service; they care about it," he says. "They know that under the current politics its survival is endangered. You offer them hope."

Again I ask why.

"Nothing ever gets done in Mexico, nothing that involves a

change in direction, unless it is provoked by the interests of foreigners, especially Americans. You don't know what power you have. You may end up unintentionally repaying us for Texas yet."

In the morning, Guido, our porter, raps us awake with knocks on our doors and serves us the ubiquitous Mexican morning train coffee. Mexican morning train coffee, not to be confused with any kind of real coffee, consists, judging from taste, of dishwater run through yesterday's grounds and sweetened with piles of the unnecessary sugar Mexico buys from Cuba in a gesture of hemispheric solidarity. But it does contain real caffeine—a second cup and I am wired for the first half of the day.

Lourdes makes an offhand comment to Guido about this train following the route of Cortés, and he says, "Oh, no. This train doesn't go that route now. It isn't usable any longer, too dangerous. This way is a much safer." Lourdes doesn't even have to say it. "Never approach anything in Latin America with preconceptions." When we press Guido to tell us more, he retreats apologetically and sends the conductor back to talk to us. Has he told us something he shouldn't? It's a question that haunts Mexicans all the time.

The conductor, Arturo Stevenson, has no problem talking frankly to us. He comes to our doorways expecting formal tourist questions, and when Lourdes asks, "What do you think of Cortés?" he smiles, melts, and says, "He was a hero and a villain—both. But for me he is mainly a villain, and I'm not even one hundred percent Mexican."

Arturo's paternal grandfather Stevenson was a black man from Detroit, and though the rest of his roots are Mexican, Arturo grew up in the United States and became an American railroad man. Twenty years ago Mexico needed people who knew how to operate modern locomotives, so he came here simply looking for job advancement. "I became a Mexican rail pioneer," he says. "My roots before that don't count. What I am is about this moment. I am a Mexican who has a life and blood here."

But Arturo has a passion about the roots he claims do not matter. "We had a civilization here that rivaled Egypt, and that man Cortés came here with one thing—superiority of arms—and changed everything, nipping in the bud what might have been." He cites Cortés's own reported amazement at the level of civilization in Tenochtitlán—the place he finally decided he had to raze in the name of God.

It seems to take forever for the train that does not follow the route of Cortés to get to the station in Mexico City. Even here with modern spring-loaded concrete ties underneath and high-tech electric catenary overhead, the salient feature of Mexican railroading prevails—no electric switch control. Thus as the train approaches each of the many switches characteristic of any big-city yard, the crew must stop the train, take verbal instructions by radio, manually throw the switches, pull the train through the joint, then hop off and manually reset the switches before the train can proceed to the next junction. How Mexican: a place where the indigenous people invented the mathematical concept of zero centuries before the Caucasians from the east, but who never quite hit upon the usefulness of the wheel until those Caucasians arrived—intuitive brilliance alloyed with lapses of mechanical application.

The Tlaxcalan alliance did hold, cool heads in the kingdom determining that more Spaniards with superior armaments would keep coming from the east and eventually would be victorious despite the setback of the *Noche Triste*. They asked only that the Spaniards guarantee them a share of the spoils and exemption from tribute. For the most part, the treaty with the Tlaxcalans was honored throughout the era of Spanish rule in Mexico, and even today the state of Tlaxcala enjoys special privileges within the federal system somewhat like the situation of Quebec in Canada.

Meanwhile the hand of destiny that always seemed to favor Cortés continued its silent work in the Aztec world. As the Spaniards were healing in Tlaxcala, the Aztecs were smitten by a plague of smallpox brought to the New World by the conquistadores. Having no natural resistance to the disease, they died in droves. Those noblemen who had survived Alvarado's massacre in the Spanish compound were now wiped out. Their armies weakened and leadership decimated, the Aztecs anointed Cuauhtémoc emperor, and the war stirred back to life. Cuauhtémoc sent Aztec armies out to punish tribes that had helped Cortés. And then more ships arrived from Cuba with men and armaments that Cortés quickly melded into his recuperating force as he had done before.

Having seen the failure of Moctezuma's policy of appeasement and guile, Cuauhtémoc was determined that this time there were to be no rapprochements—there would not even be any talk. For the remainder of the campaign, he would stubbornly refuse to respond to Cortés's overtures. Now he declared all-out war in which the Aztecs' vast superiority of numbers would ultimately prevail. But his strategy was designed for a time and circumstance that no longer existed. Weakened by smallpox, opposed now by even more tribes furious at the punitive expeditions of his armies, and faced with a reinforced enemy who knew its way around the geography of Tenochtitlán, Cuauhtémoc did not have the advantages Moctezuma had had at his disposal.

For his part, Cortés also planned to do things differently, if he had to. Still he sent out his futile envoys of peace to Cuauhtémoc, but when they were rebuffed, he vowed that in this campaign there would be no foolish bravado, no waiting for fortuitous events, no marching over the causeways into the confines of an armed and dangerous Tenochtitlán. This would be a truly military campaign with a plan of total attack.

He had his shipwrights build fourteen small brigantines that would then be disassembled and carried to Lake Texcoco, where they would give him command of the waters around Tenochtitlán. In late December 1520, Cortés marched on Mexico with his force of six hundred Spaniards, his brigantines, his fresh horses and cannons, and twenty thousand Tlaxcalan warriors. When he arrived at Texcoco, he found the city deserted. His first task was to lure the peasantry back to feed his troops. Then he embarked on a series of reconnaissance missions in force around the lake, and by keeping his forces continuously on the move, prevented Cuauhtémoc from amassing enough of his superior numbers at any one point to bring about a decisive battle in his favor. Cortés thus picked off the jewels of the mainland, one by one, sometimes through guile and sometimes through battle.

Still Cuauhtémoc had enough warriors in an aroused Tenochtitlán that any outright assault over the causeways would be a disaster for the Spaniards. And Cortés honestly hoped he could find a way to subdue the city without having to destroy it. Then, like the Federation forces in the movie *Star Wars*, Cortés found one key vulnerability in the empire's bastion. Tenochtitlán was an island in the middle of a salt lake. For centuries its water supply had come mainly from an aqueduct running from the western hills of Chapultepec. After seizing nearby Tacuba, the third city of the Triple Alliance, Cortés had the aqueduct smashed. In the meantime, his brigantines had been reassembled and launched from the shore near Texcoco, and they sallied forth on the lake with cannons and musketry blasting at the Aztec canoe flotillas. Soon Cortés was master of the waters and held Tenochtitlán in a stranglehold—no water, no control over the lake, no way in or out. He settled down for a siege.

Cortés thus hoped to capture the capital without devastating it, but his messages to Cuauhtémoc were greeted with silence and increasingly desperate breakout attempts by the Aztecs as they came to realize the strategy the Spaniards had successfully implemented. One northern causeway was left deliberately open so that the Aztec leadership and army might flee the city, and the Spaniards could then occupy it unopposed. But as Cuauhtémoc's intransigence became clear and the causeway allowed a trickle of food and water to get into the city, Cortés finally had to occupy this last corridor of escape.

Now his strategy entered a new phase. First the brigantines would sail directly into the larger canals of Tenochtitlán, blasting away. Then Cortés's troops would attempt brief forays down the causeways and into the outskirts of the city, bringing the battle to the Aztecs' home ground and then retreating to their fortified mainland positions before the Aztecs could entrap them on the island. With each incursion, the Spaniards and their Tlaxcalan allies would penetrate deeper into the city before withdrawing, cunningly ravaging the city without killing it. But with each thrust, the temptation to take permanent possession of pieces of the city loomed larger. Eventually a spirit of competition gripped Cortés's three armies, and soon each strove to maintain its hold on its corner of the city. It was during one of these moments in late June 1521 that the Spaniards overextended themselves and allowed the Aztecs their last taste of victory.

As during the *Noche Triste*, the tactical issues the Spaniards faced were narrow streets, the causeway, and most important, the watery gaps that the Aztecs could open up by lifting the bridges. In its eagerness to seize and hold a quadrant of the city, Cortés's western force bridged the final water gap by making a flimsy bed of reeds on which to cross. When the Aztecs attacked them in the narrow streets just inside the city, their retreat turned into a rout when the reed mats gave way and left them floundering in the water. Cortés himself was captured for a moment when he brought his force to their aid and only narrowly escaped as the Aztecs beheaded luckless Spaniards and hurled the heads at the desperately retreating force. Upward of sixty Spaniards were killed or captured that day. Horses and cannons were lost, and hundreds, perhaps thousands, of Tlaxcalans were slaughtered.

In the aftermath, the Spaniards and the Tlaxcalans retired to their camps at the entrances to the city while from the Tlatelolco pyramid, plumes of smoke, booming drums, and the throaty notes of conch horns announced the Aztecs' victory. Then one by one the captured Spaniards were led naked to the top of the pyramid and made to dance for an hour before the pained eyes of Cortés and his surviving troops as well as the other tribes all around the lake. Finally each was dragged screaming to the sacrificial stone.

The display hardened the already hard men around Cortés with a cold fury. Before this moment there had never been any real hatred of this enemy. All sense of competition and rivalry ceased as the grim Spaniards prepared, with another timely infusion of fresh troops from the coast, to make an end of the matter. Cortés himself decided, reluctantly but firmly, that there would be no more trouble with water gaps and canals and narrow streets. This time he would invade the city street by street, razing it and dumping its rubble into the vexatious water gaps and canals.

In July the advance began, aided, it seemed, by all Mexico as tribe after tribe sent laborers to do the muscle work of tearing down the capital stone by stone. Inside Tenochtitlán, the recently victorious Aztecs were desperate with thirst and subsisting on weeds, insects, and roots. The advance went smoothly, the walls came down, and the canals were filled. As Cortés advanced daily into a new street, he took to climbing to the top of pyramids or other tall buildings and just standing there with his arms folded for the reeling enemy to see. Slowly the Aztec leadership and their warriors were backed into the northern corner of the city, but still Cuauhtémoc hurled defiance at his attackers and made a final stand in a marketplace. In the ensuing slaughter, Cortés's Spaniards and the allies went berserk, killing twelve thousand Aztec soldiers, women, and children in one day. This was the end.

As the victors mopped up any remaining resistance, Cuauhtémoc himself was captured in a canoe attempting to escape. Still proud, he asked for death, and Cortés now returned his former silence by ignoring his request. It was August 13, 1521; less than a third of Tenochtitlán's former population of two hundred thousand survived. With Cuauhtémoc in chains, the remaining Aztec warriors threw down their weapons. The people of the ruined city fell silent, milling about the rubble of their once proud capital—dazed, utterly exhausted, emaciated, staring passively at a horizon that no longer existed. All of the prophecies of doom had been fulfilled—all but one. Moctezuma, stoned to death by his own people, did not live to see the completion of his nation's history. But Cuauhtémoc did, and for his staunch stand, his absolute refusal to talk with those who would desecrate his homeland, there would be a time in the far mists of the future when his name would be revered above all others in the great story of the end of an age.

After the arrival of fresh food from a ship on the coast, Cortés's men celebrated among the ruins and then fell quickly to squabbling among themselves about the location of the treasure lost on the *Noche Triste.* Cuauhtémoc was tortured for information but only responded with sneers and derision—the treasure might be here or there, or maybe there. It was never found.

Today you cannot visit the world that Cortés destroyed. It is buried under Mexico City, beneath the *zócalo,* in layers and layers of apocalyptic change. There are only teasing disinterments, such as the Templo Mayor beside the National Cathedral or that at the Plaza of Three Cultures, where Aztec ruins have been unearthed in front of a colonial church next to a modern office building.

But you can go where the Aztecs themselves went to witness the truth of the passing of ages. Northeast of Tenochtitlán (Mexico City) lies Teotihuacán, unearthed and preserved in all of its pre-Cortesian and pre-Aztec glory. This place was a collection of grassy mounds when the Aztecs reigned supreme; earlier, while the smaller city of Rome was building an empire half a world away, the Teotihuacanos were forging a civilization and mythology that, through the Toltecs, the Aztecs would come to adopt as their own.

It is sunny and hot as our cab driver, Francisco García, takes us out of Mexico City to Teotihuacán and talks about Cortés. In his nearby pueblo of Otumba there isn't much discussion of the past, he tells us. "People are living in the moment. In the pueblos, most don't really understand the Spanish culture. And the Aztec past has no real meaning. We are all mestizo." But when pressed he thinks that Cortés was a villain—"He came to destroy our race."

Surprisingly there is no elaborate tourist facade at Teotihuacán as we will later find in some of the less visited Mayan sites in the Yucatán, just a row of homely *puestos* where mementos are sold. And there isn't as much art—sculpture, carvings, figures, relief—as at the later Mayan sites, though much of what was here now resides in museums. Instead there is the vast, clear layout of an ancient city incredibly reminiscent of Rome. A broad central boulevard lined by stairways, temples, and shrines looks like an even grander Appian Way. To one side at the middle of its length towers the mighty Pyramid of the Sun, the second-largest pyramid in the world. At the head of the boulevard, beyond a great square, rises the Pyramid of the Moon, only slightly smaller and positioned just so its shape is framed perfectly by a mountain in the distance. Egypt and Rome combined—the impression is unmistakable.

We climb the Pyramid of the Sun in the midday summer heat. With the mile-high altitude, this is no easy task and we make frequent stops to catch our breath. The structure is hugely monolithic—an early, simple expression of the might of civilization—though to the Aztecs, it was a golden age. In some ways it reminds me of the no-nonsense construction of Spanish fortresses in the New World, though much bigger. When we see the artful Mayan ruins later in our travels, we will become convinced that something was blossoming here between the time of the Teotihuacanos and the Spanish that was indeed nipped in the bud, as the train conductor has told us.

At the top of the pyramid, we survey the ruins the Aztecs themselves saw when they wanted a glimpse into the past, and possibly the future. The Teotihuacano pyramids evince the antiquity of two quintessentially Mexican concepts, order and power. Brutally massive orderliness, sweeping from the top down—that is what is conveyed by this site.

And perhaps something else. At the top of the Pyramid of the Sun, we do feel a closeness to the sun. It has been hot everywhere we have been today, but here it's more than heat. We can't help but feel an infusion of energy after the rigorous climb. A group of visiting Argentine college-age women gathers just after we have caught our breath. We all sit, forming a circle in the sun, join hands, and meditate. "Stop all thoughts," someone says. We are silent for several minutes. The stone underneath us is warm.

The circle breaks up, and standing now, the Argentines dig big crystals out of their pockets and hold them forth in their upturned palms to reenergize them in the sun here at the proper place. That was the story when the Aztecs came here; that's what it was when the Spaniards came; that's what it is today: new powers on the platform of the pyramid, new creeds layered over old, a new age in an old place.

2

The Man with Fire
Mexico City to Guadalajara

Why should there be any mystery about Mexico's being a land where revolution has happened again and again? This is a country whose native inhabitants were conquered by foreigners who did not seek to exterminate them, as colonists had done in the United States and elsewhere. The new power did not segregate itself into a separate nation within a nation as in South Africa. Instead it intermarried and produced a mixed race of varying degrees of ethnicity with a corresponding color-based caste system. Such a society contained all of the various seeds of revolution found in other places: class conflict, racial conflict, ideological conflict, natives versus aliens, and ultimately the pivotal question of who shall really rule this land. Mexico's war for independence from Spain was just one phase of a continuing struggle as power has worked its way down through the castes—as one by one, each more numerous lower caste has achieved political consciousness and cohesion of action. And it is not over yet.

• • •

The sky is blue this Sunday in Mexico City, no sign of its famous pollution, never mind its violent past. During the cab ride from the station to our hotel, once again the María Cristina, the driver explains, "Well, it is Sunday, and World Cup Soccer Championship day. No one is out driving." People will go to mass and then stay in to watch the game pitting Brazil against Italy at the California Rose Bowl on television.

The streets of the world's most populous and ecologically disastrous city are remarkably traffic-free today—and clean. But for the political posters connected with the upcoming presidential election, you could imagine yourself in any of the world's great capitals with better reputations for aesthetics.

In the lobby of the old-world María Cristina, a couple dozen patrons settle in to watch the World Cup on the wide-screen television. Most are middle-class Mexicans, some are from Brazil, and a few are Americans. It's a partisan gathering, with everyone except the Americans cheering for Brazil. Out of sheer cussedness, five of us Americans chant "Italia!" One Mexican asks me, "What are you doing here? The World Cup is in your country today."

During one of the rare breaks (American commercial television has trouble with soccer), there is an advertisement for Corona Beer. The entire thirty-second spot focuses on a sun-drenched bench on a large yacht. On the bench stands a half-empty bottle of Corona beer while a second, empty bottle rolls languidly back and forth with the pitching of the boat, clinking occasionally with the standing bottle. In the background there is a glimpse of blue water and some deep-sea fishing poles leaning beside the bench. Finally the empty bottle rolls off the bench and the ad ends. There have been no voice-overs and no faces of people, which strikes me as significant. For if there were faces, what color should they be?

When the Italian soccer hero, Baggio, sails his shootout kick over the net, pandemonium breaks loose—"Brazil! Brazil! Brazil!" Out come the Brazilian flags and orders for lots more beer. The Brazilians march around the lobby waving their flags while the Mexicans cheer them on.

Throughout our travels so far we have been asking people where we might find food like that seen in the film *Like Water for Chocolate*. "Such food exists only in the movies," we have been told over and over again by people we have met on the trains.

"Not so," one of the Americans here tells Lourdes. He and his daughter enthusiastically recommend that we take dinner tonight at the Hostería Santo Domingo, the oldest restaurant in Mexico City, where we will find just what we are looking for. We go there when the World Cup celebration has wound down.

Once a monastery, the Hostería San Domingo is all arches and stained-glass windows. From the ceilings hang traditional pre-Hispanic *papierotes*—colorful paper cutouts repeating different festive patterns. Over floors of polished tiles where Dominican monks once fasted and prayed, there is today a cheery bustle of waiters wafting tantalizing aromas with each pass.

We sit beneath a painting of a table set with virtually all of the dishes presented in the film that inspired our visit. Our waiter, Rosindo, takes great pride in introducing us to fine Mexican wines and explaining the character and history of some of the true Mexican dishes served. "We are losing that tradition," he says. "So I try to promote it to all who come." He directs our attention to the painting, done by one Gómez Grossa of the Diego Rivera school, and points out each dish in the menu—the painting enables the diner to visualize an entrée before ordering it.

On Rosindo's recommendation, we try *chiles en nogada,* the dish that was specially prepared by the nuns of Santa Clara in Puebla for General Iturbide upon his victory over the Spanish in the war of independence. It incorporates each color in the Mexican flag: green in the meat-stuffed chili, white in the walnut-sauce glaze, and red in the pomegranate seeds sprinkled over the top. Its contrasting flavors—sweet, spicy, and salty—convey a martial impression to the palate. Afterward, we notice as we leave that the policeman on duty at the door carries a big rifle.

For three hundred years the Spaniards ruled Mexico after the fall of Tenochtitlán, the racially stratified colony straining under the heavy weight of power at the top of the pyramid. Eventually that weight would begin to crash through the barriers of class and race, one at a time, in cataclysm after cataclysm, until finally, in the 1990s, only one barrier remained.

Much of the credit or blame for the shape of Mexico today is due to decisions Cortés made in the immediate aftermath of the conquest. Against the advice of his captains, who would have preferred a more militarily secure site, Cortés decided to build the Spanish capital on the ruins of Tenochtitlán and out of its rubble. He named it Mexico City, after the name by which the Aztecs called themselves, the *México*. As he had when he displayed himself standing atop the pyramids during the final battles of the war, he possessed an intuitive sense of the Indians' respect for the sources of authority. This is where the seat of power had been. This is where it would continue to be. Thus began a national habit of cultural, political, and economic focus on one city. That's why today Mexico City—the largest city on the planet—is a potentially catastrophic experiment on an urban scale well beyond the wildest dreams or nightmares of New York or Los Angeles.

Cortés had the Aztec roles of tribute translated and continued the traditional pattern of vassalage. Neighboring tribes were required to send forces of laborers, working under their traditional chieftains, to do the work of rebuilding the capital just as they had under the Aztecs. Retaining the pyramidal structure of Aztec society, the Spaniards and their religion slipped in neatly in place of the Aztec nobility and their priests at the top.

But while he maintained the appearance of the old Aztec social structure, he also instituted the ubiquitous Spanish economic system of the *encomienda*. *Encomiendas* were realms from conquered lands granted to individual Spaniards. Within the *encomienda*, the Spanish lord could collect tribute and enforce Spanish law without actually owning the land. Ownership of these lands remained, theoretically, in the hands of the natives, who remained, theoretically, free men, although tribute could take the form of forced labor. In return the Spanish lords were to provide for the spiritual and material well-being of the natives. The system legalistically skirted the Spanish prohibition against slavery in that the Spaniards did not actually own the laborers nor could they regulate all aspects of their earthly existence. All they could demand of them was a prescribed amount of labor, material tribute, and adherence to Spanish religion and law.

That had been enough to decimate the native populations of the Caribbean colonies, so the crown looked on Cortés's establishment of the institution with disfavor almost from the start. Here began an ironic pattern of conflict pitting the exploitative drive of the colonists against the relatively liberal hand of the Spanish monarchy. Again and again, colonists would chafe under attempts by the crown to establish a "kinder, gentler" imperial policy toward the natives. Articulate churchmen such as Bartolomé de las Casas launched effective propaganda extolling the virtues of the indigenous peoples and condemning their treatment by the colonists. Such arguments provided rationale for a monarchy already intent on keeping its New World rowdies on a short leash. When rebellion for independence finally did come, at least some of its underpinnings were anything but humane enlightenment.

The crown eventually succeeded in abolishing the *encomienda*, but Indians continued to provide forced labor for "good works" under the *repartimiento* system. Again the issue of slavery was finessed by the fact that the laborers were paid a wage for their work. But every Indian owed at least forty-five days of labor as part of his tribe's continuing tribute, and with the demise of the *encomienda,* they were further held in the grip of wage peonage, requiring forced employment to pay off debts to large landowners.

The Indians responded to the ruinous change in their way of life by dying by the millions. Much of the 90 percent fatality rate in the century after the conquest was due to the predations of diseases against which the Indians had no immunity. But much of it was the result of overwork and cultural collapse. Though some tribes on the periphery of the colony retained their identities (such as the Maya and the Zapotecs), those at the heart of the territory, including the proud Aztecs themselves, simply ceased to exist as cohesive entities. The labor surplus that had made possible the construction of the magnificent pre-Cortesian world evaporated, and Spanish colonists had to face a contingency they never expected—limited resources, particularly of labor.

It wasn't long after Cortés that the colonial trough, so dependent on Indian workers, became too small for all of those who wanted to feed at it. Cortés's conquistadores, already quarreling among themselves over the spoils, were soon contending with a new class of rivals: immigrants from Spain who, because of their connections back in the Iberian peninsula, had the inside track to the colonial positions of power and wealth. Dubbed *gachupines* (wearers of spurs), they were reviled by the conquistador class, who believed it had earned the right to be the aristocracy of the New World. In any case, as the original conquistadores died off, they were replaced at the top of the pyramid by the *gachupines.* And the sons and daughters of the conquistadores (and even of early *gachupines*) found themselves labeled as an inferior class, despite their white skin, because of their Mexican birth. Whites born in Mexico came to be known as criollos; they would form the second tier in the pyramid of racial class and never forgot the insult.

Beneath the white-skinned *gachupines* and criollos emerged a new people and thus a third class: the mestizo offspring of the increasingly common sexual liaisons between whites and Indians. Though their numbers grew as rapidly as the criollos', and though they were considered to have the spark of elevated humanity due to their partly Spanish blood, they inhabited a no-man's land between whites and Indians during the colonial era, with no sense of community and shared identity. At the bottom of the pyramid languished the Indians and the Africans imported for their labor as the Indian population dwindled.

Though the original conquistadores did not exhibit a virulently racist attitude toward the natives of Mexico (they despised only their religion), the *gachupines* who dominated the colonial world brought to it an obsession with race and purity of blood that has infected Mexico ever since. They debated endlessly over where to draw the line between *gente de razón* (humans with the ability to think) and the inferior *indios*. Could an *indio* become a person of reason through education? Most believed not. Were mestizos *gente de razón*? Maybe, but probably not. Some even went so far as to claim that successive generations of criollos were turning darker of skin as a result of being weaned on the milk of *indio* nurses and breathing the Mexican air. Indians and mestizos were forbidden to wear European clothing, and early attempts to educate them were abandoned. Eventually the church and the crown grew alarmed at the vehemence of these racist attitudes, stepping into the debate to declare the mestizos *gente de razón* and the Indians "children"— eventually capable through proper Christian tutelage of reason and Christian virtue. Women existed on a plane beyond all of this—as descendants of the Virgin Mary, they were in possession of divine attributes, making reason and rights irrelevant.

Besides the *gachupines* flocking to the New World seeking

wealth and bringing with them their acute class consciousness, the colony attracted an invasion of churchmen. When the first sackcloth-clad monks arrived, the conquering Cortés himself astounded his Aztec audience by kneeling and kissing the feet of these humble unarmed friars. The clergy of the colony were motivated by the full range of human aspiration. There were plenty of hypocrites who enjoyed comfort, wealth, and sex behind the facade of advancing Catholic Christianity, but there were also dedicated emulators of the life of Jesus who evinced an intense, albeit paternal, desire to care for the Indian. In another attempt by the crown to mitigate the harm done to the indigenous population, only churchmen were allowed to go into and reside in Indian villages.

Much has been made over the years of the church's attempt to eradicate all traces of pre-Cortesian religion, history, and culture. Certainly much was lost at the hands of overzealous missionaries. But the surviving artifacts and records we do have were transmitted to us by other churchmen, such as the indefatiguable Father Sahagún, who intuitively knew that they could not successfully bring Christianity to a people whose ways were not studied and understood. For their part, the Indians did not easily give up their old practices. While generally accepting a veneer of Christianity, they still held on to their idols and figures, stashing them in double walls in their houses, hiding them in grottoes, sometimes squirreling them under the very footings of Christian altars.

The Christian clergy vacillated between aggressive attempts to root out and punish these lapses and tolerant acquiescence in the survival of the deep Mexico. The pattern of building Catholic churches on the very sites of pre-Cortesian altars may have backfired and contributed to the Indians' habit of melding their newfound Christianity with their old ways rather than replacing them.

Though much of Christianity was fundamentality at odds with the old ways, the tradition of miraculous appearances was not. The

Indians had a predisposition toward seeing manifestations of numi-
nousness, so much so that the church had to repress frequently
reported sightings of Christ or the Virgin in places of the old worship. But when in 1531 an Indian beekeeper named Juan Diego
reported seeing a black Virgin at the ancient holy place of Tonatzín,
his vision could not be squelched. Thus began the cult of the Virgin
of Guadalupe, and in a departure from the usual response, the
church formally recognized the event in a controversial decision.
Now Mexico had its national miracle and its own native Christian
shrine. Spaniards would eventually rue the day.

At the train station in Mexico City, there is a fuss out on the platform as we are waiting to depart for Querétaro. People crowd at
the windows on the left side of the train to see what is going on.
"*Rateros*," someone says—a rat, a thief has been caught. Outside I
can see a fair-skinned Mexican grasping a younger, darker, shirtless
fellow by the hair. He has been caught stealing food from the train,
someone says. The police have been called. Meanwhile the vigi-
lante yanks the hair of the miscreant as if intent on pulling it all out
by the roots. The thief is younger and physically much bigger than
his assailant, but still he passively cries that he didn't take anything
and begs to be let go. When two policemen arrive, people on the
train quickly lose interest. "What will happen to the *ratero*?" I ask.

"They will take him to jail and beat him and then let him go in a
few days," shrugs one of the passengers. "And then he will try to
steal again when he gets hungry."

The train ride to Querétaro is full of images of Mexican life
bursting from the sun-warmed earth. We pass men gathering brick
from ruins of abandoned homes, pointed maguey and rounded nopal, and trackside laughter and horseplay. We also see Mexico's
poverty—the beggar child, the crippled woman crawling on her
cracked and bleeding knees—and the power of emotion that
springs from it in the yearning faces young and old that crowd

around the train at station stops. But on this ride we begin to see a paradox. All along the route the corn grows taller even than in the American Midwest. Orchards are heavy with oranges, mangos, bananas, and pears. There is good land enough here for prosperous-looking cattle ranches. In the pueblos, market stalls are piled with fruit and vegetables and meat. Even the smallest homesteads have goats and chickens in the corral and neat gardens of beans, corn, squash, and nopal cactus out back. Except in some of the regions of the arid north and the mountains, Mexico is everywhere a land of abundance. And yet, everyone below a certain rung on the socio-economic ladder suffers from some degree of malnutrition. The government is probably correct in claiming that over the years that rung has moved lower and lower, but the fact remains that vast numbers of the Mexican people are hungry in a land of plenty. And the harsher fact is that full bellies and Spanish blood go hand in hand. After spending months in Mexico, when one pictures hunger, one sees gaunt ribs under dark skin. When hungry people are bonded together by their skin color as well as their deprivation, violent solidarity is a powder keg just waiting for a spark of leadership.

It's a rainy evening in Querétaro on the Plaza de la Corregidora. Querétaro is a pleasant city of leafy trees, gardens, and well-preserved colonial architecture. Like most Mexican cities it presents a visage of prosperity that belies the social crisis endemic to so much of the countryside. We have settled in for the evening at El Regio, one of the canopied sidewalk cafés that ring the square, where a magician moves from table to table doing his tricks. But there's not much action here on this rainy evening, so he ends up sitting down and giving us a private show. He is José Martínez Somarriba, aka "Artístico Gran Giuseppe," and his energy soon attracts the girlfriend of one of the owners of the café, Angélica Hernández Solís, who also joins us.

José lives in the pueblo of Apasio el Grande, near the railroad tracks. He leaves home around 1:00 P.M. and works here till nine in the evening, then relaxes for a while and gets back home near midnight. He was originally attracted to the city because of the bright lights and the hope of a better life, and he worked as a waiter until a magician began teaching him tricks. Then he saw his dream and sprang for it. He believes he is fortunate to have come from a humble pueblo and found this life in the city. And while his compatriots are out scratching the fields in the morning, he gets to sleep in late.

Angélica's family is also from a rural pueblo. They liked to cook, so their dream was to open a restaurant here in the city. Like José, Angélica and her family have found what they sought. They are both dark complected and of humble origins. But they demonstrate the possibility of an upward mobility that runs counter to an otherwise fixed caste structure.

Angélica says that the city people of Querétaro are regarded as "closed-minded" by the folk of the countryside. When we press her to explain what she means, she says that she doesn't use the term in a moral sense. It's not that they are closed-minded to new ideas or to modern lifestyles. If anything, what she means is just the opposite—they are not accepting of the simple and traditional ways of the countryside. They regard country people as bumpkins. She won't go so far as to say that it's a matter of race; she and José are themselves examples of the fact that it is teasingly possible for those who are adaptable and ambitious, if darker skinned, to migrate upward by moving to the city. It's a matter of the second-best opportunity for the good life. If you can't be born with fair skin, at least you can move to the city.

Angélica suggests that we visit the Temple of the Crosses, the site of a miracle that draws the true believers. There we will see the soul of the simple, traditional country people who make pilgrimages here to bear witness to something too spiritual for the sophisticates of Querétaro. At the temple there are trees growing in the soil where an Indian was martyred that have ever since blossomed with crosses instead of flowers. Today the crosses are harvested, encased in plastic, and sold as key chains.

Lourdes and I try to imagine what kind of natural phenomenon could be interpreted as such a miracle. Perhaps the flowers have only four petals, thus looking like a cross. Perhaps there is some subtle pattern in the bark or the flowers themselves that true believers see as crosses. We make our own pilgrimage to the temple the following day when the rain has stopped. In the nave of the chapel hangs a black Christ with long Indian-style hair. We see earnest peasants shuffle in, poverty showing in their worn clothing and their calloused feet. They wet their hands in the holy water, sit down, and swoon into a spiritual trance. Their features relax, their shoulders lower, their eyes glaze. Concerns about work, hunger, domestic trouble, or safety seem washed away during these quiet moments, and I think of Marx. "The opiate of the masses" may be right. But these people come here seeking peace and they find it. Despite everything else, it is the miracle of the church.

The miracle we came here to see is a little harder to get to. The convent where the trees are located is closed just now, and I suspect machinations to cloak the truth of the supposed "miracle." But as we wander the cloisters, Lourdes approaches a novitiate who takes us to see the trees. They grow only in one interior courtyard, unceremoniously sharing the space with a couple of old pickup trucks. Behind a makeshift barrier of chicken wire, stand the trees, similar in shape and foliage to small locusts, a type of tree we have frequently seen elsewhere in Mexico. At first glance we see no crosses and I think, well, this is something that is going to take some imagination.

But then Lourdes finds them, so large and obvious I missed them at first because I was looking for something subtle—all along the branches, three-pronged thorns in the perfect shape and proportion of crosses with pointed tips. Some are as big as two inches in length. The novitiate explains that the convent has attempted to transplant these trees elsewhere, but then the crosses will not grow. Only here in this soil fertilized by a martyr's blood does this tree grow crosses.

A day later, when we are waiting for the train back to Guadalajara at the Querétaro station, I wander off by myself down the street to buy some soda and snacks for the ride. The station is located in a bad part of town; there is a shady-looking pharmacy, a dirty, mean bar, a liquor store, and some grubby little grocery markets. I see drunks sleeping on stone slabs, two peeing in the gutter, and another making threatening gestures, yet there are also a few middle-class folk walking by. There is a prostitute with her kids—you often find a corner like this near the train station, says a guy in the grocery. When I emerge from the store, the prostitute gestures toward me, and two drunks sitting on the curb point and laugh. "Want to buy sometheeng, *señor americano*?" one of them shouts at me in scurrilously pronounced English.

Back at the station, I find Lourdes sitting with an old peasant woman and her daughter. The woman wears a clean black-and-gray dress with a crocheted hem. Over her shoulders lies a black-and-white shawl. Her hair is shiny white and her skin is smooth and dark. She is beautiful and her daughter looks just like her, only younger and dark haired.

But the woman is not happy. She is wringing her hands and explaining to Lourdes that she lost the money for her train ticket. She is proud—she is no beggar. She says she has only one thing to sell for the ticket money, and then she shows us a magnificent white lace tablecloth. Lourdes turns to me with a big grin—it happens I have been looking for just such a tablecloth. The deal is made, thirty pesos for the tablecloth, enough for the train tickets the woman and her daughter need.

The woman smiles and poses with her daughter for a picture.

"Life is good," she says. "You will take a piece of me with you, and I will take a piece of you with me."

Lourdes sighs, "We materialistic Americans. The piece of us is just money." But later it occurs to us that maybe it wasn't. The piece of us was also the train ride home—mobility. And as I think of this and admire the patterns in my new tablecloth, I'm reminded of the miracle of the crosses.

By the 1550s the Spaniards had found the treasure they so long sought. In the Chichimeca country several hundred miles north of Mexico City, the ground held the richest veins of silver the world had ever seen, and colonists moved quickly to establish Zacatecas, the city of silver. Within a century, the lodes of Zacatecas had enriched not just Spain but all of Europe as the world supply of the precious metal was doubled by the wealth of Mexico. There was at this point a critical moment when the silver of the Spanish empire might have beneficially changed the course of both Mexican and Spanish history. Here was wealth enough, if distributed with some degree of equity, to catapult all of Mexico, mestizos and Indians included, to an unimaginable level of prosperity with enough left over to maintain Spain at the pinnacle of European nations.

But the moment was squandered. Protective of its Iberian industry, the crown forbade the colony from using its newfound wealth to establish a viable independent economy and demanded that all manufactured items be imported from producers in Spain. In Mexico the *gachupines* hoarded the mineral wealth not exported to Spain to support a grandiose lifestyle for themselves. And in Spain the lion's share of the spoils was lavished on the monarchy's frenetic military and imperial adventurism—so much so that overconfidence in the seemingly inexhaustible supply of silver from Mexico led to national bankruptcy and, indirectly, to the defeat of the Spanish Armada by the British in 1588.

The silver boom also had devastating effects on the Mexican landscape and its indigenous inhabitants. Fantastic wealth seemed to cancel any sense of limits to human enterprise, and so the forests were denuded, the fertile lands overgrazed, and cities began to sprawl beyond the capacity of their natural infrastructure. With the hillsides barren of vegetation and the Aztecs' ancient system of hydroengineering destroyed, Lake Texcoco flooded Mexico City so badly that the city occasionally had to be abandoned. Spanish engineers responded eventually by building the Tula drainage ditch, a massive feat but one made necessary not by nature, but by her disruption.

Like the earlier civilizations of Mexico, the Spanish colony flirted with ecological disaster—and for the Indians, they accomplished it. Without the money to buy food, the Indians who had for so long lived entirely off their native land faced starvation as the landscape became increasingly stark and arid. Yet still unsated by the flow of silver, Spain's appetite for the riches it could suck from Mexico was ravenous. Besides the tax on pulque, the traditional cheap brew made from the maguey plant, the crown reaped financial harvest from its monopolies on everything from gunpowder to playing cards to tobacco. Royal income from its tobacco monopoly even exceeded that from silver! Throughout the seventeenth century, Spain and the colonists at the top of the pyramid in Mexico nursed at the two breasts of the Mexican land and its natives, creating one of the greatest gaps between rich and poor the world has ever known.

The resulting tensions sparked insurrection long before the war for independence. In 1624 an uprising over food racketeering brought together for the first time a mob of priests, criollos, mestizos, and Indians. In 1692 the coincidence of a devastating flood, a solar eclipse, and another terrible food shortage provoked the Tumult, an uprising of mestizos, Indians, and blacks that ravaged Mexico City for days.

The plight of the Indian became, by the eighteenth century, an issue that both divided and united the white power factions at the top of the pyramid, no longer a single monolithic block. Criollo resentment of *gachupines* was a long-established rift. And within the church there was a power struggle between the priests of the secular clergy—the religious arm of the colony—and the orders of the regular clergy, such as the Franciscans and Jesuits, who owed allegiance to no one but Rome itself. The Indian became the pawn in these games, his plight exploited by any faction that felt it needed him. Thus criollos and lower churchmen of the secular clergy marched with Indians in the insurrection of 1624. But following the Tumult of 1692, the struggling factions at the top settled into a grudging alliance against the Indians, whose wrath they were beginning to fear.

That's how it stood throughout much of the eighteenth century, sometimes called the Baroque Years for the high adornment in architecture and fashion, or the Bourbon Years for the increasing French influence in all things Spanish during the decadent age of the Iberian monarchy. Meanwhile Mexico's new class of mestizos grew in numbers and impact, and the distinctions between classes became even more trenchant as the acquisition of money or job skills blurred them. With a stroke of the pen in the baptismal record, parish priests made fateful decisions that charted the futures of whole families. Fair-skinned mestizos offered lifetime savings as bribes to have their children declared criollo. Spanish-speaking Indians or mulattos of lighter complexion finagled to have their offspring declared mestizo. Darker and poorer criollos and mestizos dreaded the decision going the other way.

Within the mestizo class, a subclass developed as some managed to acquire wealth and move toward the top of the social pyramid despite their sometimes obvious pigmentation. No question about it, even in race-conscious Mexico, money and property could whiten the skin. Initially these families claimed, sometimes genuinely, to be descended from Indian nobility on their native side. Eventually money and standing were enough to do the trick. As more and more mestizos gained the status of criollos, they helped to create a kind of social glue that began to link the criollos to the truly Mexican classes beneath them.

Though the fear of mestizo and Indian insurrection still bound the *gachupines* and criollos together, by the end of the eighteenth century they seemed to be parting ways in nearly every other respect. For two hundred years the criollo had nursed his grudge against the *gachupín* and had steadily forged a sense of Mexican nationality. Now mestizo intellectuals emerged with an even stronger feeling for their Mexican heritage, since they were its true sons. Despite their continuing harsh treatment of the contemporary Indian, criollos and mestizos alike began to claim their roots and derive their nationalist legitimacy from the glories of a pre-Cortesian past. And in the most radical expression of emerging nationalism, they adopted as their own the Christianized Indians' cult of the Virgin of Guadalupe. The legend was elaborated: Juan Diego had seen her standing on a prickly pear cactus, like the serpent and snake of Aztec myth. The success of the conquest was reinterpreted: God had effected it so that the Virgin could appear in this land. Christianity was brought to the New World, not by the religious orders bound to a foreign nation across the Atlantic, but by the Mother of God herself.

Other less exalted causes furthered the rift between criollos and *gachupines*. Newly arrived *gachupines* tended to claim the most beautiful of the daughters of criollos. Criollos could educate themselves in the universities and become far better qualified for the lucrative positions within the colonial bureaucracy than newly arrived *gachupines,* who often came from relatively lowly stations in the Iberian peninsula. But still it was the *gachupines* who marched past their Mexican betters and into the choicest posts. With the doors to high public office closed to so many educated criollos, they formed an increasingly discontented class that yearned to rule their own roost.

Two fuses of rebellion were lit and began to burn steadily in the late eighteenth century, one by the fickle rain god Tlaloc and one by events in Spain. In 1785 Mexico experienced its worst drought yet, at a time when population levels had so escalated that even good years stretched the food supply to the limits. What came to be known as the "year of hunger" was a turning point—never again would income match food costs. Hunger was now a permanent reality for the vast majority of souls living in Mexico.

Meanwhile the new Bourbon regime in Spain, influenced by the ideas of the Enlightenment, struggled to right the ship of state after the excesses and mismanagement of the previous century. Part and parcel of that effort was a series of reforms aimed at making the colonies more economically and politically efficient. For the first time since Cortés landed in 1764, Spanish soldiers were sent to the New World with instructions to augment their power with militias from the colonial population. As was the case in the British colonies to the north, the sending of troops to guarantee crown control only inflamed the criollos' growing passion for independence. But worse, the crown instituted a reorganization of colonial administration, giving the new posts to *gachupines,* and thus locking the criollos out of power more effectively than ever. Then the crown went even further by attempting to curtail the power of the church. In 1767 the Jesuits were expelled from New Spain, adding new insult to criollos, many of whom had turned to the Roman order for their livelihoods after being shut out of government. And finally, in 1804 the crown ordered the church, whose vast financial holdings had been the source of credit in New Spain, to turn over to the royal treasury its pious funds and to liquidate its holdings in land, with the profits to be lent to the crown. The upshot was worse than simply the evaporation of credit; suddenly the prosperous criollo and mestizo hacendados, merchants, and ranchers found their mortgages foreclosed. This was the last straw.

When Napoleon invaded Spain in 1808 and placed his brother Joseph on the throne, Mexico City *gachupines* pulled off a coup to oust the viceroy and installed a junta to hold the colony in the name of the deposed monarchy. For two years sullen criollos met throughout Mexico in "literary clubs" to consider their options as patriots. One of them was an aging priest, Father Miguel Hidalgo y Costilla, a man of complex motives and actions who came to be known as the father of Mexico. Most criollos had little interest in social justice and the plight of those below them in the pyramid of Mexican society; they just wanted to replace the *gachupines* at the top. Superficially Hidalgo's family history and personal background would seem to place him firmly in this social niche. But he had learned to speak four Indian languages, violated crown regulations in teaching Indians winemaking and silkworm culture, toiled with them at brickmaking and irrigation projects, questioned the Immaculate Conception of Jesus Christ, and developed a fiercely independent moral code that he could defend with fury. And when his moment came, he unleashed on behalf of the downtrodden a revolution so ferocious that his criollo compatriots had to defeat it before they could go on to accomplish their own rebellion for independence.

The Tren Tapatío out of Mexico City for Guadalajara is the last remaining overnight train in Mexico, besides the Monterrey and Veracruz runs, that still has Pullman sleepers. The cars are not maintained quite as well as those on the Regiomontano, and as we accelerate to track speed outside of the Mexico City yards, we note quickly that this track is rougher. It will be a difficult sleep tonight.

In anticipation, Lourdes and I have mixed up a batch of margaritas and discover that the universal Rule G (the railroad prohibition against drinking while on duty) is not rigorously followed in Mexico. Our car attendant is more than happy to join us, and soon his tongue is loose and voluble.

Miguel got his job on the railroad through a friend—he uses the term *"palanca"* (the lever) to refer to the fact that it takes connections to get anywhere in working for the railroad. He says the trains have gone downhill since they were nationalized by the government (many of those we talk to seem to believe that anything the government touches inevitably goes downhill). Still, rail employees like Miguel work to maintain the train service as a viable alternative for travelers who want to travel in touch with the land. And of course, for those of modest means, the second class is the cheapest available form of transportation.

Miguel would welcome a takeover of the railroads by foreign interests. "They are smart," he says. "That's to our advantage. It makes us stretch, learn more of the ways of the world."

I ask if he is concerned about the traditional pattern of foreign interests exploiting Mexico. He answers, "Exploitation only happens when you're not prepared. But if I'm ready and can take care of you and myself, I'm okay. I am proud of who I am as a Mexican, but if the government is not helping, I can't become a full person. If the head is wrong, the feet can't go right. So maybe I need to turn to foreigners to help set my feet straight."

As we have talked I have been fumbling around the compartment looking for something with which to cut limes. "Here," says Miguel. And he takes out his keys and uses one to deftly slice the lime as neatly as I could with a sharp knife. "Mexican ingenuity," he says.

We ask him about the upcoming presidential election. "The golden goose is going to stop laying," he says, referring to the process that has yielded easy, peaceful victories for the ruling PRI regime for so long. "I have no hairs on my tongue, nothing stops me from talking—let me tell you." It doesn't matter who wins, he believes, there are going to be problems. His sympathies would normally be with Cuauhtémoc Cárdenas and the leftists, but, voicing a complaint we will hear a lot, he doesn't think Cárdenas has much credibility anymore. "He was in the PRI and jumped to the PRD just out of personal ambition. He is fickle, like your President Clinton." The PRI is corrupt, so the only tenable alternative is the conservative PAN. "So our best hope lies with a party whose philosophy I cannot support. What will it mean to cast a ballot?" He believes lots of people will feel that way and that the election will be the beginning of troubled times.

In the morning I take my spot on the back platform with coffee in hand and again find it impossible to see this land as a site of troubled times. The passing fields, quartered so neatly by undulating stone walls, roll green and bright out across the plain to the purple mountains in the distance. In the little pueblos we pass, families milk cows and wave at the train with big toothless grins. At one stop, a pair of young lovers walk along the tracks hand in hand, both already dressed and groomed as for a night of dancing. The guy looks up at me and beams with pride and joy. I flip him the thumbs-up and he claps his hands together and returns the gesture with both thumbs. The girl blushes and tosses her hair and laughs.

In the second-class cars of the train, people are stirring and becoming sociable. The faces here are darker and more Oriental than in the first-class and Pullman sections, but crack a smile and one is returned with a friendly *"Buenos días, señor."* In the vestibules between cars, attendants make coffee and people gather to buy snacks and tamales from big baskets, and bottles of juice from buckets sitting on huge chunks of dirty ice.

At the stop for Ocotlán, we purchase breakfast tortillas from a peasant woman vending at trackside. She has eight children, she is proud to tell us, four boys and four girls. The father is absent and all of the children help to make life work. The thirteen-year-old daughter makes the cheese, the eighteen-year-old runs the house and does the cooking, and when Mother comes home from her day of work, dinner is ready and her underwear is washed. "When I ask her why she does this," the woman tells us, "she says, 'Mom, you work so hard.' " And then she adds, "You know, she doesn't want to get a man."

"Why not?" we ask.

"She says, 'So I won't end up like you, Mother.' "

The woman says this with pride, not shame. Her daughter is smarter, an independent woman of the modern world.

Guadalajara is often thought of by Americans as the most Mexican of Mexican cities. And it is, in the sense that this second-largest Mexican city is associated with so many of the traditional icons of Mexican life familiar to Americans—tequila, mariachi music, the rodeo, the *tapatío* hat dance, and revolution. We don't know it at the time of our visit, but seven months later Guadalajara will become the site of a ballot box rebellion, as the PAN will democratically overthrow the long rule of the PRI in the state of Jalisco.

Guadalajara, at one-fourth the population of the capital, is an easier city. The pace of traffic in the streets is less frantic and the air is not so badly polluted. People move about here more slowly and graciously, reminding me of southern cities in the United States compared to northern ones. Modern commerce certainly booms here, but it has produced less clutter. You can walk or drive through parts of Mexico City and not know for sure that you are in Mexico; in Guadalajara, every turn reveals a tableau that places you firmly where you are. People dress less in the American and international vogue; street vendors are more likely to be selling tamales than hot dogs; ornate old colonial buildings do not share so much of the streetscape with billboards; the music in the air of the downtown streets is more mariachi than metal. The city just seems older, though it isn't—as if time had stopped here a few decades ago.

At the Hotel Francés, just off the *zócalo*, we find a lobby straight out of a Humphrey Bogart movie. In this four-story space, a piano

player takes requests while visitors huddle at tables whose arrangement behind potted palms suggests intrigue and romance. Behind
etched-glass doors, an ancient elevator with an accordion gate takes
us very slowly to our rooms on the third floor. The corridors of the
upper floors are balconied around the space above the lobby, and
from my room I can still hear the muted echoing tones of the piano
three floors below. The whole place is rich with carved wood, an-
tique furniture, and classic pottery displayed in wood-and-glass
cases.

Back in the lobby, the piano player takes a break and sits down
with us. Martín Higareda is a rebel musician who studied at the
University of Guadalajara and then decided he didn't want to make
music the way he was being taught. "It was all just exercises," he
says. "Classical, step by step by step—no feeling, no creativity, no
passion. I couldn't make music that way. They don't really teach
music; they teach some kind of science of music."

So Martín quit the university and learned music by listening to
others play and feeling the connection between music and what he
experienced in his life. Then he would play here at the hotel and
get feedback from his audiences.

"I mistreated the instrument at first—getting blisters on my fingers trying to get more feeling out of it than I had the skill to do.
But people would criticize and praise. This place was my school."
He established his sense of validation when one of his former university professors visited the Francés and declared that, yes, this
young musician had found another way to learn music.

Martín likes to talk about music in the abstract. Sometimes it
just brings sadness, he believes. "But if we listen to the melody, we
find the way out of the sadness." It can take him as much as a week
to master a new song because he refuses to work from sheet music.
"You must remain respectful of the composer, of course, while
finding yourself in the passion of the music. Sheet music players
make it all sound the same. They are not free. Musicians like me

have made our declaration of independence." Martín recommends an excursion to the market town of San Pedro. There, he believes, we will see that the crafts of Mexico display that same rebellious form of creativity that inspires his music.

Next morning we take a bus to San Pedro, which was once a colonial town past the outskirts of the city. Today it is like a pearl surrounded by the sprawl of Guadalajara. It is a morning of sensory assault: the commuting workmen on the bus who badly need showers at the beginning of their day; the bubbly blown glass, the shining but slightly flawed silver, the crooked ceramics, and pre-frayed woven goods; a table set with all of the gifts that only very few recently married couples could hope to receive; the smoke of roasted fatty meats stacked on carted spikes at street corners; and moss-topped stone walls marred by political graffiti proclaiming that the PRI equals dinosaurs, corruption, and misery. Mexican art and life seem deliberately amiss. Somehow it is out of the very uneven texture of that life, the sense of irregular rhythm, that the urge to revolt arises. Or perhaps it is the other way around—maybe it is the urge to revolt that generates the rich roughness of Mexican reality.

Wandering Guadalajara late at night we find the mariachi bands waiting on street corners to sing in situations where no questions are to be asked. We watch prosperous, well-dressed, probably married men pick up cheap prostitutes on the very steps of a church. They make their move bowing with dignity and formality and then hire mariachis and speed away in long black cars. A political poster plastered all over colonial stone walls near the *zócalo* proclaims, "Don't stain the name of Zapata," and goes on to attack the current Zapatista rebels because they hide their faces from the sun and act more like bandits than revolutionaries. Never mind that some of Mexico's most beloved liberators, forefathers of the PRI and the status quo that the posters seem to support, began as bandits themselves. What we are seeing isn't hyposcrisy, we believe. It's just that things always seem skewed like this in Mexico, as if some great trauma has forever shifted truth and logic and harmony out of focus.

On September 16, 1810, Father Hidalgo climbed into the pulpit at the town of Dolores in the fertile agricultural region north of Mexico City known as the Bajío and raised the cry of revolt. Legend records his words as "Long live Ferdinand VII. Long live America. Long live religion. Long live the Virgin of Guadalupe. Death to the *gachupines!*" For some time he had been part of a plot to overthrow the *gachupín* junta, first to declare loyalty to the true Spanish crown and then later to claim an independent Mexico for the criollos. But when the plot was discovered and he was forced to precipitiously and personally launch the revolt that September day, he seemed possessed by his own more radical agenda. As an army of some twenty thousand mestizos and Indians rallied to his cause under the banner of the Virgin of Guadalupe, he declared in rapid succession the abolition of slavery, the end of the caste system, the restitution of lands taken from the Indians, and an end to all Indian tribute. Many criollos were aghast, including his fellow rebel leaders Ignacio Allende and Juan Aldama. They had contemplated nothing like this, though some, including Allende and Aldama, convinced themselves that Hidalgo's promises were intended merely to raise the army of the lower classes needed to defeat the crown, and so they maintained their allegiance to him. The churchmen of New Spain split over Hidalgo's declarations: the lower clergy, having struggled on behalf of their starving Indian wards for years, rallied to his banner, while the upper hierarchy damned him and eventually had him excommunicated. That action doomed the church to the wrong side of Mexican history, and in effect excommunicated it from the nationalist aspirations of the country ever after.

But even Hidalgo's most radical intentions surely did not include the ravages his unruly army performed on upper classes in the string of cities that fell before the rebels' advance: San Miguel, Celaya, Guanajuato, Valladolid (today's Morelia), Zacatecas, and San Luis Potosí. Guanajuato, in particular, was devastated—its buildings torched, its well-heeled slaughtered, its women raped, its wealth sacked. Incensed by centuries of oppression, Hidalgo's throng was taking its revenge on *gachupín*, criollo, and even mestizo upper classes alike. For the well-to-do in a regime based on oppression of the masses, it was the ultimate nightmare. And now Hidalgo advanced toward Mexico City itself.

Criollos at this point were deeply divided. Many, horrified at the excesses of Hidalgo's army, reembraced the *gachupines*. Others swallowed their compunctions and supported Hidalgo, hoping that after victory, he could somehow put the cork back in the bottle of social upheaval that he had opened.

As these allegiances settled, Hidalgo found himself with a force of sixty thousand to fight and win a bloody battle against the royalist forces in the mountains above the city. Strangely though, he failed to follow up on the victory to move into the capital itself. Perhaps daunted by high casualties or else hesitant to unleash on the capital the fury he had seen in his unruly forces in Guanajuato, Hidalgo instead turned toward Mexico's second city, Guadalajara, successfully entering and establishing his headquarters there after suffering a brief setback at Querétaro.

But his moment had passed. The retreat from Mexico City and defeat at Querétaro cost him dearly in morale among his followers, and criollos were now, by a large majority, firmly allied with the *gachupín* royalists against the social upheaval Hidalgo had led. When a royalist force of highly disciplined regulars—ironically most of them Indian recruits—advanced on his enormous but unschooled army in Guadalajara, Hidalgo and his captains were sent scurrying to the north, where the spirit of rebellion still held sway.

He was captured and tried for treason in Chihuahua. Possibly tortured, he expressed regret at the violence he had spawned but never renounced his belief in the goal of independence and social justice. Along with his captains, he was beheaded and his head hung in a cage in Guanajuato, site of his followers' worst excesses.

Following Hidalgo's defeat and death, the cause lost its fervor and former criollo allies now worked with the royalist General Félix Calleja in a conscious effort to mop up the remnants of the people's revolution before returning to their own agenda of rebellion for an independent criollo state.

But the reunion of criollos and royalists brought about by Hidalgo's revolution didn't last long. During the upheavals, the decrees concerning church wealth that had caused such havoc among criollo debtors had been repealed. Now with peace seemingly restored in New Spain, the crown initiated a new set of liberal reforms aimed at curbing the power of the church. The effect on criollos in New Spain was the same as it had been before. This time the lawyerly, conservative criollos turned to Colonel Agustín de Iturbide, of impeccable credentials as a counterrevolutionary, having fought Hidalgo and pursued insurrectionists all over the Bajío. When the Spanish viceroy made the miscalculation of sending Iturbide with a small army to finish off the last guerrillas operating out of the mountains, Iturbide met secretly with their leader, Vicente Guerrero, and invited him to join him in kicking the Spanish out of Mexico once and for all. Guerrero reluctantly consented, and after a few easy fights, it was all over.

In 1820 Iturbide declared Mexican independence in the Plan de Iguala. The plan guaranteed independence, religion, and union. The Mexican Catholic church retained its privileges and was declared the only permissible national religion. Private property was sacrosanct, though distinctions between rights of different castes were officially abrogated. But the new nation would be founded as a constitutional monarchy, with the crown offered first to young Ferdinand VII of Spain. If he declined, it could be offered to a

Mexican. Spain sent Juan O'Donojú to deal with the situation, and he prudently signed the plan for independence.

On September 28, 1821, Iturbide, dressed in full military regalia, marched into Mexico City followed by a cheering throng of criollos, mestizos, Indians, and even former *gachupines*. Mexico was now a nation. Though Iturbide had won the day and Hidalgo was widely despised at the moment of independence, history would eventually remember the fiery priest as the father of Mexico. It was Hidalgo's movement that embodied the aspirations of the nation as a whole, not those of just one class. But Hidalgo also terrified Mexico with the consequences of releasing those aspirations. That ambivalence continues to manifest itself in the way Mexico views its subsequent revolutionary heroes: Villa, Zapata, and even today's subcomandante Marcos. Revered in spirit and feared in historical apparition, Hidalgo remains a contradictory symbol of both hope and horror. In 1821 the scepter of power had crashed through the first level in the social pyramid. And because of the terrible vision that Hidalgo held forth, it stopped right there.

In the government palace at Guadalajara, I enter into a sunny stone courtyard and catch a glimpse of color flashing through an archway over a grand staircase. As I approach and begin to climb the stairs, one of the palace's famous murals wraps around overhead and draws me into its world.

Looking up and about from the first turn of the staircase, I feel as though I have been kicked in the gut and I have to sit down on the steps. This is José Clemente Orozco's painting of Father Hidalgo, *The Man with Fire*, commissioned by the revolutionary government in 1921. I never imagined how much more than a portrait of a founding father it would turn out to be. Its violence soars in four directions of angry movement—up the back wall behind the staircase, around the two side walls, and up and over the vault above so that I have to lean my head backward to see where it all goes.

The travel guides describe the mural as "enigmatic," but there is nothing mysterious about it. In reds, oranges, yellows, and browns it tells the entire story of Mexico's frenzies of blood and woe, reaching back to the coming of Cortés and forward to the twentieth-century revolution, mingling images of these cataclysmic moments with icons of the nineteenth-century war for independence. On the left wall crumbles the rubble of the church, where serpents crawl through tumbled crosses. On the right fools' faces wearing swastikas and hammers and sickles carry on their ideological idiocy while more important things happen in the lower center, where peasants writhe on the ends of bayonets, amid blood and fire. Looming hugely above it all, the beatific face of Father Hidalgo turns eyes upward in a spasm of tragic passion. His long white hair suggests wisdom and love, but one hand is clenched in a fist and the other takes a torch to everything that is happening around him. The face and the torch dominate the entire mural, as if in the moment after this one captured in paint on plaster, everything will be consumed in flames and only the suprahumanness of the face will remain.

That a government would commission such a painting in its halls is astounding. This is no cozy portrait of a flag-wielding founding father crossing a river in some safely past corner of history. Its moment is just as much now as it is then; its place is anywhere; its heroes are nonideological; its significance is universal. This is a dangerous painting.

Late that evening in the lobby of the Hotel Francés I meet a Mexican-American businessman who has been frantically trying to place a call to Los Angeles. "What a place to do business," he grumbles in English as he sits down beside me at the bar to nurse his bourbon and water. José Ramírez migrated from Mexico to Los Angeles as a child and eventually studied business at UCLA, "becoming fully Americanized in the process." He thought he could make some money while providing a service to his people by setting up an HMO that catered to migrant workers in the fields of places like the Salinas Valley, California. Now, though he still operates out of L.A., his business has expanded into ninety Mexican cities, and he is a successful man.

"You'd be crazy to have a startup HMO in the U.S. these days," he says. With its growing population and its friendly government, Mexico is the new place to make money in his field. Though José found his fortune through his U.S. education and contacts, he is increasingly drawn economically and emotionally to his home country. He is considering moving back here with his wife and kids, but he has worries about instability. "That's what America offers besides money these days, safety. With our inflammatory politics and rebels openly operating in some parts of the country, a man in my position just doesn't feel the same security here, no matter how much he loves his homeland."

I tell him that I have just today seen the mural *The Man with Fire*, and he says, "There you have it. That's the legacy of fear that the Mexican lives with, especially the Mexican who has much to lose." I ask if he believes his worry is one that is widely held by Mexicans already rooted here. "Oh, they rarely show it," he answers. "The stolid, inscrutable Mexican—he thinks his best defense against trouble is to deny that it's out there. But don't let him fool you. He sees blood and fire in his nightmares."

Nonetheless José Ramírez has just about determined to take the risk and make the leap back home. Most of his business is here anyway. "The more you get out of life," he says, "the more you understand that you can't have it all." He is going to choose Mexico and settle for a degree less security.

I ask why the recognition that you can't have it all makes him choose Mexico.

"Because even if you can't have it all, you can still have your first choice," he answers. "That's what success means, being able to have your first choice. And, after all, I am a Mexican."

On New Year's Day of 1994, revolution erupted again in Mexico when a ragtag band of ski-masked peasants calling themselves the Zapatista National Liberation Army, or EZLN, marched into San Cristóbal de las Casas in the state of Chiapas and declared war on the government. A mysterious leader known as subcomandante Marcos proclaimed the uprising to be more than just regional strife: He would take his movement all the way to Mexico City. Though the government of President Salinas called for a cease-fire just twelve days after the outbreak, land-hungry peasants already had taken over thousands of hectares of Chiapas hacienda lands while nervous hacendados armed themselves to defend their property.

Meanwhile, at a night political rally on March 23, Luis Donaldo Colosio, Salinas's hand-picked successor, was gunned down in an assassination no one believes was the work of a lone crazed gunman. While the Zapatistas threaten on the left, people believe that a putsch from the right side of the PRI itself doomed the establishment candidate who had begun to talk a little too liberally.

As Mexico lurches toward its August 21 presidential election and beyond, our travels throughout Mexico are dogged by these two ragged events. Even as NAFTA is signed and journalists and observers from all over the world gather to witness what just might be Mexico's first honest election, and even though foreign travelers like us feel comfortable, welcome, and secure, Mexico has not truly changed. People here don't like to think about these two events and what they might portend, but they do. And those who know their history are worried, no matter how cheery the mask they wear for the watching world.

3

So Far from God

Guadalajara to Mexicali

As the Tren Pacífico pulls out of the Guadalajara yards bound for Mazatlán and eventually Mexicali on the U.S. border, we already see signs that we are entering into a different environment that will remind us more of home. The graffiti scrawled on the passing factories and warehouses show more interest in LSD, pussy, and gang tags than anti-PRI slogans. Though the eight-car train has only coaches, its *primera especial* section is cleaner and more orderly than anything we have seen on all-coach trains so far. The rest rooms have toilet paper and the concession-aire sells Diet Pepsi.

The family riding in the seats behind us is bound for Arizona, where they will visit two generations of their children. The older woman and her incredibly young-looking seventy-one-year-old husband will visit a son in a town outside of Phoenix, and their daughter, who is traveling with them, has two children in Phoenix.

Lourdes and I are fascinated by the old man's secret of youth—with his dark hair, taut skin, and barrel chest, he could easily be a man in the prime of his forties. When he turned sixty, his wife tells us, he had a hard time getting retirement because of his appearance. "He's worse than a woman," she says. "Borrowing my creams all the time, dying his hair. And he's always finding medicines for youth. Our daughter-in-law runs a beauty salon and he drives her crazy."

The man, who has moved to the seat across the aisle from us, leans over and confides to us that even his wife doesn't know his secret, but he will tell us: "It's just black clay and cream of milk and avocado on the face every day." He suggests to us that we should try it; we are just getting to the age where we will be needing it.

He made his first trek to the California vegetable fields as a young man with the intention of staying just the legal forty-five days on his temporary work visa. "I cut celery and made good money. Sure, they treated us like rented merchandise, but we had good food, a decent climate, and the ranchers were nice people. I ended up staying on a year as an illegal."

He went on to harvest chilies near Oakland and had his first encounter with racial problems. "It wasn't the Americans; it was the Filipinos we worked the fields with. They were good workers but we had character differences and didn't get along. I learned to be nice to them though; they were the cooks."

Asparagus was his least favorite crop. "It grows too fast. You cut it one day and think you're finished with that part of the field and the next day it has grown up again. Change me to a different plot, I said. I'm tired of this one."

He believes American employers like Mexican workers because they are hard workers. He eventually settled in, picking tomatoes at twelve cents a box, and learned to work fast enough that he could do a hundred boxes a day. He learned quickly that you were paid by quantity, not by quality, so he dispensed with picking clean. "Just pick and pack, pick and pack, and don't think or fuss."

Over the next fifteen years he made ten more of these yearlong illegal forays into California; it became part of a way of life. This was during the years of César Chávez's activism, but he never took part in union action. "I was just hired to do my job and I did it. My real life was still back here in Mexico." So when an American woman asked him to marry her, he politely declined and came home to marry his Mexican sweetheart.

He was aware of how poorly Mexican workers were treated, despite the friendliness and easygoing nature of their American employers. "If you got hurt, they would send you to the hospital, but once there, you weren't taken care of very well. 'He's a Mexican. Let him die.' " He once fell fifteen feet from a ladder in an orchard and hurt his knee. He was lucky that he was a good healer. They gave him aspirin and a bandage at the infirmary and sent him on his way.

In the old days you could work this way, save money and send it home to the family, because the cost of living was so much cheaper in Mexico. Not anymore. He doesn't know how a guy earning twenty-five dollars a day in the California fields could support a family of ten back in Mexico these days. That's why so many now end up moving their families north and living there.

He's glad he didn't have to do that. He has managed to accumulate a little property; he even ran a restaurant for thirty years. Still he has to work, despite his retirement income. "If I don't work, all I have to eat is tortillas and chilies. So when my son calls from Arizona at ten in the evening and asks, 'Papa, why are you still working?' I tell him I work to eat well."

His four sons and two of his grandchildren have all moved permanently and legally to the United States. One son earns eighteen dollars an hour as a roofer, more than his father earned in a day at the same age. The wife of another runs a beauty salon. "They are making livings I couldn't imagine when I was young." But he and his wife have no intention of joining their children in Arizona. It's not home. So they just make these occasional visits.

I ask him about American concerns about illegal immigrants and California governor Pete Wilson's Proposition 187, banning government assistance to illegal aliens, and he rolls his eyes. "Why do they want to do that? They need our work. And can you imagine what would happen here if there weren't the opportunity to work in America? And what will happen to those Mexicans who have made a life there? They have houses and cars. They don't want to come back. What will happen?"

As we have talked, the train has left the Guadalajara yards far behind and now winds through the agave fields surrounding the town of Tequila, where José Cuervo is made. You can smell it in the air from the open platforms as the sun bakes the aroma of tequila from the millions of blue plants laid out in neatly textured patterns in all directions. Now the train winds up narrow ridges into the highlands of Sierra Volcán Transversal, through tunnels and around precipitous curves affording views back over the city. Across the valley in the distance looms the Volcán de Tequila. Up close in the pueblos along the tracks we see men making bricks from red clay and women hanging laundry while the children play in the dirt. The rail route roughly parallels the old Camino Real all the way to California. It is a beautiful route full of Mexican fecundity—but also a gateway beckoning to a vision of a better life up north.

Four and a half centuries ago their Spanish ancestors marched up this way to settle an empire and save the natives from heathenism in California. Today Mexicans ride these rails or hitchhike on Highway 15 to earn a decent living illegally picking vegetables on lands that were once part of their country. It is particularly galling to Mexicans to hear American complaints about illegal aliens working in the states that were taken from Mexico during the era of Manifest Destiny. The anti-immigrant demagoguery of American politicians adds insult to long-standing injury.

Mexicans know it's politics. From their experience with governments on both sides of the border, they understand all too well the politics of exploitation and neglect. But they don't understand the politics of scapegoating, division, and hate-mongering. At its clearest, they see it as proof that, despite NAFTA and the proclamations of North American solidarity from our side of the border, nothing has changed in the unequal relationship between Mexico and its giant northern neighbor. Despite the corruption and cynicism that bedevil Mexican society and politics internally, there is nothing that so galvanizes Mexicans into unity as the image of Governor Pete Wilson trumpeting the righteousness of Proposition 187. It's the one thing they all can agree about. But then, mistrust of the *norteamericanos* is one thing Mexicans have always agreed about.

The United States had gained its independence just forty years before Mexico, and a clash between the two young nations of North America soon became inevitable. For centuries the frontier of Mexico, its lands of new opportunity, lay to its north. The frontier for the *norteamericanos* lay to their west—both looked to the same area for continental expansion. But the Mexicans got there first.

Exploration and colonization of the northwest began within a few decades of Cortés's triumph, as wealth-seeking conquistadores and newcomers from Spain sought to cash in on the conquest. In 1542, Beltrán Nuño de Guzmán established the realm of Nueva Galicia, comprising today's Michoacán, Jalisco, Zacatecas, and Culiacán, and initiated a reign of terror that Indians in those parts still remember. The "man of the noose and knife" ruled with such arbitrary cruelty that he instilled a spirit of rebellion in the natives of the region that eventually made it a hotbed of revolt during each of Mexico's subsequent upheavals.

In these same years, Francisco Vázquez de Coronado explored as far north as today's Kansas, seeking the Seven Cities of Cíbola and their legendary cache of gold. Guided by the stories of Álvar Núñez Cabeza de Vaca and the African slave, Esteban, who had wandered these lands and reported sighting the mythical cities, Coronado mapped out a region that eventually would be colonized by Juan de Oñate when he founded Santa Fe in 1609. Otherwise, much of northern New Spain was colonized in defensive maneuvers to prevent other European powers from establishing a foothold in North America. In response to French encroachment in the Louisiana territory, San Antonio and Texas were founded in 1718. The California coast was charted by Juan Rodríguez Cabrillo as early as 1542, but it wasn't until the 1740s that fears of British and Russian explorations of the far northwest led to the occupation of Alta California.

In 1769 the Spaniards put into effect an ambitious plan to settle California and convert its Indians with the building of El Camino Real, a royal highway connecting Mexico City to the far northwest. Twenty-one missions and four presidios were established along its length, followed by numerous pioneer ranchos and developed pueblos. The argument by later American proponents of Manifest Destiny that Mexico was not serious about governing California founders on this project. The Spaniards, unlike the Romans, were not great road builders. Nowhere else in New Spain did they build such a road. Furthermore, the government sponsored the pioneers who manned the presidios and missions from Texas to California with the clear intention of settling the frontier. Ironically, the Mexican provinces of the north were established in the same American spirit of pioneering that motivated westward-moving *norteamericanos* a century later.

In the immediate aftermath of independence, Mexicans were divided in their attitudes toward their neighbor to the north. Some liberals wanted to mimic the philosophy of government embodied in the U.S. Constitution and even went so far as to suggest emulation of *norteamericano* cultural habits—so alien to Mexico's Indian and Spanish heritage but seemingly so successful for nation-building in the Americas. Certainly achieving U.S. diplomatic recognition of Iturbide's empire was a primary goal, and when Washington swallowed its compunctions about the appropriateness of monarchy on this continent and acknowledged the Iturbide regime in 1822, there was a collective sigh of relief throughout Mexico. But some of Mexico's founding fathers warned from the start that the Americans' belief in Manifest Destiny would lead to war with the United States. Particularly galling was the oft-repeated yanqui statement that all adjoining lands not effectively governed by Mexico should belong to the United States.

By that standard all Mexico might have been annexed to the United States in the early years of independence. For four decades after the crowning of Iturbide, Mexicans proved themselves inept at governing themselves, though expansionist designs of the yanquis and interventions by European powers hampered whatever progress might have been possible. The first empire accomplished a few things, such as abolishing racial categories and colonial restrictions on trade, reducing taxes, and dismantling the paternal system of Indian government (though this also removed protections the Indians had enjoyed). But otherwise the feud between liberal and conservative criollos at the top levels of society, the ambitions of tinhorn military adventurers, and the total neglect of the mass of Mexicans at the bottom led in the next forty years to coup after coup and social conditions as bad as at any time in the colonial era. The hunger and poverty that had rallied the lower classes to Hidalgo's banner worsened as Mexico City became a scene of hellish squalor for anyone below the highest tier of the pyramid. The streets and neighborhoods and churches of Mexico City thronged with the begging poor, *lepreros,* as many as twenty thousand, clad in rags and suffering all manner of deformities and skin diseases. Crime became rampant, with dozens of unidentified murder victims displayed daily on the steps of the capital prison. Robbery was so common that the well-to-do simply stopped carrying large sums of money. Even the affluence of the capital was of a Potemkin village variety, with aristocratic criollos hiding their indebtedness behind gaudy displays of magnificence.

This is what the people got for their war for independence. It is small wonder then, that when yanqui armies came calling, a majority of states and masses of the Mexican people failed to rally to the cause of defending their nationhood against the invader.

I have traveled on trains all over North America, and this ride on the Pacífico is the first I have seen during these Mexican journeys that ranks with routes like the *California Zephyr* or the *Canadian* for scenic qualities. Beyond Tequila we continue to wind up a sharp ridge, through hairpin after hairpin, tunnel after tunnel, the yawning gap of the Río Grande de Santiago Valley to the east and volcanoes looming behind it. The landscape is similar to the eastern arid side of the southern Sierra Nevada: lots of ragged rock with clumps of evergreen and cacti.

At the summit we stop at the town of Barranca, elevation five thousand feet. Though it's a sunny summer day, the air is cool, as it is in so many of Mexico's semitropical high-altitude places. Beyond Barranca we roll out onto a high plateau where the farms are now more northern in character. We see horses instead of oxen, cowboys instead of dirt farmers, range instead of cornfields.

But after the stop at Tepic in the late afternoon, we witness the truth of the adage that in Mexico it is altitude, not latitude, that matters. We have traveled hundreds of miles north; but as we descend to the lower elevations of the Pacific plain, the air again becomes hot and sticky and the landscape tropical. Now we see jungle vegetation—sugar cane, papaya, tangerine, lime, and banana trees. The land is wetter. The people along the tracks wear their shirts open or not at all. When the train stops, mosquitoes invade through the open windows.

There are two Americans on this train today, and the tropical setting now galvanizes my curiosity about where I think I have met them before. Jim and his wife, Dorothy, are looking to make a living out of their wanderlust in Mexico. We start with pleasantries and the usual commentary among "alternative" American travelers about how so many tourists bring nothing, see very little, make no contact, and take away only photos.

The couple tells us about the three hundred pounds of luggage they carry, all lashed together with cable for security. They travel with every kind of survival gear imaginable. When they tell us they have just bought land on the Mosquito Coast of Honduras I know why I think I recognize them. He is Allie Sherman, from Paul Theroux's *The Mosquito Coast*, made real in the flesh. This gives me the shivers, as I recall Allie's end with the seagulls plucking out his eyeballs. They are planning to build a homestead somewhere south of the border to survive the holocaust they believe is imminent in the United States. Jim likes to invent things. And he is sure that his American entrepreneurial talents will enable him to sell something to Central Americans that will guarantee him a good living.

Meanwhile Lourdes has befriended another Mexican traveler to the United States, and I am relieved to turn my attention back to some sane Mexicans. Manuel lives in San Diego and works in a cement plant. He went in as an illegal in 1982 and then took advantage of the 1985 amnesty to acquire dual citizenship. He has come to Mexico now to take his two daughters back with him to the States. It has been a hard decision. His extended family would like him to be here to help work their subsistence farm, but he wants more for himself and for his daughters. He came down here with a truck, and a hitchhiker offered him more for it than he thought it was really worth. So he sold it with the idea of always building toward a better life with his daughters back in the United States. Without the truck now he is traveling with them by train back to the Mexicali border crossing where he will find some way to get to San Diego.

As the train speeds out across the Pacific plain, nearing the resort city of Mazatlán, a fine sunset develops and it draws a group of riders out to the open platform. Manuel is here along with two young fellows from Mazatlán, the conductor, and a brakeman. Mazatlán is a booming place, they all agree. It's full of *norteamericanos* spending lots of money, and more than ever before, Mexicans with enough money to play at the beaches the system created for foreigners' pleasure.

"We're a country that is tied to the other side," says the conductor. "We recognize that, and so we treat U.S. citizens well when they are in our country." But he can't understand the underpinnings of Proposition 187. "Isn't the labor our people bring to your country just as valuable to you as the money your people bring to our country is to us?" He waits for an answer; his question is not rhetorical, but I have none to give him.

"They're already starting to come back, you know," he says. "I see more and more Mexicans on this train who have left the U.S. and are coming back home because of Proposition 187."

At Mazatlán, I ride in the back of a pickup to our lodgings at Los Sábalos Hotel on the beach while Lourdes squeezes in front with the kind fellows who picked us up at the train station when no taxis appeared. We pass a cacophony of Mexicana along the route: food vendors, mariachi bands, craftsmen. There is also neon and rock music, tank tops and Ninja Turtles, McDonald's and Dunkin' Donuts. Our hotel is a beautiful beachfront place with pools, tropical gardens, and a great oyster bar. But this could just as easily be Fort Lauderdale as Mexico.

At independence the Mexican empire was one of the largest in the world, extending from Panama to Louisiana to Oregon. It didn't last long. In just two years the imperious emperor Agustín Iturbide managed to alienate all of the power centers that had once supported him. Thus when a young criollo officer in Veracruz called for a republic with power vested in the congress Iturbide had dissolved, the emperor was easily dethroned and sent packing—with a proviso that if he ever returned he would be executed. Somehow in his haste to depart, Iturbide never received this final instruction, so that when he made an ill-considered attempt to return a year later, he was arrested and summarily shot. Meanwhile the central American provinces revolted and went their own way.

One of the first acts of the provisional government following the fall of Iturbide sounds familiar today: the negotiation of a sixteen-million-peso loan from Great Britian to get the country back on its feet again. Besides the obvious need for capital, it was a shrewd international maneuver (one of the few by the young nation) to establish a vested interest by an outside power to help guarantee independence against the expected designs of the United States. But it also helped establish a pattern of Mexican dependency and the overinvolvement of foreign governments in its internal affairs.

The new republic boiled over with contending philosophies and power centers. At its simplest, the controversy was over whether the Mexican republic would be centralist, with most power vested in the government in Mexico City, or federalist, with powers reserved for the states. Though the liberal federalists won the first round in shaping a new constitution rather like that of the United States, one look at Mexico City today shows who won in the long run. In a sense Mexico's liberals of that age were hamstrung by the same contradictions as they are today. While advocating freedom of the press, an egalitarian society, curtailment of privilege, and secular public education, they were committed to a foreign economic model of laissez-faire capitalism that didn't fit the reality of Mexican society. Further, they had no more interest than did the conservatives in bringing social justice and economic well-being to the millions of mestizos and the indigenous at the bottom of the pyramid. Then, as now, they espoused an order that could work only in a population more like that of Pennsylvania.

Conservatives, on the other hand, had no such confusion. They favored a centralized rule by the elite, preservation of privilege, Roman Catholic monopolies on religion and education, and censorship of inflammatory speech. They knew exactly who they were. They still do today.

Beyond this dichotomy fermented the never-ending intrigues of military strongmen interested in nothing but their own advancement in power. Despite all the sound and fury from contending philosophies of government, it was this factor that really dominated Mexican politics during the era of confrontation with the United States. Though there were aspiring caudillos galore, no one stood out so much as Antonio López de Santa Anna, a man at least as despised in Mexican memory as he is in American. During his lifetime he ruled Mexico no fewer than eleven times. He was alternately a patriot, a traitor, a liberal, a conservative, a hero, a goat. In the end, Mexicans remember him as a colorful fool who orchestrated much of Mexico's humiliation at the hands of the yanquis.

Santa Anna was the officer from Veracruz who initiated the revolt that overthrew Iturbide, though his associates very quickly and wisely cut him off from power in this first instance. His second chance came in 1829 when Spain attempted to seize upon Mexico's turmoil and reconquer the lost colony with a force of three thousand men landed at Tampico. At the head of a Mexican army, Santa Anna defeated the Spanish force and was dubbed "the hero of Tampico." Thus when liberals had had enough of the conservatives installed in a coup shortly after the Spanish misadventure, they turned to Santa Anna in Veracruz to pull off a countercoup in 1832. After his inauguration as president, however, he showed little interest in the business of actually governing, instead retiring to his Veracruz estate and turning the conduct of the nation's affairs over to his liberal activist vice president. When conservatives rose in high dudgeon against the reforms the new regime initiated, Santa Anna came out of Veracruz, tossed his vice president and other liberals out of the government, discarded their legislative reforms, established a conservative, centralist regime, and then again retired to Veracruz, letting his new vice president run things, emerging himself only to put down occasional liberal revolts. The new leadership quickly established a conservative counterreform, most notable for requiring specific levels of wealth for congressional and presidential candidates.

It was in this climate that Mexico faced the challenge of the Americans in Texas. In the 1820s Mexico had encouraged the colonization of Texas by whoever would settle on the land. Though the government would have preferred primarily Mexican settlers, the energy and capital brought to the colony by *norteamericano* pioneers seeking to establish a cotton economy had appeal. So intent was Mexico on settling the region that it suspended the prohibition against slavery (Negroes only) and offered a ten-year suspension of general taxes. These incentives, along with the abundance of good land, attracted the likes of Stephen Austin, who led three hundred families into Texas in the first year. Soon the Anglo population was triple that of the Mexicans, and the two groups did not meld as the government had hoped. Mexicans gathered tightly in the towns, focusing on the local Catholic parishes, while the Anglos settled on rural plantations. Initially the Anglo settlers had little interest in wresting the land from Mexico. The ill-fated revolt of Haden Edwards and his attempt to declare the independent Republic of Fredonia in 1826 was never the big deal that Texan lore makes it out to be. Even Austin himself opposed it, seeing the tax advantages of continued allegiance to Mexico at the time.

But by 1830 it was a different story. Growing alarmed at the number of Anglos in the colony, the Mexican government closed the border to immigration and trade—though to no avail. The long border along the Sabine River was impossible to patrol, and the Americans kept coming—the first illegal aliens to cross the U.S.-Mexico border. Austin, still seeking accommodation with Mexico, went to Mexico City and appealed for Texas statehood within Mexico and its own capital (Texas was at that time combined with Coahuila, whose capital was in distant Saltillo). Only when he was rebuffed and the centralist government of Santa Anna's second presidency moved to tighten control over the wayward province by sending in troops, did Austin contemplate insurrection. Independence was declared in March of 1836 for the Republic of Texas under an Anglo president and a Mexican vice president.

Santa Anna emerged from the seclusion of his Veracruz estate and marched north with an army of 6,000 troops. At San Antonio, with half of his army, he encountered William Travis and 186 defenders in the old Alamo mission. After a ten-day siege, Santa Anna demanded unconditional surrender. Travis refused and the Mexican army assaulted the little bastion, killing all of its defenders, including American frontiersmen Davy Crockett and Jim Bowie. Santa Anna had another victory over foreigners and the Texans had a battle cry. A month later a Texan force of nearly 400 was defeated by another Mexican army and surrendered, expecting to be treated as prisoners of war. But Santa Anna ordered the surviving 365 prisoners to be shot. It was a grim turning point for the remaining 800 men in Sam Houston's army. Retreating toward the Sabine River but looking for their chance at revenge over the vastly more numerous Mexican forces, they found it one afternoon when the victorious Santa Anna, preparing for a triumphal return to Mexico City, neglected to post sentries around his encampment. Houston's forces attacked and whipped the reveling Mexicans and captured Santa Anna a few days later. Santa Anna negotiated his release by promising independence to Texas. When he returned to Mexico, he and the promise were discredited, and again he withdrew to his Veracruz estate.

But Santa Anna was still not done. In 1838, the French, seeking to slice their piece of the pie from the reeling nation, called for restitution of six hundred thousand pesos for damage done to a

French pastry shop. Thus began the short "Pastry War" and when French ships and troops threatened Veracruz, Santa Anna emerged from retirement to lead a force to defeat the invaders, losing his leg in the battle. Again Santa Anna was declared the national savior, named president, and allowed to return to Veracruz and administer the government through his vice president.

Throughout all of these presidencies, Santa Anna established a threshold of corruption and bad government that became an institutional habit in Mexico. By 1844 Mexicans of all persuasions had become disillusioned by their independence, their leaders, their serial constitutions, and the squabble between liberals and conservatives who seemed to be making war more on the populace of the nation than on each other. Another coup broke out and the upshot of this one was Santa Anna's exile to Cuba. Maybe he was the problem.

But Santa Anna wasn't the sole problem, and he himself was not done with Mexico. This was the state of affairs when the United States began its move to realize the dream of Manifest Destiny. And in that historical chapter, Santa Anna would play his most despicable role yet.

Actually, you wouldn't mistake Mazatlán for Fort Lauderdale. The hotels don't rise as high and glitzy as they do in Florida, or in Cancún, for that matter. And they charge far less for first-class accommodations. The vendors prowling the beaches sell real Taxco silver and Tarascan blankets at reasonable prices. You can rent a catamaran sailboat for five pesos an hour, and the owner will throw in an extra hour because he doesn't take accurate note of the time. You can order shrimps Mexicana for breakfast, and you have to ask if you want toast instead of tortillas.

The beach here is coarse, tan Pacific sand, and the breakers aren't big enough for surfing because of the string of islands just offshore. Though there is no boardwalk, the beach itself links a series of little merchant arcades in between the hotels just off the Avenida del Mar. At night out on this traffic-clogged strip, the street life is hot and hybrid—Latin American and Euro-Anglo with hints of Asian influence. *Norteamericano* college kids on permanent spring break have discovered this place, Japanese businessmen work their cell phones here, Germans marvel at how far their marks can stretch, and in the winter there is a massive invasion of Canadian snowbirds. Mazatlán is really neither Fort Lauderdale nor Mexico. It's a province of that zone of indistinct nationality that forms an archipelago of beaches in this latitude from the Pacific through the Caribbean to the Atlantic.

You don't have to ride far beyond Mazatlán on the Tren Pacífico before you are back in the real Mexico. Thirty kilometers to the north, the pueblo of Mármol was founded fifty years ago as a site for a cement factory. The factory closed five years ago but people had been planted here and some haven't left. The first-class train blasts through this dusty little whistle-stop at sixty miles per hour, but the second-class train stops and there are always people getting on and off. Perhaps if the town hadn't been on a rail route, the departure of the cement factory would have taken all the people with it.

Right beside the tracks (there is no station) stands the town's only grocery store, the Súper Mármol. It is one tiny adobe room crammed with soaps, lightbulbs, cornflakes, chilies, soda, beer, toilet paper, cookies, bags of coarse sugar, coffee, canned vegetables, pots of dried beans, tortilla flour, and a meager assortment of fresh bananas, mangoes, potatoes, avocados, tomatoes, and peppers. For meat, people go to the butcher shop down the street, and there are a tortilla store and a fish market out by the water.

The proprietors of Súper Mármol, José and María López Hidalgo, came to this town when they were young, bought a house, and opened the store. That was when the cement factory was booming and the town's population was ten thousand. Their children, along with about eight thousand of the former population have moved out, mainly to Mazatlán. "Why should we move to Mazatlán?" María asks Lourdes as I make my inventory of what is on the shelves. "What would we grown-ups do in a place like that?" The children actually come here for vacations, she says, because the air is cleaner, the nearby beach is uncrowded, and you can get such a restful night's sleep in this quiet place. "A good place to sleep. That's important. It's half of your day," she explains not at all facetiously.

It's the pensioners who have stayed on here primarily and a few younger people who work on the ranches or for the state on the highway. "Young people used to marry here in town," María says. "But now they go to Mazatlán to find husbands and wives. Those who have stayed are here for the tranquillity. That's what we got in return for the loss of the factory and all those jobs."

José, a hulking, friendly, white-haired fellow with big hands, says it wasn't always so peaceful. There was trouble at the factory, corruption. And the factory closed because of a nasty union fight. Rather than give the workers more money, the owners took the business to Mazatlán.

As we talk, people come and go, most just to chat rather than to buy anything. One young fellow comes in to boast about riding a bronco for fifteen seconds, his longest yet. A pretty young mother stops by to buy her four-year-old daughter a lollipop. A man brings José a basket of avocados, and José pays him from the cash register. A pickup full of armed and sweating policemen stops briefly, and José says they don't have much to do here because "they rule with an iron fist. Thank God, it's always peaceful here now."

A short, dignified elderly woman wanders in, and it's clear that she commands special respect. María introduces Doña Carmen as "*la presidente*," though she actually is not an officer of the town. Her qualification for the title is that she is eighty-one years old, and that means a lot in a place of dwindling vitality. Her mother lived to be a hundred and ten and occupied the same post on the social ladder of Mármol.

Doña Carmen is proud to tell us that she has nineteen children and is a great-great-grandmother. Only one of her progeny is single, a forty-eight-year-old son who "fishes for corn" when he should be "fishing for a wife." They have all dispersed themselves elsewhere, and so she has time to be mother to everyone in the village.

She invites us to come to see her house, just a few yards down the dusty street from the Súper Mármol. It's the first time we have been invited into a Mexican peasant home. The house itself is just three rooms: one with simple living room furniture (a couch, a chair, a table with a kerosene lamp); a kitchen with a sink, a wood stove, a long cutting-board table, and two beds with magnificent woven blankets in an L-shaped alcove off one end; and a bathroom with buckets of water carried from public taps still supplied by the departed cement company. The floor is dirt with rugs scattered here and there. Pictures of family hang on the concrete block and adobe walls, and the whole place is rather dark (there are only three windows) and cool considering the heat outside.

But the real essence of Doña Carmen's home resides in the shaded porches, breezeways, and gardens that surround the actual house. Her home seems less a house with gardens than it is gardens with a house in their midst. She has put the same energy into growing profusions of flowers as she has into cultivating the vegetables that are part of her subsistence. She also grows herbs for their medicinal value—the town has no drugstore. When I cough, she makes me a tea of *navio* bark and cinnamon that soothes the throat. She grows basil not for seasonging but as a treatment for gas and earaches—bodily disturbances that call for the relief of pressure.

Under a *palapas* roof, she has hung up all of the plastic quart bottles from the milk she has drunk since her children left the house. "It's a way of telling the months and years," she says. And the plastic bottles entertain her when the wind blows.

"I am considered one of the richest women in the town," Doña Carmen boasts, gesturing to her gardens. "People here live modestly off the land; we don't need a lot and we have what we need. Just live long enough like me and see how easy it is to be considered one of the richest women in town."

But *"presidente"* Doña Carmen has suffered her own loss in this place. "What about your husband?" Lourdes asks her with a gentle, circuitous Latin diplomacy. "He was killed," she answers without hesitation. "He was a guard and some money was missing from the factory; he was blamed and was killed. It was a bad time. But it's quiet and peaceful here," she insists. The managers of the factory discovered that he had been unfairly blamed, had actually attempted to do his job in the robbery, so they gave her money shortly afterward.

"But I didn't care about the money," she explains. "It wasn't until eleven years later that it was made right." That's when someone killed the corrupt man from the factory who had killed her husband.

"Who killed him?" we want to know. "The courts? The police? Factory officials?"

"No," she says. "It was someone from the town. Justice was done. You can't kill someone and get away with it. Sooner or later someone will set it right."

The long stretch of the Tren Pacífico's route from Mazatlán to Hermosillo is a night run with no Pullmans. Before these travels are over we will eventually ride at night in coach, even in second-class coach, but we're not sure that we're ready for that yet. So following a good session of soul-searching, we decide to fly Mexicana Airlines from Mazatlán to Hermosillo, where we intend to again pick up the train.

The Mexicana flight is a pleasant surprise. Unlike the trains, the airplane (a new 757) is cleaner and better maintained than its American counterparts. Whereas the introductory announcements on American Airlines during our flights to Mexico stressed that the real purpose of the flight attendants was to provide for our safety, here the emphasis is on our comfort. Pillows are brought to us. During our midafternoon flight, we are served fine hors d'oeuvres: little tortillas in several different shapes, some with jalapeños and cheese, others with pork and salsa. Beer and mixed drinks are free, and all this in economy class. The flight takes off and lands precisely on time.

Hermosillo, the capital of Sonora, contradicts our expectations of a western cowboy kind of town. Rather it is a late colonial city with much of its Gothic-inspired architecture intact. Many of the buildings in the central city are dazzlingly white, conveying almost an Arabic impression. Though the heat is abominable, the omnipresent rubber and lemon trees in shady green plazas scattered throughout the city and the low humidity lessen the sense of oppressiveness. A warm desert wind seems to sweep the tiled walkways of the *zócalo*—there is a surprising sense of freshness here.

The museum pricks our curiosity. Its central courtyard is filled with mural art and, more interestingly, a series of inscriptions that present a cycle of Mexican creation and life. From Einstein, "That which you see was made from things you don't see." From Indian chief Cuauhtitlán, "It was said that then there were four lives and this was the fifth age when the sun came out." And other Mexican poets and seers: "Cities were beginning but already music existed in them"; "For you no longer will there be warmth"; "Nothing can frighten you any longer, no joy, no sun, no warmth."

Lourdes explicates for me the creation story running through all of these. Something happened in the infinite. It brought happiness into the confines of the world, and this joy engendered flowers and the sound of the land—a day of dance began. But the cycle moves from joy in the creation to woe in its perpetuation. All ends in sorrow. "It is like the lyrics of so many Latin American songs," says Lourdes, "I loved you. You left me. Now I'm sad."

I ask her, "How can a culture thrive so on sorrow?"

"That's the way it is when you've lost everything," she answers. It's the story of the Latin world, whether it be the ancient Indian life lost to Cortés or the Cuban life of Lourdes's childhood lost to Castro.

We find our way to the office of museum curator Ana Sylvia Laborín Abascal, who shows us around and explains that these murals are recent, not like the Orozcos or Riveras found elsewhere. They were painted under a state commission between 1979 and 1984. "Sonora was very poor with murals," she says, "not like Mexico City or Guadalajara with their great traditions. We were trying to found a tradition here."

In one of the murals there is a large, bare-breasted female figure in a heroic pose. Ana Sylvia is flattered and embarrassed to admit that it was she herself who posed as model for the painting. This and other aspects of the murals were greeted with mistrust and concern by the very traditional locals at first. "People here are not like the *gauchos* [city people] south of the river. They are more traditional. It's a case of city versus country."

But she and the other museum directors went to great lengths to ensure that the depictions in the murals were historically accurate and that their purpose was to give the people of Sonora a sense of identity. As time has gone on, Sonorans have come to accept the project, even to cherish it, as they have come to understand how it speaks to their experience.

Ana Sylvia tells us the stories depicted in some of her favorite murals depicting Sonoran history. One shows José María Leyra Cajeme, a chief of the Yaqui tribe made famous by Carlos Castañeda in the sixties. José María was at first considered a traitor because he had been raised by whites. But he left them to become a merciless leader of his own people against the whites. "He was called the man with no liver, for his hardness," Ana Sylvia explains. "When you have a long memory for offenses done against you or your people, you are said to be like a Yaqui." José María was imprisoned by the whites and shot. But despite his apostasies and his cruelty, he was a cultured man who made civilizing laws for his tribe that they still follow. Ana Sylvia concludes, "He lost his youth, then he lost his life. But he left something for his people, and they will revere what he has left forever."

A poignant mural of an old woman who represents both mother earth and the ancient Seri tribe catches Lourdes's attention. The woman's hands preside as midwife over the birth of the earth—all green and joyous before the coming of modern history suffuses it with blood, pain, and loss.

Another of Ana Sylvia's favorites depicts the mother of winds and earth holding a ripped map referring to the loss of northern Sonora to the United States in the Gadsden Treaty. "The Pápago tribe was split in half by the new border," she explains. Families and friends were cut off from one another. "This is a picture that really means something to our people." Even in Sonora, so far from the land of the Aztecs, of the Maya and of Cortés, the story is of a brilliant creation marred by the coming of whites—though here more often Anglo than Spanish.

It wasn't really Texas that the American expansionists in Washington were after, but California, Oregon, and the dream of a nation stretching "from sea to shining sea." Texas actually was a problem in American politics because of the issue of slave versus free states. In California, however, as early as 1842 an American naval commander seized the port of Monterey, mistakenly informed that war had broken out with Mexico. When news arrived that no such condition yet existed, the chagrined officer sheepishly apologized and sailed away. But the incident left no doubt in Mexican minds about Washington's ultimate intentions.

With the 1844 election of James K. Polk, who campaigned on a platform promising not only Texas but Oregon too, war became guaranteed. Even before Polk's inauguration, Congress voted to annex Texas. With the divisions that would eventually lead to the American Civil War now fracturing deeply, Manifest Destiny seemed like the last remaining bond that might hold the United States itself together. And virtually every one of the great compromise efforts of those years somehow involved expansion to preserve the delicate congressional balance of slave and free states. Mexicans paid the price.

Polk, it has always appeared from the Mexican perspective, entered office with a grand strategy for dismembering Mexico. One of his first acts was to order General Zachary Taylor to occupy Texas "in order to defend it." In the Gulf, naval squadrons were dispatched to stand offshore at Mexican ports. Another flotilla was sent to California. Agents provocateurs traveled to California to incite rebellion among American colonists there. The Slidell mission was sent to Mexico City offering $20 million for all of the northern territories, despite the clear reality that no Mexican government could afford to sell land to a foreign state and hope to stay in power. To defuse the situation and deflect larger designs, the desperate Mexican government offered to recognize the independence of Texas. The upshot was another coup bringing to power a government more determined to defend Mexican soil against the Americans.

Meanwhile Polk ordered Taylor to occupy the land beyond the Río Nueces, the long-established border of Texas, as far south as the Río Bravo (Rio Grande) on the pretext that the border was not really clear. When a skirmish occurred in the process and a few Americans were killed, Polk had his Gulf of Tonkin incident, and war was declared over the shedding "of American blood on American soil." During the debate before the vote for war, young Congressman Lincoln from Illinois argued against the justice of the declaration and earned for himself permanent standing as one of the few yanquis ever held dear in Mexican memory.

Taylor invaded from Texas and soon captured Monterrey and Saltillo. General Philip Kearny swept through New Mexico and headed for California where the U.S. Navy occupied San Francisco and the Bear Flag revolt kicked in right on cue. General Winfield Scott and his prototype marines prepared to land at Veracruz and follow Cortés's route to "the halls of Montezuma."

This was a messy, confusing, and shameful war. From his exile in Cuba, Santa Anna offered his services to Washington, promising to sell the northern territories to the United States for $30 million if the Americans would help him regain his presidency. Simultaneously he negotiated with the Mexican government for a return from exile and an opportunity to save the country once again. Polk shrewdly played along and allowed Santa Anna to sail through the naval blockade, confident that his return to Mexico would benefit American designs one way or another. Upon his return, another coup installed Santa Anna in power and authorized him to organize the defense of the nation.

Polk's stratagem paid off as Santa Anna completely mismanaged the defense of the capital, allowing his troops to be mauled in a retreat from Veracruz and then attempting to declare victory as Americans marched deeper into the heart of the country. Meanwhile in the Yucatán a Mayan revolt so terrified the criollo masters that the criollos actually asked American occupation forces for help, going so far at one point as to offer the Yucatán for American annexation in return. On the American side, there was the odd incident of the Saint Patrick's Battalion, seventy-two foreign-born Americans (mostly Irish) who crossed over and fought with the Mexicans.

Not until Scott's troops actually entered Mexico City did Americans anywhere face a truly spirited defense. But at the military academy on Chapultepec Hill, young cadets made a heroic stand and fought to the death rather than surrender. It was the only moment of Mexican pride in a war of ignominy.

When representatives of the United States presented their terms for peace—the annexation of all of the northern territories in return for $15 million and the assumption of Mexico's debts—there were Mexican patriots who urged guerrilla-style resistance and a popular revolt against the American presence in the spirit of Hidalgo. But Mexico's criollo leadership, more fearful of the portents from the Yucatán than of American hegemony, chose to give away half of their nation rather than risk losing their place at the top of the pyramid in a social upheaval.

After the signing of the peace, Santa Anna was invited to occupy the presidency of a much diminished nation for his eleventh term. In 1853 he negotiated the Gadsden Purchase of the wedge of land forming the southern tier of today's Arizona and New Mexico and promptly embezzled the $10 million proceeds. This led to his last and final fall from power.

It had all come to ruin: the dream of Hidalgo, the aspirations of independence, even the criollos' hope to comfortably rule in the Spaniards' place at the top of the pyramid. Mexicans knew that their politicians, their generals, and even the class structure of their society had betrayed them. Only seven states had actually contributed forces to the defense. Criollos in the Yucatán and Indians in central Mexico alike stood on the sidelines while the new invader duplicated the feat of Cortés. A wave of nostalgia for the staunch stance of Aztec Cuauhtémoc swept the nation after the defeat. But despite the knowledge that they had been betrayed at home, Mexicans also emerged from this chapter of their history with no doubt about who was the enemy abroad. No longer would liberals seek to mimic the model of the colossus to the north. And not until the 1990s would any Mexican government openly acknowledge to the people an alliance with the yanquis. Even Porfirio Díaz, the dictator overthrown by the 1910 revolution largely for selling the nation to foreigners, once declared, "Poor Mexico. So far from God, so close to the United States."

• • •

The Tren Pacífico from Hermosillo northward is many hours late. No one at the station can tell us just how many, and we feel vindicated by our decision to fly. But yesterday's train, we are told, is due to arrive at the northern town of Benjamín Hill and then stand there long enough before departing for Mexicali that we should be able to catch up with it if we ride one of Mexico's excellent, fast first-class buses from Hermosillo. With misgivings over how much of the route of the Tren Pacífico we have missed, and serious doubt on my part that a bus can be fast or excellent, we take the proffered advice.

What a surprise. The bus is a modern Mercedes, as clean and comfortable as the Mexicana flight. For twenty-six pesos we ride one hundred miles in air-conditioned comfort at sixty miles per hour. During the ride we are entertained by a Mexican movie on individual screens hanging above each pair of seats. The film stars Vicente Fernández, a current popular Mexican heartthrob, whom we get to see several more times in subsequent bus rides. He wears a hugely oversize sequined hat and is always the romantic leading male. In some of his films he is a white knight come to rescue a damsel and her distressed family from the clutches of exploiters. In others he is a passionate man caught in a vicious tragedy in which he is very nearly a villain. He pays with his life in those, along with that of his love interest. A lot of blood is spilled, often from great pulsating spurts as characters are shot in the chest, the head, or the genitals. But in each film we see, the central scene occurs in the ring of a cockfight where Vicente sings a song laden with romantic or tragic meaning for his beloved, who sits shocked and mortified at ringside.

The town of Benjamín Hill does not convey the grandeur and romance of Mexican life depicted in Vicente's movies. It is dusty, dirty, and, since we arrive after dark, threatening. Drunk young men cruise the main drag accosting the few daring young women who are out. As I loiter at the bus station considering what to do, Lourdes disappears without warning for maybe a half hour or more. When she returns there are stern words. She: "I was finding out what we need to do." I: "Please don't make me have to rehearse how I will tell your family that I have lost their mother to rapists or kidnappers." What she has found out is that the train will not depart until the morning. We have to stay the night.

It is a relief to board the Tren Pacífico and head out across the desert in the morning. Our air-conditioning is working and the train is not in bad shape, but we can't seem to find out what time it is. We're pretty sure we're in the equivalent of the mountain time zone; this route begins in the central zone and ends in the Pacific. But some Mexican states do not recognize daylight savings time, so you can cross a border and there may be no change, or a change of an hour, or even a change of two hours. When we ask a passenger and a train attendant for the time this morning, we get different answers. It's either 9:00 A.M. or 10:00 A.M. The conductor should know. But when we ask, he disagrees with both of the others—it is 8:00 A.M. Not so, says another seemingly articulate and intelligent passenger. "They don't change their watches when they should," he explains. "They only know the correct times for the starting and end points of their section of the route. It's 10:00 A.M." Surely this passenger is wrong and somehow the conductor is right. The central necessity of train travel on single-track lines is accurate agreement on times.

We have seen this pattern before in cities when asking for directions. There is often disagreement between the first couple of people we ask. Sometimes we have been heading in the direction indicated by the previous person we asked, and when we ask another, his or her first move is to turn in the direction from which we came and aggravatingly start to point before saying a word. It has given rise to a phrase we chuckle over but take very seriously in these travels: take a poll. So we do that now to find out what time it is.

In taking a poll to find out the truth in Mexico, you cannot rely on numbers. The majority in your poll will very often turn out to be wrong. Our experience has taught us to listen carefully to the explanations offered for why each person's view of the situation is the correct one. After taking the poll we determine the truth based as much on the plausibility of the explanations as on how many people agree.

It turns out that the articulate passenger is correct, at least concerning the space in the universe we currently occupy. We are on mountain time, normally one hour earlier than central or Guadalajara time, which everyone agrees is now 10:00 A.M. But Sonora does not recognize daylight savings time, so the actual time at this geographical spot in Sonora is 10:00 A.M. (though it would be 9:00 A.M. if daylight savings time was in effect here as it is in Guadalajara).

But concerning the running of the train, we are assured that it will not collide head-on with a southbound train running on different time. Southbound trains run on the time of their point of departure, in this case Mexicali. Northbound trains run on the time of their point of destination, also in this case Mexicali. For his purposes and our safety, the conductor knows what he is talking about. In Mexicali it is now 8:00 A.M. Pacific daylight savings time. We decide not to discuss this further with him.

As we roll across the sun-scorched Desierto de Altar, we can see the heat waves rising from the low dunes. There is nothing but sand and mesquite as far as we can see in any direction. We see no sign of wildlife, though we are told there is more than there appears to be, more than in many parts of Mexico because here no one hunts things to extinction. If we could venture out into the sands we would find tarantulas, scorpions, sidewinder rattlers, lots of lizards, desert tortoises, and perhaps some creatures no one knows are there. But as far as humans are concerned, this land is absolutely uninhabited for great stretches. The temperature today will easily top 110. When the train halts once at a highway stop and someone opens the door, we can feel a blast of heat wipe out all of the work done by the air-conditioning for the past hour.

A man wearing a white cowboy hat tells us that this is just one of the obstacles that migrant workers must cross to get to the work fields in California. Rogelio (Eddie) Hernández makes his living taking Mexican workers "over the fence" to find work north of the border. He is not at all shy or apologetic about his illegal business, and he is taking some that way right now, though he won't tell which of the other passengers are his crew.

He first climbed the fence in 1979 into Texas and had a very hard time of it. He spoke no English and was taken advantage of by the gringos he worked for. He was robbed at fast-food joints and beaten up just for being a Mexican north of the border.

He went back again, subsequently to California, and learned English and the ways of the gringos so that would never happen to him again. It was in that state, where he would see wave after wave of new migrants going through the same things he had gone through, that he found his calling. He could make good money for himself while providing a service to his green comrades.

"It was pathetic to see them coming with such high hopes and then just wandering around aimlessly, wasting half of the time they had just finding steady employment. I take them now and teach them how to say 'Where's the boss?' 'Who is the owner?' How to talk friendly and ask, 'What's for work?' How to go to McDonald's and order and count their change right."

Eddie has done well enough with the commissions he charges to workers and employers that he now owns a ranch back in Veracruz with horses, chickens, and goats. He spends every winter there tending to the work and his family. "The California economy wouldn't work without illegals like those I bring," he argues. "And you can't imagine how hard it is for those brave fellows who go over the fence just to earn a decent living." I think of where I would be here in Spanish-speaking Mexico without Lourdes, and I think I can.

Late in the afternoon the desert begins to give way to occasional irrigated fields and then more of them until the landscape fills up with greenery—young corn and orchards of miniature fruit trees. We are approaching the Colorado River crossing, we are told, and had better watch carefully or we will miss it. There isn't much of it left when it leaves the United States, which has long showed itself to be a bad neighbor where water is concerned. As we are looking for the river, we note outhouses with handles attached. When the hole fills up, the house is simply picked up and moved over a new one. Homes in this region are especially ramshackle, often made of nothing more than vertical sticks, cardboard, and scraps of corrugated, rusted metal. There are power lines but no sign of plumbing. What water is available here is channeled into the irrigation ditches.

Finally there is a long muddy stretch and we watch for the river. We aren't sure that we ever do see it—just two small streams passing under the tracks—but later we are told that was it. The mighty Colorado.

A man wearing a white hat with an outrageous purple feather corners us on the vestibule and asks what we think of Proposition 187 and the American politicians who blame so many of the United States' problems on Mexican immigrants. We answer that there are many Americans like us who don't share those politics. He says he hopes we know that Mexican labor is the reason why California is so rich.

Francisco is a legal migrant grape picker who works seasonally in the Fresno area and returns to Guadalajara because he can't stand the winter cold. He earns thirteen thousand dollars a year, enough that when he is home with his family he does not have to work. His wife earns additional income as a schoolteacher, and though they have to budget carefully, the long separations are really the only hardships in their lives. "We don't need much to be happy, so we have a good life in the winter," he explains.

But despite the fact that he is not an illegal himself, he has more anger toward Governor Wilson than anyone else we have encountered. "The man is either crazy or a racist or both. He is looking for racist votes. Your country doesn't need politicians like that." Francisco believes that the taxes paid by legal workers like himself more than cover the minimal services given to nontaxed illegals. "It has nothing to do with money, and everything to do with ugly politics," he says.

Under such unfriendly circumstances, Francisco is afraid that any Hispanic going to work in the States—whether legal or not— will be somehow attacked. "We have an important role to play in California agriculture. If all Mexican workers got together for one week on a strike, we could close down the California economy." He goes on: "California, New Mexico, and Texas were once our land. Now they want to expel us from the land of our ancestors."

He regrets that he sees no one on the horizon these days like the César Chávez of old. However, he claims that when a new Chávez emerges, perhaps Chávez's son, he will get help from the Mexican government if for no other reason than that the government now fully recognizes the catastrophe it would face if the pressure-release valve of migration across the border were shut off.

Francisco thinks a better California proposition would be one that set up rules allowing qualified workers intent on working to cross legally. "If there are people who abuse your welfare system, deal with the offenders."

"What else could California do to be a good neighbor?" I ask.

"Declare another amnesty," he answers. He himself was once an illegal but jumped at the opportunity presented by the previous amnesty. Now he has a resident alien card good as long as he registers each year, which he does not mind doing. "The American politicians who made that program were the good neighbors," he concludes. "Where are they today?"

We can tell we are approaching the border town of Mexicali as the train slows and the landscape turns to factories, refineries, billboards, and trash, trash, trash. In the train station, apparently undergoing major renovations, a Mexican customs official pounces on us because we walked the wrong way off the train. "Come with me, sir, you come with me," he says in totally unfriendly English. Visions of Mexican jail cells fill my head as he leads me around a corner and out of the sight of the crowds. It turns out he just wants to look in my bags for drugs. When he has finished he smiles and apologizes. At least he speaks English. I think of the encounters our Mexican travel buddies have had with officialdom on the other side of the border and shiver.

The newspapers of Mexicali are full of Proposition 187. It has been called a violation of basic human rights by Mexican government officials who have otherwise been downright obsequious to the United States during the era of NAFTA. Editorials call it a racist policy showing the shallowness of American cant about multiculturalism. There is talk of boycotting the border, and businesses are banding together in cartels to aggressively keep prices on this side of the border lower than those on the other side.

It's an uncomfortable place to be an American, and after my brush with the customs agent, I am relieved to board the Mexicali flight that will take us out of here. But just when the plane is about to become airborne during its runway roll, the brakes are slammed on and the jets blast into reverse thrust as the takeoff is aborted. It's a scary moment; no explanation of what has occurred is ever given. Then the plane taxis around back to the beginning of the runway and this time lifts off without incident.

4

In the Silence of the Canyon

The Copper Canyon Route, Los Mochis to Chihuahua

The train is already rolling when I wake up and pull back the covers and then the curtains to look out the window. It's rainy and brilliant green outside with splotches of orange— we're passing an orange grove. On the vanity sit a bowl of candies, a vase of carnations, and an empty wine bottle from last night's welcome aboard party, and as I hear English spoken in the corridor outside, I remember that I am in Mexico but not on a Mexican train. This is the private luxury train run by the Sierra Madre Express of Tucson. After all we had read about these excursions into the Copper Canyon, we had to break away from National Railways of Mexico for our sojourn through Mexico's most primitive and spectacular country.

Lourdes is already waiting for me at a table in the dining room, located in a dome car looking out above the train. Breakfast is a fine *huevos rancheros* with ham and excellent coffee—no hyper-sweetened Mexican train coffee here. After our meal we linger with well-dressed American vacationers identifying the passing flora: lavender Japanese orchids, kapok plants with their white downy tufts so beloved by backpackers and campers, the white-blossomed napa. This is the rich Sinaloa Thornforest life zone full of cactus and thorn trees—a strange combination of desert and jungle. But since the train runs uphill all day—six hours from sea level to over eight thousand feet—it is not long before the tropical landscape gives way to something more like chaparral with ranches of horses and Brahma bulls.

We are entering a land of dissonance on a gargantuan scale. Recently discovered by travel buffs and writers as one of the hottest venues for luxury train travel through spectacular and remote scenic grandeur, the Copper Canyon is not really one canyon but a network of canyons far vaster and deeper than the Grand Canyon of Arizona. Crannies of it have literally not been explored by modern human beings. It is also home to the long-forgotten and endangered tribe of the Tarahumara, among the most primitive peoples in the Americas. Participants in our excursion will quaff margaritas and dine on quail in a cliffside luxury hotel just a few hundred yards above the homes of people who live in caves.

Our tour guide, Perla Taylor of Colombia, has a special fascination with the Tarahumara and sits down with us to tell us why. "They are very shy, perhaps even terrified of white outsiders. If you can get them to shake your hand, it is not really a touch but something more like the brush of a feather." Like other primitive peoples in remote places, the Tarahumara have been recently "discovered" by the outside world, and the contact has not been beneficial to them. Perla believes their shyness springs from an instinctive awareness that even the most well-meaning intrusions by the modern world carry danger. Perla gives us a packet of articles on the Copper Canyon and the Tarahumara that she says is required reading for anyone wanting more than a superficial experience of the trip. As we read into it, she warns, we may lose some of the feel-good aura of our journey—we will discover that the austere spaces of the canyon harbor dark secrets about the human heart.

The enormous network of the Copper Canyon was first discovered by the conquistador Francisco de Ibarra in 1564. Gold and silver had already been discovered in Zacatecas, and his expedition was part of the continuing effort by the Spaniards to realize the riches that inspired their conquest. When Ibarra first saw the ragged topography of the canyon lands, he was ecstatic with hope—surely such a spectacular display of radical geology would yield treasure such as never had been seen before.

But his hopes were largely dashed. Though he established the town of El Fuerte on the plain at the entrance to the canyon and made some minor discoveries, the canyon itself yielded nothing that even approached the scale of the strikes in Zacatecas and elsewhere. Additionally, the canyon lands were so enormous and forbidding, even the valiant conquistadores despaired of ever being able to fully explore all of them. Food was sparse, and the natives Ibarra encountered offered no help. The Tarahumara would not engage, submit, intermingle, or even offer to fight the way Indians did elsewhere in Mexico. They simply fled deeper and deeper into the recesses of the canyons. They learned that confronted with such tactics, the whites would go away when the Spaniards eventually departed the canyonlands hungry and frustrated at the apparent lack of precious minerals. Though the Spaniards founded successful mines in the nearby Sierra Madre, they did not return to the Tarahumara's domain for more than a century. Meanwhile the fort at El Fuerte became a base for Spanish operations against more aggressive mountain Indians, such as the Mayo, Sinaloa, Zuaque, and Tehueco. The history of Mexico swirled on elsewhere, but the canyon lands of the Tarahumara were simply beyond the pale.

The second invasion of whites occurred near the end of the

seventeenth century when Father Juan María de Salvatierra founded a Jesuit mission in the canyon at Cerocahui. Attempting to make contact with the elusive Tarahumara, Salvatierra explored the territory more thoroughly than had the earlier conquistadores and became the first white man to reach the bottom of the main chasm in 1692. But his mission was not much more successful at saving heathen souls than Ibarra's had been at finding gold. Again the Tarahumara simply retreated from the white intrusion, like a snail into its shell, even more deeply into the remote corners of their world. And again there were limits to how far the whites would pursue them. Twice now they had learned the pattern of withdrawal, but at a price that would be paid by future generations. As they confined themselves to ever more inaccessible parts of the canyon lands, they were losing their hold on much of their arable land.

Interest by the outside world again focused on the region in 1872 when American Albert Kinsey Owen proposed a rail line from Kansas City to the Mexican port of Topolabampo. Colonel Cyrus Holliday, builder of the great Santa Fe Railroad in the United States, had similar thoughts during the years when American rail pioneers dreamed of rail access to the Pacific. The Topolabampo scheme would offer such a route four hundred miles shorter than that of existing U.S. lines, and in Mexico new railways would not have to fight the internecine battles with already established competitors that sometimes led to gunplay and sabotage in the United States. Like previous ventures into the canyon lands, nothing much came of these ideas at first. But by the middle of the twentieth century the old dream was rekindled and work actually began. Finally the Mexican government itself, intrigued by the possibility of developing a major Pacific port at Topolabampo, took over the project and finished it in 1961. It was a massive engineering feat accomplished in an age when labor costs had come to make transcontinental railroad building a thing of the nostalgic past.

Thanks to the railroad, the long isolation of the Tarahumara now came to an end. Besides rail construction, logging, prospecting, and tourism have brought them and their lands firmly to the attention of the outside world. The contact has been devastating; their population has dwindled from more than fifty thousand to fewer than ten thousand. It has been partly the result of disastrous drought and poor harvests of maize. But it has also been the result of corruption by modern ways they are not prepared to cope with and encroachment on their lands by loggers, miners, and unscrupulous exploiters.

By midmorning we have reached the Río Chinipas Bridge, 1,000 feet in length and 355 feet above the river below. Looking down, the Sierra Madre travelers gasp to see the wrecks of freight cars at the canyon bottom. After the bridge begins the serious climb, at a grade of 2.5 percent for the next several hours. The route winds up the side of the sharp Río Septentrión Canyon, a tributary of the Copper Canyon system, and frequently we round curves with the impression that there is nothing between us and the airy chasm a thousand feet below. We plunge into tunnel after tunnel, each time emerging with a new prospect of the tributary canyon and the higher rising Sierra Tarahumara beyond. Occasionally the virgin chaparral gives way to Tarahumara cornfields, some of them the steepest agricultural plots in the world, according to Perla.

At the head of the canyon, we stop at the village of Temoris, elevation 3,365 feet. Here legend has it that the Tarahumara discovered a cure for leprosy. A handsome man married to a beautiful young woman learned that he had leprosy and wanted to kill himself. But suicide is forbidden by the Tarahumara religion, so instead he took to drinking *sotol,* the ceremonial Tarahumara corn beer, for his physical pain and emotional torment. A pitcher of it was always near his bed so that when he awoke from his fitful slumbers he could immediately drink. One day as he slept, a spider crawled into the pitcher and drowned in the *sotol,* lacing it with its venom. The man continued drinking from the pitcher and was miraculously cured within a week. To this day the Tarahumara claim to be able to cure leprosy with a mixture of the spider's venom and *sotol.* But they have not revealed to inquiring pharmacologists the species of the spider.

High above the station stop for Temoris, the tracks turn sharply through three switchbacks and climb up a cliff face to the plateau at the top. At one point we can clearly see the three levels of tracks crisscrossing the face of the cliff. Then we roll out across the plateau and begin another climb through towering peaks. Occasionally the forbidding high chaparral landscape gives way to small pueblos, like Bahuichivo and Cuiteco, where apples are grown. Missions were established in these pueblos as far back as 1691, and yet they slept in obscurity until the coming of the railway in 1961.

By early afternoon we have climbed out of the chaparral zone and into the evergreens of the high-altitude region. The air has cooled, and pockets of freshness waft past the observation platform as if we were approaching an unseen ocean shore. At seventy-five hundred feet, the train slows for the stop at Divisadero. Here the Sierra Madre travelers detrain and the guides simply point past the little stone station toward a yawning chasm of light to the east. Passing the ramshackle sheds of trackside vendors cooking tamales on smoking oil drums, the travelers venture in that direction and then stop short, dropping their bags and satchels.

There it is—the massive abyss of the upper Urique Canyon, the main chasm of the Copper Canyon system, plunging nearly straight down from a fenced overlook just beyond the station. The vertical drop from here to the canyon base is more than six thousand feet, the distance to the opposite walls more than ten miles. The change in altitude from the top to bottom is so radical that the base of the canyon is desert, the sides are chaparral, and the top, where we stand, is an evergreen forest. The temperature on the canyon floor will be more than one hundred degrees when it is a cool seventy-six here at the lip. Rain that may drench us here during a passing shower will evaporate before reaching the bottom, where it never rains in the summer.

The walls of the canyon are sharply undulating, varied in color and texture from smooth green to rugged brown to ragged black and purple in the distance, and it takes a few minutes to realize that even the Urique is itself a network of smaller canyons, peaks, rims, and little plateaus, so dwarfed by the scale of the whole that they might be overlooked. It's easy to see how pueblos of Tarahumara could be so lost in this strange terrain that the outer world would never find them.

We will stay two nights at the Posada Mirador, a deluxe hotel perched right on the canyon rim. Because of the altitude, the Mirador is a rambling thick-walled adobe building with functional fireplaces in every room. Though it gets its share of North American tourists like the Sierra Madre travelers, it is also a destination for well-heeled Mexicans. Five cultures meet and mingle in its spacious, windowed main lobby—American, Canadian, Mexican mestizo, Asian, and Tarahumara. Drinks, dinner, and the warmth of the fireplace combine with the high altitude to send guests off to bed at an early hour. The place is quiet by nine o'clock. A solitary Tarahumara man hired by the hotel sweeps the tile clean and then takes up his night watchman's station by the front door, where he too falls asleep.

In the morning it is raining, and the Sierra Madre travelers gamely board a bus to visit a nearby Tarahumara *ejido* and mission. We bounce over muddy, potholed roads to the *ejido,* where we see maize fields, a school, a store, and the mission chapel. We do not see any clusters of Tarahumara homes and our guides explain that the Tarahumara do not live in neighborhoods but are dispersed in individual homes, mostly caves or log houses, out across the canyon countryside. The mission has become the only social gathering place besides these individual dwellings, even for those who have no intention of adopting the religious teachings of the missionaries.

In the square formed by the chapel and the store, there is a handful of Tarahumara hanging out. Most of the men are dressed in denim—as Mexican peasant men are everywhere—though a few wear the traditional rope-belted "pajamas" of the tribe. The women and children are wrapped in colorful serapes and blankets. But as predicted by our guide, Perla, the most notable feature of these people is their eyes. They are dark and almond-shaped, with a gentle curve to the lid, and a sparkle of something like love and hurt in them. Maybe it's the way they look at us—Lourdes says they rip your heart out.

They are loath to speak and more so to touch. Even the eyes turn away when you speak to them or offer your hand. It is silent in the square except for the crying of one small child standing holding his older sister's hand just outside the door to the chapel. Is he hungry, or in pain, or has he been rebuked?

The air is cool and clammy this rainy, high-altitude morning, and Lourdes is not dressed right and fears she is getting a cold. So while I go into the unheated chapel to listen to the guides, she disappears seeking warmth.

The tour has arranged to have Pedro, a Mexicanized Tarahumara man, tell us about his people, and Perla translates from his Spanish. Before the coming of the mission, he explains, the members of the tribe led a largely solitary existence, coming together only for harvesting, planting, and the *tesquinada,* when the men drink *sotol* to have visions in the central sacrament of their religion. Word would pass through the woods telling when a gathering would happen.

The trait for which the Tarahumara are best known to the outside world grew out of these gathering times. The main event, after the work was finished, was a footrace on which the men would bet sacks of corn, woolen blankets, goats—anything except their wives and children. Two communities would compete, with their teams kicking a wooden ball as they raced through the woods. The winning community would take all of the wagers.

The race might last for days; at night, the teams would have torchbearers as well as kickers. Energizing themselves only with *pinole,* a mixture of corn and water, they would run the race nonstop until one team had moved its ball, with feet only, the required distance across the rugged countryside.

Though hunting is not the main source of their diet, the Tarahumara would periodically turn their formidable endurance on local game and run deer—killing them by literally running them to exhaustion. Five years ago the outside athletic world discovered the Tarahumara's remarkable long-distance running skills. Two men were recruited by the Nike shoe company to compete in a marathon in Colorado. They were given expensive Nike shoes for the race, but after they had run just a few miles and were lagging behind the pack, they traded the fancy footware for the tire-soled sandals they have come to use in modern times. They took first and second place going away.

Concerning the other trait that intrigues the outside world, Pedro is anxious to dispel myths about the *tesquinada.* No, the men don't use it as an excuse to stay drunk all of the time. Traditionally it takes one hundred days to prepare spiritually for the event. Sometimes a man would hold a *tesquinada* at his house as reward for the friends who helped him in his fields. But usually the import of the *tesquinada* is religious.

Tesquinadas are most common in the seasons when there is no planting or harvesting and then the *sotol* is made by the women, who seldom drink it. But once the men gather for the *tesquinada,* they take it very seriously and spend a whole day becoming extremely intoxicated. The goal is to arrive at a state where they have visions that serve as both spiritual and practical guidance for the tribe. Pedro insists that peyote is not an essential ingredient of the *sotol,* as outsiders' gossip has it, but acknowledges that it may occa-

sionally be used. After the *tesquinada* the men take days or weeks
to recover from their hangover while the women keep the house-
hold and fields in order. Then they relate their visions to the
women, who listen and mnemonically record the stories in songs,
chants, and sayings.

Emerging from the chapel and Pedro's monologue, I find
Lourdes curled up, wrapped and sitting on the stone porch against
the adobe wall of the store with a Tarahumara woman whose
warmth-retaining posture she has mimicked exactly. As we leave
she tells me that she was able to talk to the woman, perhaps because she was the only one of the *norteamericanos* to adopt the
physical position of these women while the rest stood or paced
around.

The woman's name is Lupe and she has six children, ages six to
fourteen. While she talked shyly and hesitantly with Lourdes, she
kept her face hidden, showing only those soulful eyes. She came to
the store to buy some cornmeal; there's not much to eat right now
because the harvests failed due to lack of rain. But the cornmeal
was too expensive, so she wasn't able to get any.

"Do you need something to feed the children?" Lourdes asked,
and the beautiful eyes sparkled in reply. Lourdes went into the
store and bought ten kilos of *maseca* for ten pesos. When she came
out and handed the woman the package, the eyes sparkled again
and then there were more eyes, as several other women material-
ized seemingly out of nowhere. They did not beg; we never do see
Tarahumara with their hands out as we have seen so often elsewhere in Mexico. They just stood there.

I ask Lourdes if she found out anything about the crying child.
"He was cold," she says. The woman would not tell her that the
child was hungry, but Perla explains later that is how hunger
shows—the run-down malnourished bodies simply can't keep
themselves warm.

Back at the hotel that afternoon before dinner we are entertained by a group of male Tarahumara dancers performing their traditional imitations of the creatures with whom they share the canyon. They were supposed to be here the first day of our visit but did not show up because they were drunk. Perla says, in contradiction of Pedro, that it was a *tesquinada,* which has become casual and perhaps even alcoholic in nature in recent years.

To the delight of the Sierra Madre travelers, three fellows dressed in bloodred ceremonial "pajamas" play very unmusical accompaniment on a guitar, a primitive violin, and a drum while the fourth does a shuffling dance, the dried *ayocote* beans strapped to his ankles adding to the rhythm. When he is a bull he lowers his head and makes little charges at the spectators; when he is a rooster he mounts one of them (me); when he is a pig he squeals and thrashes. There is none of the polished sense of performance one often sees in native dancing done for tourist visitors. In fact, there is little spirit. I can't tell whether this is because what we are seeing here is more authentic than what one sees in more sophisticated presentations for tourists elsewhere or more pathetic in the sense that their heart is not really in this. Lourdes sees it too, and thinks it is the latter. She has gotten ahead of me in reading Perla's file of articles. "Sit down with that stuff after dinner," she advises me. "There is more trouble in these people's lives than just drought and bad harvests."

The Tarahumara never had a golden age anything like that of the Toltecs, Maya, Zapotecs, or Aztecs. Throughout their history they lagged further behind these peoples than the advanced Mesoamerican societies lagged behind the Europeans. They are not alone. There are a number of tribes in isolated pockets throughout Mexico living today in primitive conditions who have never evolved to the high societal state of some of their brethren, especially in the north and in inhospitable mountain, desert, or jungle environments in other parts of the country.

But the Tarahumara have been here for two thousand years and, because they speak a kindred language, may be related to the mighty Aztecs themselves. They are one of the tribes once known as Chichimecas—northern barbarians—as were the Toltecs and the Aztecs before their arrival in the Valley of Mexico. What separates the more and less advanced tribes would seem to involve environment. Virtually every tribe that managed to find its way southward into the Valley of Mexico flourished and developed a high level of civilization, no matter how barbarian its origins.

Deeply conservative in nature, the Tarahumara tell advanced outsiders, "If the knowledge you bring does not produce corn, we do not need it." They believe profoundly that their survival depends on their isolation, though their habits over the years may have made this an inauspicious self-fulfilling prophecy. But to this day they have never taken up arms against white intruders; they would never do what the Chiapas Maya have done (though they have recently sent a delegation to meet with the Zapatistas to discuss the general situation of the indigenous). Their life is a spiritual one, dominated by the *tesquinada* and the harvest.

Though they have lived for a long time on the edge of subsistence, the recent drought and new economic realities have suddenly brought them near extinction. The railway and NAFTA have made logging and mining in rugged capital-intensive regions now profitable. And President Salinas's amendments to Article 27 of the Mexican Constitution in 1993 have put these simple people at the mercy of the economic interests eyeing their lands. For centuries the *ejidos*, the communal lands on which the indigenous grew their crops, were actually owned by the government on behalf of the people. This prevented individual tribes or persons from being able to sell these lands to investors and effectively secured for the Indians' posterity those lands that were not taken by force or legal subterfuge. Spurred by current revisionist economic thinking, which maintained that the *ejidos* were Mexico's least productive lands, the amendment privatized the *ejidos,* making them the property of the tribes and thus opening the door to their sale to rapacious investors.

Now the availability of these lands has cleared the way for major development. Two hundred thousand mestizos from other parts of Mexico have moved into the region, threatening to overwhelm the dwindling Tarahumara with sheer numbers.

The government, despite official pronouncements about saving the Tarahumara, applies subtle pressure to them by regulating carefully the amount and kind of aid they receive from outside charitable efforts under the guise of protecting them from cultural contamination. There are many who believe that the government's real intention is to subtly use hunger to control them and thus to open up the possibilities for development of their land in a patronage of shame similar to what the Canadian government once did to its proud Sioux.

The Tarahumara are confronted with a choice as Mexican as the color of mestizo skin: conform to the Mexican melting pot and be looked down upon as *indios* forever or fight for identity and probably die. Rape or death.

But there is an even darker horror story in the lives of the Tarahumara. The rich biosystem of the Copper Canyon has begun to attract entrepreneurs far worse than the loggers or miners—international drug families looking for new, secure, remote places in which to grow poppies. They need land that they can clear of both people and natural vegetation and where they can build secret airstrips. The Copper Canyon, far from the centers of a government with a penchant for winking at such activities anyway, is a natural. When cleared and cultivated for poppies, the land and climate at certain elevations here can produce heroin on a scale comparable to that of the Asian locales that have dominated the trade for so long.

In a scenario that locals have already seen enacted a number of times, the drug people come in with their choppers and AK-47s and begin killing off the Tarahumara in targeted areas, far from the eyes of tourists and legitimate developers in the thin line along the railway. When the remainder of the terrified residents of the pueblo leave, they take over the land and set up operations. In this way, the trade was quietly headed toward rivaling that of Pakistan, Afghanistan, or Iran when Mexican and American environmentalists began to publicize what was happening here in just the past few years.

Though their intervention may save the day in the long run, for the time being it has mainly served to increase the level of violence and fear. Tarahumara are now on notice from the drug lords that cooperation with outside environmentalists will send them to the cemetery. In a particularly appalling recent episode, a Tarahumara man who worked with the environmentalists was ambushed while at prayer in his chapel and tortured with bullets fired into all of his joints for over an hour. He survived the attack to tell his story, which may have been the drug lords' intention; his jaw and neck were the only joints on his body that weren't destroyed.

The invaders are not just foreigners. A well-known Mexican is reported to be the father of a particularly violent Copper Canyon drug operation. Environmental activists had succeeded in getting a warrant for his arrest, but he was included in a state blanket amnesty and now operates openly out of Chihuahua. Two environmentalists who have been leading the charge, Mexican Edwin Bustillo and American Randall Gingrich, have been repeatedly attacked and beaten. But they press on with a passion to save what they regard as one of the world's richest biosystems whose varying altitudes produce a diversity of flora and fauna that surpasses even that of the rain forests.

Meanwhile infant mortality among the Tarahumara has risen in the past year to more than 50 percent. Missionaries familiar with Tarahumara traditions who look in on the *tesquinadas* report a drastic change in the nature of those sessions. Where once they were characterized as much by horseplay, joking, and laughter as by spiritual visions, today the participants have become grim, watchful, silent.

Perla has informed the Tarahumara performers that I would like to try some of their *sotol,* and later in the evening they return with a small jug of it. While they watch with wide eyes and big smiles, I sample it with one of the other men in the tour group. It is sweet, has no carbonation, and clings to the tongue. It reminds me of corn silo drippings, which I suppose is exactly what it is.

I only partake of about a cup of the stuff. But a half hour after the Tarahumara have left and I am talking with the few Sierra Madre travelers still awake at 9:30, I feel wired. I am intensely alert and feeling a rush of energy. There was also a glass of wine at dinner and a margarita earlier. But I am a pretty conscious and deliberate drinker. Something different is going on.

Sleep is out of the question, so I sit up late in a rocking chair by the fire with Pancho, a mestizo from the nearby village of Areo-ponapuchi who speaks English, and the mestizo bartender, Mario Luna, while the Tarahumara night man does his sweeping. Pancho thinks my condition is funny. "They put peyote in it," he says. "They always do." He tells me that the *tesquinada* goes on virtually every day now. "The men only work during the planting and har-vesting time. The rest of the year they go from house to house drinking to get strong." I ask how drinking makes them strong, and it turns out that "strong" means drunk.

According to Pancho, it is the women who keep the tribe alive, working all day every day while the men get drunk. The women never drink. Pancho seems to admire them a great deal.

He runs a little general store in Divisadero. His pueblo of Areo-ponapuchi has a population of six hundred, about half of which is mestizo. Though he has personal friends who are Tarahumara, the two peoples live on opposite sides of the road. The mestizos work in forestry or for the railroad, while the Tarahumara grow maize or make baskets, violins, pottery, and corn beer.

As I finally begin to settle down, Pancho suggests that one of Mario's margaritas might help me be able to sleep. Mario, who has been making a drawing of the Roadrunner and Wile E. Coyote, jumps up and returns shortly with the best-tasting margarita I have ever had. He says it is his own recipe: a shot of tequila, a shot of orange liquor, freshly squeezed grapefruit juice, the juice and pulp of a whole lime, and a splash of soda over crushed ice—"stirred, not shaken, like James Bond."

Mario returns to his drawing while Pancho and I drink. Mario's girlfriend will soon be visiting him from Mexico City for three days, and the drawing is a present for her. In it, he is the coyote and she is the roadrunner.

The Tarahumara night man has stopped working and has been leaning on his broom while we talk. Pancho offers to buy him a beer and asks him to join us. He hesitates at first, fearful that he might get in trouble, but when I also offer him a cigarette, he awkwardly sits down and sips on the beer Mario brings for him.

Rosario Pillado has some mestizo blood in him—his grandfather married a Mexican woman. He will not talk about the troubles of the Tarahumara. So as men will do the world over during late-night drinking sessions, our talk turns to women. Rosario loves his wife, mother of his six children. Though he is only forty-eight, his oldest is twenty-five. His youngest is now older than he was when he became a father.

Mario loves his girlfriend and positively wiggles in his chair when he talks about her. Pancho does not love his wife. He loves other women who are not married. But he wants to keep his wife for the sake of the family as long as he can continue to be with the single woman who lives down the street.

We talk about age. Rosario and I are the forty-somethings here;

Pancho is thirty-seven, and Mario is twenty-three. Pancho says that the secret to youth is having a job you love. He loves to play his guitar and sing. Rosario says that it is women who make men older, and Pancho seems to agree. But I point out that Rosario looks very young for his age and has been married a long time. He says, of course, that it is because he has a very rare good woman.

I ask Rosario if it is true that Tarahumara men drink a lot. He answers that they are often "strong." I ask how many drinks it takes to make them strong, and all agree that the magic number is three, of any kind of drink. "Three drinks and you are strong." I try to get at the use of the word "strong," wishing I had linguistically literate Lourdes here with me (she by now is sound asleep). Rosario is no help, but Pancho suggests that it may mean lacking shyness, because the Tarahumara when drunk lose all of their characteristic timidity.

"Do they become aggressive and violent?" I ask.

"Oh no," Pancho answers, and he translates to Rosario what I have said. Rosario too shakes his head emphatically. It is the mestizos like himself, Pancho concedes, who react to drink that way, never the Tarahumara. And Rosario goes on to tell of how common it is for a participant in the *tesquinada* to dream that he has become violent with his friends and then exert himself for weeks afterward to apologize for affronts he never committed.

By the time Pancho and Mario go home, Rosario is already asleep by the door. I am able to sleep, but wake in the morning feeling as though a steel rod were being shoved through my forehead and out the back. Lourdes has little sympathy for my condition. She has a genuine cold, and Perla and others insist that the Tarahumara do not put peyote in their *sotol*. I must have gotten a little too "strong." I go back to bed while Lourdes hikes off to check out Areoponapuchi.

I have dreams. I see my ex-wife and my teenage daughters standing on the lip of the canyon. I want to shout to them that it's not true that women make men old—at least not me. I want to tell them how much I prize the years we all had together, just as Rosario does, even though I have chosen another life. But the words won't come. I wake up sweating and shaking. The dream is gone but the vision remains—the *tesquinada* has done its work. There is something I will tell these three women when I return from this journey. I have never said it before.

Lourdes returns from her hike after I am finally up and refreshed and human again. There she saw Tarahumara men working to fix a roof, carrying rail ties, chopping wood, and repairing a car, while women did domestic chores, laundry and cooking. She thinks I should take what Pancho has told me about the Tarahumara men with a dollop of skepticism.

Today the rain has stopped and the sun is bright. We follow a path leading down into the canyon from the hotel to the cave dwelling of a Tarahumara family whose men were part of the dancing group last night. As we hike, the grandeur of the canyon explodes around us. Above tower black crags while below a carpet of green velvet softens the rugged geology at middle altitudes. In the distance we can see the thin silver plumes of waterfalls, and when we get a glimpse of the bottom of the canyon, there lies the Río Urique meandering like a gray ribbon through the tan desert floor. Closer at hand, tropical oak and pine and flowering cacti rustle in a mellow breeze that blows upward from the depths below.

The opening of the Tarahumara cave is walled off from the outside with mud brick. It has a door with a glass window at its entrance. Several little sheds of scrap boards just outside the cave serve as bedrooms for children—we can hear a baby crying in one of them. A chicken coop is mounted on stilts out front to protect the chickens from coyotes at night. The ground is scattered with toys, metal trucks, and stuffed animals. Down another path beyond the cave we find human feces.

The entire homestead sits tucked under a high cliff overhanging the cave. Water runs off the cliff and is collected in a pool made of more mud bricks. A rubber hose leads from the pool to a spot a few yards away where a woman does her laundry the old-fashioned way—scrubbing it on a rock. Lourdes tries to speak to her in Spanish, but the woman is either very shy or does not comprehend very well. Finally one question gets through, "Where are the men?" The woman answers that she does not know. They will be back late in the day.

We board the Sierra Madre train for one last ride on it farther up the line to the town of Creel, where we will depart from the tour group and continue on to Chihuahua on the regular Mexican train. During the ride we are treated, along with a few of the other Sierra Madre travelers, to an interview with Father Verplancken, a Belgian-Mexican missionary who has probably done more for the Tarahumara than any other single person in recent years. He is a soft-spoken, intense man with piercing eyes and graying dark hair. He carries himself with a sense of one who knows exactly who he is, and cares little about that self. He has his mission.

He had read about the Tarahumara as a boy in Guadalajara in 1952, when their mere existence was just being rediscovered. When he became a novice, he asked to be assigned to the Tarahumara, and has been with them ever since. His main task was to build a clinic for them in Creel, though to accomplish that task he also had to do such things as engineer a water pipeline, develop electric power supplies, and so on. As a result he has become part engineer and doctor as well as a missionary.

He disagrees with the view that history has made the Tarahumara shy of outsiders. "It is in their very nature," he argues. He asks us to compare the way they sell their wares to what we have seen anywhere else in Mexico. They do not hawk or haggle. They do not try to hustle. If you want to buy something, you have to ask them. After they name a price, you either take it or they look away, seemingly losing interest if you try to negotiate. Commerce is not their forte.

The Tarahumara are facing a calamity, he says. In recent years the ground has been so dry that the men could no longer even break the soil. Fatal starvation rates are up to 20 percent, and by the time many of the children come in from the hinterlands to the clinic, it is often too late. Because of their culture and their religious beliefs, the clan tries to cure them first with their shamans. They come to the clinic, only as a last resort, if at all.

The issue of the Tarahumara's religious beliefs is a major problem for Father Verplancken. "They believe in multiple souls," he explains. "The head, the chest, the stomach—each has its own soul. They believe that when a part of the body is sick, the soul of that organ has departed. When all the souls have departed, or when the soul of the heart is gone, the body is dead."

But the problem is that the souls don't stray far. They linger in the ether of the place where the patient lives. It is the job of the local shaman to entice the soul back into its organ and thus cure the patient.

"That's what causes the dilemma," he continues. "The parents in the remote areas will not bring a child here because they believe they are taking him farther from the missing soul and thus he is less likely to be able to recover here. It strikes them as insane that anyone would suggest taking a sick child far from his home."

He relates a particular case. There was a child he became aware of who was suffering from the third degree of malnutrition in a family cave far across the canyon. When one of Verplancken's assistants visited the cave and examined the boy, he found that the child had been strong and healthy before his nutritional crisis and thus was a prime case for saving—if only he could be brought to the clinic for intravenous feeding and round-the-clock monitoring. The mother agreed to the trip, but just before departure the grandmother put up a fuss. The Tarahumara defer to their elders. So the child died.

I ask if this does not spur an impulse to convert them from their beliefs and he demurs, "They have so little; their way of life is so endangered. Even as a missionary, I struggle when I am up against their beliefs. But I cannot take away from them this one thing they have, their identity."

Lourdes wants him to talk about what else threatens the Tarahumara besides hunger. She tells him that we have read Perla's file. Verplancken is cautiously optimistic concerning some of the dramatic things we read about. He is worried about the privatization of the *ejidos* but actually thinks the Tarahumara will do better in this respect than Indians elsewhere. "They have a tremendous peer pressure not to sell that may protect them. Plus their traditional fearfulness of whites. High-pressure buyers just scare them away." He also sees a change in the danger from drug lords. "Their activities are publicized by environmentalists and journalists like you. The government can only wink when nobody sees it wink."

He is concerned with more subtle threats. The first generation of children educated in government schools is now approaching adulthood and rejecting their culture as a result. The values brought into the canyon by the mestizo influx are eroding the Tarahumara identity. "There is coming to be tremendous pressure on them to conform. If they do that, then maybe they will start to sell the *ejidos* and go to work for the sawmill and then they will be lost."

The hope for the Tarahumara, besides better rainfall, is their talent for learning crafts. "They are good at seeing something done and learning how to do it through imitation." That's how they pass on their own crafts and how they successfully learn new ones. Many are actually making a little money selling crafts; some even have their own shops. "This is better employment for them than working at the sawmill," Verplancken says. "So it may be said that some tourism is a benefit, but tourism is of course a double-edged sword. It can also corrupt."

After detraining at Creel, where we buy some of the delicate, thin-walled pots the Tarahumara have been making without the wheel for thousands of years, Lourdes and I say farewell to the Sierra Madre travelers and guides and board the northbound FNM train for the ride to Chihuahua. As we pull out of the little mountain logging town, we pass the strangest train I have ever seen. It is a half mile of flatcars with recreational vehicles strapped down on them. This is not a delivery of new cars but an innovative new form of tourism. The people are in the RVs on a tour that takes them and their vehicles into the Copper Canyon. We shudder at the implications for the Tarahumara.

The FNM train is another manifestation of the tourism coming into the region. The *primera especial* car we ride in, including its bathrooms, is the cleanest, most carefully attended we have encountered—better than Amtrak coach. We notice that everyone in this car is a tourist, and most are whites speaking English or German. A quick train walk confirms that the attendants segregate their touring riders from the usual Mexican travelers, even from other *primera especial* ticket holders.

The conductor explains that this train was privately run until 1985—the Chihuahua Pacífico Express. That plus the fact that the FNM knows that here they have a profitable tourism route explains the very different regime we have noticed.

Shortly after Creel we have climbed to the Continental Divide at more than eight thousand feet. The alpine evergreen zone here just begins to stunt toward treelessness before our descent down the east side of the divide brings us back firmly into it. But soon the green gives way to browns and tans, and the log houses of the Tarahumara are replaced by sod brick. This is vaquero country, and as we roll out onto the now treeless high plain toward Chihuahua, we see lots of them, along with their horses, cattle, and tractors.

The land is mostly open, fenceless range, though occasionally interrupted by an orchard with its smudge pots, antibird netting, and spraying irrigation systems. This is the dry side of the divide, but here we see what an economy that can afford irrigation can do. The ranches and orchards are clearly prosperous and there is plenty of water. But just a few score miles to the west, the Tarahumara are dying because of drought on the "wet" side.

The sun sets a beautiful orange as we approach Chihuahua, and then the range darkens quickly. We pass a dell where I see two white horses running wildly under a full moon, and I am possessed by an aura of epiphany recalling that of my *tesquinada* dream. Who are the two horses, and why do I know the tableau under this full moon has some personal meaning? A recent New Age song runs through my head, "Long ago, white men came in the name of God. They took their land; a New Age had just begun." I think of the Tarahumara, the people with no promised land, and how their stubborn clinging to their place and their souls may have doomed them as much as the march of history. And what has all this to do with me, I keep wondering all the way until our arrival at the station in Chihuahua.

Travel addicts know the experience I have just felt. We poke our heads into stories of human drama in far-flung places and somehow, by some chemistry of curious connection, we find links between the mysteries we uncover and the issues and traumas in our own lives. Why should the story of the Tarahumara so quake the foundations of my soul? In Chihuahua I have no idea. But by journey's end there will be an answer.

5

Yesterday's Train
Chihuahua to Aguascalientes

The Tren División del Norte runs from Ciudad Juárez on the Texas border opposite El Paso, southward through Chihuahua, Torreón, Zacatecas, Aguascalientes, and Querétaro to Mexico City. Our intention is to ride it from Chihuahua to Zacatecas in time for the presidential election and then beyond Zacatecas to sample what people on board are saying in the aftermath. But we are told we will have trouble meeting any kind of schedule along this run. Because of the rail connections to the United States at El Paso, it is Mexico's most heavily traveled freight route. The passenger service here is given a lower priority than anywhere we have traveled so far, and thus the trains are notoriously late.

We chose Zacatecas as the site from which to watch the historic election of 1994 for several reasons. It has been described to us as one of Mexico's most beautifully preserved colonial cities, with a strong sense of its identity. It is also a prosperous place, a city with a thriving middle class whose historic economic health, deriving from the local silver mines, has been translated into a diversified modern spectrum of enterprises. But most important, Zacatecas is off the pathways of *norteamericanos,* despite its material success. People say it is like San Miguel without the gringos.

Our first stop in this journey is the city of Torreón, which sits at the top of the central plateau that was long the source of Mexico's wealth. Besides the mines between here and Zacatecas, cotton was king when a different climate prevailed. But the weather has changed so much that cotton no longer grows here. The driver of our taxicab taking us from the station to our hotel says, "The rain has stopped coming because we haven't behaved well." Water was once free; now you have to pay for it. Property owners used to be able to divert the river; now they are on a metered pipe.

It is Saturday, August 20, the day before the election, but life in Torreón seems unexceptional. Children dressed in spectacular first Communion outfits pose for pictures in front of the cathedral while beggar women in brown rags stoically maintain their stations just a few feet away on the steps. One beggar man whispers that the bishop has given him special permission to take alms this day, but no one seems particularly impressed. In the *mercado* the usual market day scramble for fresh produce and imported electronics goes on unabated. We are especially fascinated by the action around a vendor of freshly made tortillas, whose cooking operation is set up in plain view of the customers, who seem entranced by the process of manufacture of Mexico's oldest staple food. The raw corn is cooked for an hour, then cooled and rinsed clean. Still moist, it goes through a grinder that turns it into the tortilla flour, the key characteristic of which is its varying degrees of fineness— the finer part serving as the glue for the tortillas, the more coarse grains giving them body and texture. The glutinous corn flour is next run into a mechanical tortilla maker that cranks out the flattened, partially cooked disks. These are stacked and bagged in plastic and a kilo of them is sold for about one and a half pesos, or thirty-seven U.S. cents under the current exchange rate. The tortilla machine of course could be replaced by the traditional method of hand-patting and quick pan grilling.

The tortilla stand is located hard by one of the entrances to the *mercado*. Just outside gather several beggars—standing hungry right in the mouth of the horn of plenty. Occasionally someone takes a few tortillas out of his fresh purchase and places them in outstretched dirty hands. This too is considered part of the everyday scene.

But it's not quite normal here today, as we discover when we order margaritas with our lunch at the hotel on this hot summer afternoon. There is national prohibition during the weekend of the election. No alcohol is being served or sold legally anywhere in Mexico from Friday through Monday. At one time the ban applied only to election day itself, but this year, in response to alcohol-related troubles in the past and as part of the Election Commission's attempt to make this Mexico's cleanest election ever, the ban lasts four days.

The Mexicans we talk to seem resigned to the enforced teetotaling regime. "Why not let the whole country dry out every few years?" says one. "Mexicans drink too much anyway." As Americans with certain preconceived notions about how one relaxes in the heat of Mexico during a hot, dusty summer weekend, we are not quite so sanguine about the prospect. So it seems a fine opportunity for us to explore the possibilities inherent in one of Mexico's time-honored traditions, *la mordida.*

Lourdes suggests we might be able to put the bite on someone at one of the liquor stores, flash some pesos and see if he will flip us a bottle. No dice. The liquor stores we find are locked, and uniformed patrols linger nearby. The liquor sections of grocery stores are darkened and plastered with signs announcing the electoral prohibition. Too many people are around. It seems this thing is being taken fairly seriously.

Back at the hotel, whose name we will not mention for obvious reasons, I find a friendly English-speaking bellhop and explain our plight. We are visitors I point out. We will not vote. Surely something can be arranged.

It just happens that the bellhop has a friend who works in a bar across town. He is sympathetic but wants me to understand that there is some risk of someone being arrested or losing a liquor license, so there will be some extra cost. But he thinks the thing can be done. We haggle a price (about twice the usual for a bottle of tequila) and he disappears, promising to meet us in the restaurant in an hour.

As we linger over dessert and coffee, we see him pass by once about an hour later, maybe just checking us out. And then suddenly he is there beside us saying the deal is done. The bottle is in my bag in the coat check room. I pay him what we have agreed upon, and he demurs that he maybe should also have an extra tip for his trouble. Final price, eighty-five pesos for a bottle of tequila normally priced at about twenty-five pesos. The bottle is indeed carefully tucked in a brown paper bag inside my suitcase.

It's ninety degrees in the shade when we arrive at the station to catch the southbound for Zacatecas. There's a big crowd waiting here today, a festive one, with blankets and pillows, baskets of fruit and jugs of juice. Vendors are doing a brisk business in cold sandwiches, ice cream, flavored ices, and frozen fruit bars. Every time a light appears down the tracks, the crowd rustles in anticipation, but it's always just a freight rumbling through. No one really expects the train, in the middle of a long slow route, to be anywhere near on time.

A friendly, well-dressed man in his late twenties is eager to talk to us, the only Americans present. Pedro has a company that extracts minerals, but business is slow now, as investors are waiting for the results of the election. So he is using the slack time to travel to visit relatives.

He thinks everything about the upcoming election is colored by the fraud of the 1988 election. "Everyone knows Cárdenas won," he says, and he explains that he personally witnessed the ballot count at one polling place and saw with his own eyes that the government later announced the wrong candidate the winner for that site. "When the count was going against them, the government cut off access to the counting machines. Ballots for Cárdenas were burned and dumped in rivers," he says, voicing what foreign observers would conclude a year later. "Now they know that people will not stand for another fraud like that. So they are doing everything possible to make this election look cleaner. Whether it really will be is anybody's guess."

He is not optimistic. Echoing the sentiments of dozens of Mexicans we talk to, he stresses that the economic barons of the country will not allow the PRI to let itself lose. "Somehow, the government will find a way not to relinquish power. Of course none of it really matters. The PAN has already made a deal with the PRI. And Cárdenas no longer has any credibility. The best thing will probably be for the PRI to win in a clean election."

The train is late and not air-conditioned. Out in the scorching desert, we find we can open the windows and then it's merely unpleasant. But when we make interminable stops at stations, the heat in the cars becomes suffocating. Rolling through the arid juncture of the states of Coahuila, Durango, and Zacatecas, we see ragged mountains in the distance and irrigated desert agriculture up close. Oases of green orchard haciendas surrounded by barbed wire fencing and angry-looking signs saying PROPIEDAD PRIVADA, ¡PROHIBIDO EL PASO! suggest the wealth of this region as well as the strife underlying the land issue throughout the country.

Just when our sweaty clothes have begun to stick to the hot plastic seats, a blessed man comes through the car selling bottles of beer in buckets of steaming ice. After making a quick purchase, I question Pedro about this apparent violation of national electoral prohibition. He shrugs, "I guess they don't think we vote on the train. Maybe the law doesn't reach the train."

As I quench my thirst, Pedro wants to talk more about the election. If the PRI wins cleanly, he thinks no one will say anything except for the far left. If the PRI wins through fraud, there will be big trouble. If the right-wing PAN wins, many people may be willing to give them a shot at it, and the election will be historic. If Cárdenas wins, there will very likely be a PRI or army coup and the biggest trouble of all. "If there is honest change, foreign investors will see it as progress, democracy, and stability, and it will be good for the country. Everyone knows this—almost everyone. It's only the very rich Mexican interests who don't want change," he explains. "They think it will damage their business. But they are the ones who always call the shots." Again here is the paradoxical theme in this historically exploited country of outsiders' sometimes being the key to progressivism while native reactionary forces work to thwart it.

In the 1860s, after the debacle at the hands of the *norteamericanos*, Mexico experienced a superficially schizophrenic crisis, lurching first to a period of true reform under a pure-blooded Zapotec Indian president, enduring another foreign invasion as a result, then leaping into a reactionary escapade that installed a European as emperor, and finally returning to a "reform dictatorship" under the Indian president. But the apparent craziness made perfect sense. Both sides in the ongoing liberal-versus-conservative struggle had come to view compromise as the cause of the nation's trouble, and so polarized themselves into opposite extremes. Liberals, now heavily influenced by a rising and striving mestizo middle class, wanted to reach as far as they could toward Hidalgo's ideals of social justice without endangering private property or unleashing social upheaval. Conservatives despaired of Mexico's ability to govern itself and yearned for a blue-blooded European man on a white horse to save Mexicans from themselves.

First it was the liberals' turn, their revolution of Ayulta being the violent vehicle that sent Santa Anna into his final exile, initiating the period in Mexican history known as La Reforma. Social justice for those at the bottom of the pyramid now became at least a subject for fine words along with a fervent belief that capitalism held the key to Mexico's salvation. And in the new atmosphere of admiration for Cuauhtémoc and the glorious pre-Hispanic past, it was possible for a Zapotec Indian, who, like Abraham Lincoln, had come from humble origins and educated himself as a lawyer, to rise through the ranks of power. Benito Juárez participated in a legislative and constitutional assault on the power of the church and the military that, while not toppling the pyramid of social power in Mexico, at least removed some of its key underpinnings. As minister of justice, Juárez ended the exemption of church and military personnel from civil court trials. The liberal establishment then went on to force the church to divest itself of its peso-generating holdings in real estate beyond what was needed for actual religious purposes. Finally it curtailed the clergy's power to charge exorbitant fees for sacramental services, thus opening up the heart of religion to the masses of the poor.

It may be difficult for Americans today to grasp the revolutionary impact of these reforms, particularly the first and third. The effect of both was to initiate a momentum toward secularizing the state and disengaging the link between church and military that had always placed them both beyond the reach of historical evolution. On the other hand, the second reform, which might seem so progressive to us today, removed the church as the friendly lender of low-interest money. Now money lending became the province of capitalist enterprise. Never again would poor Mexicans deal with a bank as forgiving as the church had traditionally been. Worse, the Indians' *ejidos,* their traditional communal lands, were included in the legislation, opening them up to sale and exploitation by non-Indians. La Reforma had ironically succeeded in planting a seed of future discord and social upheaval that haunts Mexico yet today.

Still the clamor from conservatives led to civil war, especially after the constitution of 1857 separated church and state, allowing the legal practice of religions other than Catholicism. The pope himself called for insurrection against "everything that the civil authority has done in scorn of ecclesiastical authority and of this Holy See." Again the Mexican countryside was ravaged by the pope's war until Juárez's victory in 1861. Juárez celebrated his presidency by launching the most anticlerical movement the nation had ever seen, exiling bishops, closing "superfluous" churches, forbidding the wearing of clerical vestments on the street, and banning the ringing of church bells at times other than for mass. In subsequent swings of the national politic, Juárez's anticlerical bent to Mexico's evolution took root and grew.

But when Juárez took on the foreign interests, he met the limits of progressivism in the nineteenth-century world. In 1861 he declared a two-year moratorium on Mexico's debts to foreign countries. He made no attempt to cancel those debts; he just wanted time to pay them. But the reaction of the debtor nations spelled his doom. Although Britian, France, and Spain certainly had no history of working together, the new international monetary order had changed the rules of the game. And the American Civil War offered a rare opportunity to meddle militarily on this continent without having to confront the United States. Jointly the three nations sent an expeditionary force to compel Mexico to pay the debt. In Mexico the church and archconservatives connived at the invasion, which was successfully headed toward its limited objective until the Spanish and British discovered that the French, under Napoleon

III, intended to stay and attempt to establish a French colony on Mexican soil. Embarrassed, the Spanish and British withdrew, and the French invasion, openly supported now by the Mexican church and conservatives, continued. On May 5, 1862, Juárez's generals won a spectacular victory at Puebla, thus enshrining a date that American bars and vendors of tequila have today turned to commercial advantage. But the defeat enabled Napoleon III to recruit a much larger army in defense of French national pride that eventually won the day and drove Juárez from the capital in 1863.

Victorious conservatives in Mexico now faced a baffling muddle they had seen before—the progressive liberalism of European monarchs, products of the Enlightenment, that they had championed to restore their own place at the top of the pyramid. The occupying French maintained most of the reforms of Juárez while relentlessly pursuing his person across the northern countryside. But the conservatives pushed on, working with the French to hold a successful plebiscite on the question of inviting Hapsburg Maximilian, younger brother of Emperor Francis Joseph I, to occupy a Mexican throne. Besides the belief that only a European monarch could effectively govern Mexico, patriotic conservatives were also moved by the consideration that the Hapsburg connection to the great powers of Europe would help ensure that Mexico would have allies against any further encroachments by the United States. Maximilian and his empress Carlota arrived with great fanfare in Mexico City late in the spring of 1864, traveling part of the route from Veracruz over Mexico's first railway.

The honeymoon of this marriage between Mexico's reactionaries and European monarchy did not last long. Conservative Mexicans were again appalled at the liberalism of their new rulers when Maximilian affirmed the reforms that had passed muster with the French before him. As a gesture of national reconciliation, he appointed some followers of Juárez to his cabinet, outraging both liberals, who viewed these men as traitors, and conservatives, who viewed Maximilian himself as a traitor. Meanwhile the Juaristas gained strength, moving from guerrilla operations to full-scale civil war, aided after 1865 by weapons shipments from the United States, which had never been happy with the imperial goings-on in Mexico during its civil war. When the French forces retired in 1867 after diplomatic pressure from the United States (so much for the thought that the European connection would counterbalance the yanquis), Maximilian was quickly defeated by Juarista forces at Querétaro and sentenced to be shot. European monarchies, as well as the U.S. government urged clemency, but Juárez was adamant. Never again, if anything he might do could ensure it, would a European aspire to rule Mexico. Maximilian was executed on June 19, 1867.

Juárez occupied the presidency until his death by natural causes in 1872. During his tenure he launched programs to promote public education, attract industrial investment, and build a national railway system to unify the country. He had succeeded in smashing the power of the church and the conservative cabal. The new mestizo middle class flourished and found entry to the doorways of power. But Juárez could not bring order to a country that had not seen it since colonial days. The economy lay in tatters and crime was rampant. Mexicans, even the poor, craved order above all other things as they never had before. They wanted now as their ruler a homegrown strongman. Juárez responded by organizing police in the countryside, the *rurales,* and becoming more autocratic in office. But he was not the man. After his death one of his generals would rise to meet the challenge and establish a regime that would last longer than any in Mexican history since colonialism. There would be peace for a while in Mexico, the railways would be built, and the trains would run on time. True democracy and social justice could be put on hold. Though the social boundaries between criollo and mestizo had been breached and classic liberalism had triumphed, the crash of power through the next tier of the social pyramid would have to wait until another day.

In the late afternoon a bulky man with heavily slicked-back hair wearing a dirty white lab jacket and carrying a battered briefcase comes through the car selling his salves. He calls himself "the pharmacist" and claims his ointment will cure backaches, headaches, PMS, rashes, fevers, halitosis, flatulence, cancer, and infertility, among other things. He doesn't seem to find any takers but prowls the cars for a good hour making his loud harangue before detraining at an unscheduled stop in a canyon in the middle of nowhere. Looking out the open window I can see that we have stopped to meet the northbound train, just pulling slowly into the siding next to us. The pharmacist detrains and ambles to the open door of the other train. Just as he is about to get on, two pretty teenage girls dressed in tight shorts, sandals, and red halter tops detrain from the northbound. He gives them a hearty greeting, and they shortly board our train.

When we are rolling again, the two girls stroll past, flashing eye contact with all of the men, and there is a stir in the car. The married men awkwardly avert their glances while the women stare daggers. I question Lourdes: "Prostitutes?" "No," she laughs. "You have been riding in the desert too long."

But shortly Pedro leans over to us and says, *"Ahí va la picardía"* (There goes some spice). Indeed the two girls, seventeen and nineteen years of age, are regulars who work this train every day. There is an electricity that positively charges the car when the girls saunter through, and at the next stop, they do detrain with two young, well-dressed men in tow.

As the train meanders through the Cañón de Jimulco, Pedro tells us that his family lives in Chiapas and has no sympathy for the Zapatista rebels. "There was peace in Chiapas and they have ruined it," he says. "By killing people and wearing masks they are not winning hearts and minds." Neither has the radical church, he thinks, which has abetted the rebels by hiding caches of arms and offering support. His Catholic family is very angry over "revolution theology." "Who said the clergy should be doing politics instead of religion?" he asks.

Pedro insists his family is not rich but describes them as typical of Mexico's rising middle class. And the politics of traditional leftist revolution does not speak to those like him at the center of the new Mexican reality. Even the students and academics in the universities who might be expected to support a leftist agenda prefer peace to revolution. "The rebels are simply out of touch. But they are going to cause a problem anyway," he says, referring to a rumor going around that something terrible is going to happen shortly after the election. Merchants, teachers, and professionals are gathering supplies—canned food, fuel, gas, wood, medicine, beans, rice, tortillas. "We are preparing for the worst."

The train is very late getting into Zacatecas, well past dark. We wind into the highlands surrounding the city through horseshoe after horseshoe with tableaus of the front of the train doubled back in tight curves beside steep streets, neighborhoods, streetlights. We rush to a crummy Best Western hotel and fall in for some serious sleep.

It's sunny, bright, and cool the morning of election day, but the desk people at the hotel say it will get very warm as the day goes on. Traffic clamors in the street out front, unusual for a Sunday. Under the constitution, Mexicans must vote and have their voting card punched to verify it. An unpunched card can have employment consequences further down the road. So today everyone is out to vote, go to mass, and have a large family meal.

There would be a big turnout for this election anyway. After the stench of the stolen 1988 election, the world's spotlight is on Mexico, and today the country is crawling with observers from foreign governments and media. For the first time the Electoral Commission is a truly independent, nonpartisan body staffed by people who have never been members of any party. All candidates have signed on to a set of rules to be rigorously enforced. People will vote today just to see for themselves the success or failure of the process.

The choice they will make is also important. Though polls have shown the leftist PRD and its candidate, Cuauhtémoc Cárdenas, have slipped dramatically since they were denied their victory in the last election, the right-wing PAN seems poised for a possible upset. Certainly the PAN stands to gain in the congress at the least. And several of the small leftist parties hope to make gains at the expense of the flagging PRD. Even if the PRI wins again, the actual size of its victory will matter—if the election is clean and people believe it to be so.

Though the streets are draped with political banners, as they have been everywhere in Mexico for the past several months, there is no campaign hoopla near the polling place at La Casilla across the street from the hotel. It is not allowed. Instead a line—maybe ten deep—waits quietly at the door to get in to vote.

Inside, the atmosphere is very different from that at polling places in the States. For one thing, the party representatives, wearing their campaign buttons, mingle here rather than outside. It's hard to tell the Electoral Commission officers apart from the politicos. Instead of the businesslike mood we know, here there is a sense of casual, social ritual—you don't just go in, have your name marked on the checklist, and enter the voting booth. We follow the progress of one woman in a yellow dress who has been waiting about fifteen minutes.

First she gives her voter card to the president of the polling place, who has the checklist at one end of a long table. The president matches the card to the checklist and holds it while the woman goes through the remainder of the process. A second electoral official, the secretary, hands her the three ballots, one for president, one for senator, and one for deputy (equivalent to our representatives). A PRI observer makes friendly small talk with her as she is asked to pause while observers from each of the other parties check her name off their lists. The PRI observer doesn't seem to be concerned about the checklist. Then she enters one of the two voting booths set up in the center of the room. When she emerges she places her ballots in the appropriate ballot boxes (with transparent sides to prevent the abuse of "pregnant boxes" stuffed with PRI ballots ahead of time) while a man wearing a PRI button looks on to make sure she places each in the right one. But he is not allowed to touch her ballots. The crowning moment of the ritual occurs when a man applies a red dye to her thumb from a container that looks like a large felt marker. This is a big deal and he takes a few minutes to make sure that he has left a wide red band that is continuous all the way around the thumb. The dye is indelible; it won't come off for weeks and of course is intended to prevent people from voting early and often. Once the thumb is marked, the voter card is returned, now punched to verify that the woman has done her constitutional duty.

Voters emerging from the polling place are fascinated by the dye. They sniff it, taste it, make thumbprints with it on the outside walls, and try to rub it off on scraps of paper or tissues. While it is wet, it will transfer a stain, but it will not come off. As the day goes on, it seems as though the population of Zacatecas is rapidly succumbing to some kind of thumb-attacking virus till by nightfall all are infected.

Movement through the polling place is a chaotic swirl. The entrance and exit lines cross each other; children go into the polling booths right along with their parents; the man who applies the red dye lounges on the arm of an overstuffed chair, and when he turns toward us for a moment, we are surprised to see that he is wearing a PRI button—he is one of their poll watchers.

We look for opportunities to draw the observers from each of the three major parties aside and ask them how they think things are going. The PAN poll watcher, a chubby, friendly middle-aged woman, cheerfully tells us the PAN is going to do well today, and that this election will be historically taintless. The parties have all had their say and signed off on every facet of the process as it has unfolded over the past year. Everybody has the same checklists now, and everything will be conducted out in the open all the way through.

The PRI poll watcher is equally upbeat, though he says there have been rumors about leftist violence. I ask him about his role in applying the red thumb dye: Isn't that the kind of thing someone might object to? He says, "Oh no. We just try to help out. We know the process, see, so we can assist to make things run smoothly." And then he moves to greet a hesitating voter with a backslap, a smile, and a gesture toward the voting booth.

The PRD representative is in a sour mood. "To tell the truth," she says, "it's not as clean as it looks." She objects to the PRI representative's helping out with the red dye and the way he tends to guide people through the process; it creates a subtle pressure to vote for his candidates. "And they shouldn't tell voters which box to put the ballots into," she continues. "If there is a mistake, it should stand and the ballot would be thrown out. Voters should have been educated before today. It shouldn't happen here."

We check another polling place on the *zócalo* later in the morning. Here there is a lull in the voting, and the president is happy to explain some of the rules to us. Everything from the marking of the checklists to the counting of ballots and posting of totals is to be done publicly this time. Citizens cannot abstain and have substitute voters as in the past. Party observers are to watch and to file written protests concerning any observed irregularities and are not to be involved in the voting process in any way. The boxes are transparent. No campaigning or proselytizing is allowed anywhere near the polling places. Party organizations are not allowed to transport people to the polls. The number of ballots available at each polling place is set ahead of time and cannot be changed even in the case of alleged shortages.

But perhaps most significant is the fact that the electoral authorities are nonpartisan volunteers, as we have been told before. The Electoral Commission called for people to sign up months ago, their backgrounds were checked for lack of political affiliation, and they were trained in the process. Those who qualified were then chosen through a lottery of people born during certain months also chosen at random. So it is no coincidence that all of the officials at this polling place happen to have birthdays in November and December, though it is a striking coincidence that in this case they all turned out to be relatively young women. These regulations were laid down by legislation passed February 28, 1994, and signed on to by all nine parties participating in the election.

We ask about the PRI poll watcher who "assisted" by applying the thumb stain at our previous stop. "Absolutely forbidden," says the president of this polling place. "If that's what happened, you have witnessed at least a serious irregularity, if not an outright violation of just the type we are trying so hard to avoid this year."

We talk to a reporter from a Zacatecas newspaper who has been lurking and taking pictures. When we tell him of the "irregularity" we witnessed he brushes it off, either oblivious to the implications for him as a newsman or biased as a representative of what is known as a progovernment paper. "That is nothing," he says. "Look at the people here expressing their democratic rights. Isn't it wonderful?"

Don't rock the boat. Don't look too closely at the mechanism by which order is maintained. For nearly forty years following the death of Juárez in 1872, that was the creed of Mexico under the longstanding regime of Porfirio Díaz. Order and progress were the words of the day during the era known as the Porfiriato, just as they are today under the PRI. Díaz was a mestizo and his political base was the liberals, now triumphant over the conservatives on the one hand and revolutionaries in the mold of Hidalgo on the other. Because of the liberal faith in constitutional law, Díaz's government learned to operate as nothing less than a constitutional dictatorship. He was duly elected for each of his terms in office. And his most repressive measures against political opponents, recalcitrant newspapers, land-hungry Indians, or striking workers were always cast in the guise of law. In this he was a man ahead of his time, heralding the strongmen of rising states in the twentieth century.

He prefigured modern leaders of developing nations in other ways. Economic growth—in great leaps forward—was the foundation of the order he so successfully established. That meant industrialization, railways, foreign investment, and exploitation of raw materials. And while the Porfiriato seemed prophetic of the developing world of the twentieth century, it was also right in step with the developed world of the nineteenth. In particular, Díaz and his liberals latched on to the European philosophy of positivism, the belief that the application of science, technology, sociology, and statistical analysis could achieve material progress, which in turn would guarantee social progress. In this system, capitalism would create more wealth for more people to strive for. Private property, theoretically distributed to ever-greater numbers, would offer upward mobility. Make the pie bigger, and more people would naturally get a piece.

Díaz and his court philosophers also believed Mexico had solved its ancient caste and racial problems. Was not Díaz himself, the man at the top of the pyramid, a mestizo? And had not his predecessor been a Zapotec Indian? Though the whites could still count on their skin color to hold their place in the upper tiers of the pyramid, social Darwinism offered opportunity to those of darker skin. The Porfiriato did not truly enfranchise the lower mestizo and Indian classes, not by a long shot. But education and progress, it was believed, offered the fittest of those people the chance to rise into the burgeoning middle class. And those who couldn't, still the masses of the Mexican people, deserved their station in life as surely as the dinosaurs deserved their doom by natural selection. Certainly there were more people feeding at the banquet table during the Porfiriato than in the past. But due to rapid population growth, their places rested on the shoulders of greater numbers of the desperately poor than ever before.

Originally liberal supporters of the privatization of church and *ejido* lands intended to see those lands in the hands of numerous small property owners who would become the backbone of the nation—Jeffersonian agrarianism south of the border. But in practice land became concentrated in great haciendas whose owners were limitlessly resourceful in finding legal mechanisms to acquire the property of campesinos. When Indians would protest, the *rurales,* now an arm of Porfiriato repression, would charge in and restore order. The campesinos' brief hope of owning their own lands under La Reforma was quickly dashed as most were forced into debt peonage by the powerful hacendados.

The liberal philosophers of the Porfiriato adapted deftly. Small plots held by Indians were inefficient, they said. The nation as a whole would be more productive with lands administered more effectively by the big hacendados. Ultimately everyone would benefit because there would be a bigger pie. The same thing happened with capital. Like the land, it was concentrated in the hands of the few or the foreign. As the pie grew, it was foreigners, the elite, and the most fortunate of the middle class who got the extra slices.

But Díaz made sure that those were the people who mattered politically. The traditional alternative power centers that the disenfranchised had turned to in the past, the military and the church, were emasculated and placated. Díaz radically reduced the size of the army, dispersed the remaining generals throughout the country, and then lavished on them the blessings of his regime. Frustrated, ambitious, and underpaid generals, to which the poor had once turned for revolution, were now a thing of the past. And while officially maintaining the anticlerical legislation of La Reforma, Díaz left it unenforced. Under his regime the church enjoyed a resurgence of prestige, if not actual power, and Díaz never failed to have a priest by his side in all his public acts.

But for most of his tenure, it was the middle class that was the most powerful force in the new demography. Railroads, industry, trade, and law created jobs and modestly comfortable positions in Mexican society that had never existed before. The bourgeoisie had money and they had numbers—enough that Díaz could maintain throughout most of his age the illusion of immense personal popularity. No one dared raise a hand against him because, never mind how many people still languished in abject poverty, there were more people enjoying prosperity than ever before.

So when revolution broke out in 1910, much of Mexico and most of the outside world were shocked. Wasn't Porfirio Díaz one of the great men of the age? Wasn't Mexico the miracle of the international marketplace? The reasons for the sudden collapse of the Porfiriato edifice have been debated endlessly. Certainly liberty and land reform, the rallying cry of the great revolution, were the issues. But how were the powerless so quickly empowered? Reading the histories while traveling Mexico today, one can't miss the implications of structural changes in the nation's demography and landscape that occurred during the Porfiriato.

First, Díaz, his government, and the thousands who occupied the choicest places in Mexico simply got old. Long before the American youth rebellion of the 1960s, Mexico experienced a generational crisis. In the three decades leading up to the year 1910, the Mexican world had changed radically. The cities had become industrialized, with all the attendant evils of the industrial revolution elsewhere in the world—slums, pollution, and inhumane scale. The countryside was no longer an expanse of open opportunity but instead was fenced off and chartered into the sprawling haciendas. To the new generation of the twentieth century, their Mexican inheritance looked very different from the bright promise of the early Porfiriato. And worst of all, the gerontocracy had re-created the same reality that had sparked the war for independence a century earlier. Now the new generation of the rapidly growing middle class was shut out from the best positions of power, wealth, and advancement just as effectively as the criollos had been by the *gachupines*—only this time age, rather than place of birth, barred the door.

Second, the superficial order of the Porfiriato landscape was shredded, long before the first revolutionary raised his weapon, by the coming of a new machine. This was not the first or the last time that there would be blood in the streets and smoke above the roof-tops because of the convulsions wrought of new technology—the printing press had done it before in Europe, and telecommunications would do it later in Iran and Asia. In Mexico it was the rail-road, built by Díaz as an engine of progress, that ripped up the old map of the country and smashed the hand that unleashed it.

Between 1876 and 1910, twenty-five thousand miles of railways were built in Mexico. Initially the liberal planners foresaw a grid linking all parts of the country, creating a national market and rein-forcing national unity. But the railroads ended up going where money, usually foreign, would be invested, and that meant the U.S. border, the mines, the larger agricultural centers, and the ports. Each line ran from these points to the capital, which was fine with the Porfiristas because it accomplished the more hardheaded objec-tive of centralizing power at Mexico City. In the bargain, the rail-roads created jobs and guaranteed delivery of raw materials for export.

But virtually every other effect of the railroads was unintended and thundered, unseen in the dark of night, toward a red dawn of revolution. Whatever complacency Mexicans might have felt in their newfound stability and prosperity, they still despised the thought of foreigners dominating their land. The railroads were built and supervised primarily by Americans and British, who constituted a new class of foreign bosses flourishing at the top of the pyramid where ambitious, educated, middle-class Mexicans thought they themselves ought to be.

The railroads exacerbated the land crisis by making possible commerical agriculture and cementing the hacendados' power over the land by serving only the largest of agricultural outlets. They opened up once remote areas to exploitation and drove up land prices as the mobility they offered attracted Mexico City investment to land holdings that previously would have been overlooked. They disrupted the map by fostering the growth of cities far from the capital, ironically confounding the Porfiristas' expectations of a railroad-based centralization of power. And in particular, the three states of the ever-independent north—Sonora, Chihuahua, and Coahuila—experienced economic boom times as a result of the coming of the railways and the development of their land and natural resources. Eventually the rails would be responsible for making Sonora the richest of all Mexican states.

The rails further disrupted the patterns of society in more subtle ways. Despite the continued growth of the capital, the population of Mexico otherwise began to shift northward and westward. Campesinos whose ancestors had never traveled beyond their own parish discovered mobility, and as they rode the rails in search of a better life, they found instead solidarity with others just like themselves living in other parts of Mexico. Information became more current—if the *rurales* were bashing campesinos in Michoacán, their brethren in Sonora would hear about it. Rail strikes brought the reality of modern class struggle to Mexico and infused the country with ideological rhetoric. Economic dislocations resulted from growers' discovery of international markets for the produce that previously helped feed Mexico.

Mexico became structured, populated, and interconnected in ways different from the past. New power centers emerged. Old bonds were gone and new ones the Porfiristas couldn't understand had taken their place. Past grievances were swept away by new ones or rekindled into new incarnations by historical changes effected through the laying of rails and the aging of the men who planned them.

Because of structural changes caused by the railway era, the aging functionaries of the late Porfiriato were simply not governing the country they thought they were. And when revolutionaries on the periphery finally did raise their rifles, they knew exactly what the railways could do for them. The old regime had conveniently built steel corridors right from their provincial redoubts into the soft belly and beating heart of the center of power.

During the middle of the day, Lourdes and I have to attend to the fact that the hotel we landed in last night is horrible—like something located at an interstate exit back in New Jersey. We check out several Mexican-owned hotels downtown but aren't completely satisfied with any of them. Just as I am tiring of the search and getting itchy about catching a little siesta, Lourdes spots a tiny sign on a side street no bigger than an alleyway: Mesón de Jobito and an arrow. Something has spoken to her; we must follow these arrows.

They lead us a block behind the main street to a little park with a gated entryway opposite. The Mesón de Jobito turns out to be a recently established four-star hotel complex set up in a renovated old barrio, where the old street has become the courtyard, and the former apartments, the rooms and suites. The place is haunted by the ghost of Jobito, the man who was once landlord of the barrio, we are told by the desk people. I can stay in a suite that was once his home, if I like the company of ghosts. Lourdes will stay in the room next door but makes me promise to rouse her to witness any apparition. She is a believer.

For the time being, however, I receive no unexpected visitors and enjoy a peaceful siesta. Afterward when we venture out again, the mood of the city has changed; there is now an electricity and tension in the air. Trucks carrying armed soldiers roll through the streets, and the lines outside the polling places are long and fidgety. We take a bus to the city's electoral headquarters, located in a little shopping mall where kids Rollerblade to loud heavy metal music blasting throughout the arena. Again we see armed soldiers and then pass a doorway that closes just a little too late to keep us from seeing the rows of stacked automatic rifles inside. Some kind of trouble with the election is being reported on the TV screens that hang from the ceilings in the mall. There is a scary, surreal feeling in this moment, like an LSD trip gone bad.

Besides reports of minor troubles at polling places scattered throughout the country, the big issue seems to be that there has been a shortage of ballots at what are called the "special" polling places, and people have been denied the opportunity to vote. The special polling places are for people who are not currently located in their home district on election day. Absentee balloting has been banned this year, as it leaves too much opportunity for fraud.

No one at electoral headquarters will talk to us now—the soldier won't even let us in the door to the main office—so we hop a bus to the special polling place for Zacatecas, located out at the bus station.

The station looks like any typical bus terminal, with a concourse lined by glass-fronted shops facing various fast-food eateries. Soldiers and police hang about in little groups sipping coffee and not appearing to be on any kind of special alert. By now the polling has closed and the ballots are being counted—here the polling and counting place is a little bookstore behind the glass walls. Outside the glass a small crowd watches every move. No one is allowed inside except for the electoral officials, who are just now beginning to count the ballots. A soldier bars the door with his gun. Even Lourdes's most charming efforts won't make him budge to let us in.

An independent poll watcher outside (there are nonaligned citizen poll watchers at these special polling places besides the usual party reps) tells us how the fiasco unfolded here. The independent observers saw that presidential ballots would run short at about noon and so requested the officials to call Mexico City to ask for more ballots. The Electoral Commission officers in Mexico City sent back a fax showing that all parties had signed the February agreement limiting the number of ballots for each special polling place to three hundred. There had been a larger number allowed in the last election, and the huge numbers of unused ballots led to charges that they were used to stuff the ballot boxes.

Presidential ballots ran out at 1:10 P.M. and the polling place was temporarily closed while officials pondered what to do. After receiving further instructions from Mexico City, they reopened the voting at 2:10 P.M. for senators and deputies only, since there were still enough ballots for those elections (only people who actually lived in this state could take those ballots). Two hundred people were turned away without an opportunity to vote for president. There was a small ruckus. The observers have a ten-page list of names of those who could not vote. Opposition party observers have filed formal protest notices.

Ballot counting begins and the party observers are allowed back into the glassed room. Some of the ballots are torn, some are in the wrong box, others are scribbled with "none of the above," still others have more than one candidate checked. All of these are disallowed with the assent of all of the party observers present. Then one by one each ballot is counted out loud, signed on the back by one of the party observers (they take turns), and stacked in the appropriate piles.

When the ballots for deputy are totaled and matched with the number handed out, there is a difference of one ballot unaccounted for. "Close enough," all agree, and the ballots are put in envelopes, sealed, and sent off to Mexico City. The results are posted on a board, the PRI candidate just edging out the PAN candidate. The PRD candidate is way back. There is a similar result with the senate ballots, including the disparity of one ballot. Everyone concludes one deputy ballot must have gotten mixed up with one senate ballot, and again the verdict is "close enough," the ballots are sealed, and the outcome is posted.

When the officers attempt to open the box of presidential ballots, no one seems to have the strength to break the seal. A man in the crowd pressing with us at the window whips out his Swiss Army knife and brandishes it so that the officers inside can see it. They laugh and one of them comes out to take the knife inside to cut the seal. Problem solved.

Now the mood in the little audience outside grows intense. Since voters at the special polls are not necessarily from the local region (in this case a PRI stronghold) but instead represent a smattering of opinion from all over the country, it is thought that special poll results will have particular early significance. I can see dark-faced men and women biting their lips as the PAN pile of ballots seems to keep pace with the PRI pile. The PAN observer is positively rapturous with delight.

The total count is 298; somehow two ballots were not given out despite the fact that officials turned away two hundred people. "Human error," everyone says, but we note that the PRD rep starts to fill out another protest form. Lourdes and I have been keeping our own tally during the counting of the presidential ballots. There are several ballots that are thrown out and several more where the voter's actual intention is unclear, but somehow the officials and observers find consensus about which pile to put them in. Some confusion ensues about the exact totals, with observers like us now holding our counts and notes about what went wrong and where up to the window. The officials finally agree that the PRI has won by seven votes, with the total off from the count of ballots actually handed out by three. Amazingly, everyone again seems to agree, "Close enough." And more amazing to us, our very careful count showed the total to be off only by one, with the PRI winning by seven votes.

We return to the first polling place we visited earlier in the day. The count here is taking place on the floor with ballots spread out all over the place. Here too there is counting confusion—this vote count off by thirty-seven or thirty-eight from what it ought to be. But then someone points out a mistake in how many ballots were received. They had started out thirty-five short, so the final vote is only off by two or three: "Close enough."

Later we check out the *zócalo* polling place. Here PAN wins 158 to 131 and also wins the deputy and senate seats! We go back to the hotel wondering—is an upset brewing?

At breakfast we think at first that the PAN has won. It's unclear on the TV news. Zedillo is speaking, saying it's not about who lost but who won, sounding almost like a loyal defeated candidate. The commentators intone that he has moved from being an economist to being a politician—the first step toward the royal presidency. Then we hear that the PRI is leading in the vote count, but narrowly. After the Zedillo interview, there is a palpable sense of relief among the commentators that nothing bad has happened. But the story of the ballot shortages at the special polling places won't go away. There were riots as a result in some locations. No one has yet at this early hour figured out how the government might have used the arrangements for limited ballots at the special polling places to skew the election.

To occupy the time while the results take shape, Lourdes and I tour the Mina el Edén, located deep inside a hill in the heart of the city. It was mines like this that drew the Spaniards and that put Zacatecas on the map back in 1586. Though this one has been closed for causing sinkholes underneath the city, the region is still the world's largest producer of silver.

A guide takes us down through four of the seven levels of what looks more like a great cavern than a mine. Precipitous drop-offs plunge hundreds of feet to pools of water, and dark shafts tower above. The passageways open out here and there into huge vaults whose walls are marked with colored stains from drippings that the miners used as clues to find mineral lodes. At some points we step gingerly across hanging bridges made of rope and boards above black holes that seem to have no end—though the guide tells us there are two hundred meters of water far down there, submerging the bottom three levels of the mine. There is no way to retrieve anything or anybody that falls into them.

He explains that no dynamite was ever used here; these monumental excavations were all accomplished with manual tools. The Indian miners usually lived to about thirty or forty years of age before succumbing to various lung diseases. Their only protection was spiritual—an altar still stands in a cranny of the mine with flickering votive candles remembering some of those who died.

No one knows the total value of gold, copper, zinc, and silver taken out of here over the centuries, first by the Spaniards, later by the French, and finally by the Mexican government after nationalization in 1917. But there are legends about individual attempts to profit from the mine's riches. In one a miner discovered a stone loaded with gold and silver when his supervisors were not around. He hid the stone, planning to steal it away later and escape from the mine forever. But when he returned he could not find it. Furious, he cursed God loudly throughout the echoing caverns until God's ears had just about all they could take, and he petrified the man into rock. The guide shows us the image of a face in the stone wall. That is the man, and there he will stay until someone finds his rock.

"And what happens to that person?" we ask.

"He will be petrified himself unless he shares it with his guide."

Later we return to the election headquarters, where armed soldiers stand guard over piles of used voting booths and scores of now empty transparent boxes. We talk to Señor Hector, supervisor for electoral education, who is relieved that here, at least, things have gone peacefully. All of this election material will be stored until everything is verified, and then it will be burned. No one can take any of it away for souvenirs or "someone might think evil."

And the process is not over yet, he points out. At this very moment burros are carrying ballots in the remote areas to central tallying places. That's why the alcohol ban went beyond the day of the election—there could yet be trouble with these burro trains.

We ask him about the issue of the ballot shortages at the special polls, and he reminds us that all parties signed off on the three-hundred-ballot limit last February. The agreement was precipitated by complications in previous elections when the specials had been given as many as seven hundred and fifty. Hundreds went unused and then the PRI was accused of stuffing ballot boxes with them.

Hector has never had an affiliation with any party—that's one of the requirements for his position in the process. He is a mining engineer from private industry; his assistant is an agricultural engineer. He says it has been very interesting to see all the work that goes on behind the scenes for something as simple as putting a ballot in a box: "Democracy is a complicated thing."

By the evening of the day after the election the real story behind the ballot shortages at the special polls has begun to emerge clearly, even in Mexico's highly unreliable media. Report after report confirms that army troops voted early on at special polling places throughout the country. One of the functions of the specials is, of course, to allow soldiers stationed outside their home districts the opportunity to vote. But when whole battalions showed up at the very opening of the polls in a situation where the number of available ballots was fixed and was likely to run out before the end of the day, a pattern of possible manipulation emerged—especially since there were polling places where soldiers, likely to vote en masse for the PRI, accounted for more than half of the ballots that were given out.

Left-wing oracles are already calling it fraud, but their complaints run up against the fact that all parties signed off on the three-hundred-ballot limit. If the scheme was in fact planned, the opposition was itself duped into becoming unwitting accomplices.

In the ensuing weeks, the vote tally will show the PRI to be a clear but not overwhelming winner. International observers will proclaim the election clean. But as we have seen, it was slightly soiled. Rules were not rigorously followed at all polling places. And if the election had been closer, the government's victory would have been stolen rather than legitimate, and the ballot limit at the special polls is how it would have been done. The number of soldiers who got to vote at polls where thousands could not would have been the difference. Perhaps no one will ever know for sure that the election wasn't compromised anyway, but a consensus emerges eventually that the numbers involved at the special polling places don't quite add up to a stolen election. But it was close.

We end the day at a café called the Acropolis, where a group of university professors is discussing politics. The lights keep going out, prompting nervous comments—"It's the Zapatistas, here they come." But otherwise there is a sense of relief and an air of things finally returning to normal. The alcohol ban has been lifted a few hours early, but most of the people in here, including families with children and grandparents, are more interested in ice cream, juices, and coffee.

The professors, one of philosophy, the others of physics, are not surprised at all by the apparent outcome of the election for a simple reason—even in a "clean" election, the state has too many ways of keeping itself in power. "They had the backing of the church, they had the backing of the big businesses, they control the largest media and the communications systems, and the system institutionally divides the alternatives to power," says the philosopher, a white-bearded fellow named Sostenes Segura Dorante.

I ask him to elaborate on that last issue. There are nine parties on the ballot, some of them there only because of legislation that legitimizes parties drawing an incredibly tiny fraction of the vote in the previous election. At least a couple are in existence only because the government encourages them in order to splinter the vote on the left. So the PAN has the rightist vote, still not quite a large enough plurality in this country to be a threat; the larger true leftist vote is splintered or nonparticipatory; and the PRI occupies the huge left center, whether it deserves to be there or not.

"Who can know if there was fraud on top of everything else?" he says, throwing up his hands. "As long as there isn't a better information flow in this country, we cannot know when we need to know. You have to wait until more information sifts out, and then it is often too late, as was the case of 1988." But he agrees with the prevailing leftist complaint that the special polling place issue looks very suspicious. "Even though the military went dressed as civilians, the first one hundred fifty to two hundred votes out of the allowed three hundred went as a bloc to the PRI." He shrugs.

It doesn't really matter though, he believes, echoing others we have talked with. There weren't many significant differences between the platforms of the major candidates. "Everyone has listened to the 'song of Salinas' as he sacrificed social concerns for the glitter of foreign investment and the illusion that he had marched us out of the third world. But twenty million Mexicans still live in misery. What NAFTA market will help them?"

He invokes a statistic that we have heard before: Each year one hundred thousand Mexican children die before reaching their fifth year. What Salinas did was to focus attention on the overall wealth of the country, a vast amount of which is in the hands of the few. "If you average the income of the rich with everyone else, it creates the illusion that things aren't so bad," he explains. And it's not just an internal problem. "There are overdeveloped countries whose comfort is paid for by the pain of our people," he says jamming his finger into the table as Lourdes winces with the verbal jab.

"When you hear Salinas's song, think of those twenty million Mexicans who have always been losing for five hundred years." He goes on to talk about the Tarahumara, whom we have just seen. "They lie in their caves and vomit blood till they die because their lungs have been totally destroyed. Hunger plus work plus suffering equals tuberculosis. Just a few kilometers from here there are Huicholas in the same condition and meanwhile Professor Salinas sings economic democracy. It is the vision of the yuppies."

He spits out this last sentence with disgust and lets us catch our breath for a moment. But then he charges again, though now in a more tranquil tone. "True democracy is the answer. Civil society has already shown it is ready—look at the huge voter turnout yesterday. It is only the state that holds us back, like an old engine that can't take us now to where we want to go."

He has spent all of his passion for politics, and now the conversation turns more convivially toward life in Zacatecas. The city's prosperity has always been based on the silver mines, the professors tell us. With its semiarid climate and single-industry economy, there has never been any agriculture or heavy manufacturing that might attract people desperate for work. It has become a rather comfy, gracious Mexican place, its demographic mix devoid of both poor Mexicans and rich foreigners.

But that is starting to change as foreigners begin to see the tourism possibilities inherent in its well-preserved colonial infrastructure. "Outside money is beginning to find Zacatecas. It could be the next San Miguel," says Sostenes, "and we don't want that to happen." So he and other community activists have been energetic in opposing the development of a proposed retirement center for *norteamericanos*. He fears that tourism would cause Zacatecas to lose its identity. His hope is that the tourists who come here will not be looking for beaches, drugs, or prostitution "because we don't have those things here. And we're too far away from Mexico City to get the Mexico City yuppies, so maybe we will attract only those with a certain attitude."

It's a quiet town, they tell us as we get up to leave, where a woman can walk empty streets at midnight and feel no fear. "Everybody is asleep; there is no one around to bother her." Later that night after Lourdes has gone off to bed, I venture back out to the main street. There is no one there except a policeman and a priest pulling the cathedral bell rope. It is only midnight.

Between 1910 and 1920, Mexico was wasted by the worst paroxysm of violence in its bloody history. Mexicans call it the revolution, but it was at first a simple rebellion against a specific dictator, Porfirio Díaz, and then turned into something more aptly called a civil war—perhaps the most devastating civil war ever experienced by a civilized nation. The American Civil War pales in comparison. By 1920 nearly two million Mexicans had died at the hands of their fellow Mexicans. In the words of Octavio Paz, it was a "feast of death."

Most of the world's revolutions have eventually wrought a profound change, a new order built around a different enfranchisement. People suffer and die, but most of the carnage is aimed at a specific evil the revolutionaries hope to supplant—a class or a segment of the body politic. The great horror of absolute dissolution and indiscriminate terror that threatens at the advent of revolution never fully materializes. Amid the disorder of conflict is the order of war, shedding light on the faces of the combatants, making clear who is on this side and who is on that, and delineating what it will take to make an end of the carnage one way or another.

In the Mexican Revolution, the worst fears of order-loving people were realized; the nightmare of social apocalypse became reality. For more than ten years Mexico resembled the black vision of Matthew Arnold's poem: "a darkling plane, swept with confused alarms of struggle and flight, where ignorant armies clash by night."

It all began when Porfiro Díaz changed his mind, deciding at the age of eighty to seek another term as president after declaring in a newspaper interview that he was ready to step down and turn Mexico over to truly democratic processes. The interview had provoked an outpouring of published articles and books on the subject of the succession. When Díaz reneged, that energy, largely a product of the young middle class, was channeled into rebellion. Thirty-seven-year-old Francisco Madero, scion of a wealthy family in Coahuila, was the author of one of these books, but initially he was no revolutionary. Madero eschewed violence, calling only for an orderly succession to Díaz that would guarantee democratic political processes: the right to free speech, freedom of the press, security for opposition parties, universal suffrage, and observance of existing constitutional protections. In the election of 1910, he ran against Díaz, spent election day in jail, and was declared the loser, of course, when Díaz supporters brazenly stuffed ballot boxes and burned the tallies.

Freed on bail, Madero fled to Texas, where he now issued a call for an armed revolt against Díaz, declaring himself provisional president. Nothing much happened for a while—Díaz put on an obscenely lavish celebration of the centennial of independence and incidentally his own eightieth birthday; the Mexico City elite carried on their social life; the foreign community continued to live high. But by the end of the year, what had appeared to be garden-variety banditry in Chihuahua became insurrection. A twenty-eight-year-old muleteer named Pascual Orozco assembled, with the help of some very well-heeled rebel money, a small army of peasants and workers that began attacking federal positions. Another bandit named Franciso "Pancho" Villa assembled a similar force and raided the Chihuahua countryside in the mode of Robin Hood, stealing from the rich and giving to the poor, who happened to be his followers. When Madero returned in 1911 to preside over these groups, a true rebellion in the northern states began.

Meanwhile, to the south of Mexico City, the state of Morelos seethed with a rebellion initially unrelated to the goings-on in the north. Here a handful of haciendas had expanded to occupy all of the best land, reducing the mestizo and Indian population to peonage or worse. The absentee hacendados lived in the fast lane of Mexico City, and their foremen ran their estates with brutal efficiency. When a thirty-year-old mestizo, Emiliano Zapata, was elected municipal president of the town of Anenecuilco, he organized an armed constabulary of peasants to physically reclaim lands that had recently been illegally absorbed by several haciendas. At the beginning there was no connection between the northern and southern rebellions. But eventually there would be, and their simultaneous appearance marked the beginning of the great revolution.

Then, for a moment, it looked as if it might all be over before it had really started. Under Díaz the army had shrunk dramatically, partly due to his deliberate program of demilitarizing the country to ensure his security and partly because of graft allowing generals to pocket money budgeted for troops that simply did not exist. Under these circumstances, the Porfiriato army and *rurales* were quickly overextended by the rebellions in the north and south. Díaz at least had the acumen to see what was coming with or without his opposition. In May of 1911, he signed a treaty of succession with Madero, resigned from office, and fled to Europe.

Madero, hardly a radical revolutionary but fervently and honestly committed to the moderate political reforms he did espouse, installed a provisional president while he embarked on a campaign to become duly and democratically elected. During the campaign, Mexico enjoyed a brief period of genuine democracy, its newspapers and public orators exercising a freedom never experienced before or since. With the revolutionary cat out of the bag, they used that freedom to vilify Madero and advance their own ideologies or favorite sons. By being true to his moderate democratic principles, Madero allowed ideological as well as simply ambitious rivals to build constituencies during the campaign, so that after his victory, he took office presiding over a nation already out of control.

Despite his honesty and integrity, in the revolutionary air of 1911, Madero just didn't get it. He negotiated with the southern rebels from Morelos as if their leader, Emiliano Zapata, were a defeated enemy. He expected the rebels of the north, his onetime allies, to lay down their arms while the largely Porfirista federal army still remained intact. And he allowed a duplicitous general, Victoriano Huerta, to take charge of bringing order to the country. Soon intrigue swirled around Madero, and treachery was everywhere.

Enter the despicable American ambassador, Henry Lane Wilson, who played a role that should make Americans damn his name, as Mexicans do, to this day. If any American should ever wonder why the people of Mexico or any other foreign nation distrust the United States, let that person read the story of Henry Lane Wilson.

Lane Wilson didn't like Madero, who never gave him the stroking he expected as ambassador of the United States. His dispatches to Washington portrayed the moderate Madero as an insane enemy of American interests throughout the country. When Porfirista counterrevolutionaries General Bernardo Reyes and Félix Díaz (son of the deposed dictator), appeared on the scene, Lane Wilson offered his residence as a haven for the conspirators. On February 19, 1913, counterrebellion broke out in Mexico City, pitting the young Díaz's forces against those loyal to President Madero. For ten days the artillery of the two forces blasted back and forth across the very heart of the capital, including the *zócalo*, slaughtering thousands of civilians and shutting down the city's economy. Madero's treacherous General Huerta negotiated secretly with Díaz while bombarding his positions, and Lane Wilson sent telegrams to Washington claiming that Díaz had the support of the nation. After Washington turned down his request to threaten Madero with American intervention, he did so anyway, coercing Madero into meeting with Díaz and thus conferring on the counterrebellion a semblance of legitimacy.

On February 18, the Huerta-Díaz coup, to which Lane Wilson was privy, unfolded. Madero was taken prisoner and his brother Gustavo, who had been the one voice in Madero's naive entourage to warn against Huerta, was tortured to death by Díaz's drunken soldiers, now allied with Huerta. Latin American and European diplomats urged Huerta to safeguard President Madero's life, but Lane Wilson took it upon himself to mute Washington's intentions of a similar appeal, offering instead unauthorized recognition of the new Huerta regime. Huerta, viewing Madero as a threat whether in jail or exiled, took Lane Wilson's hint. On the night of February 22, his thugs rousted Madero and his vice president from their sleep and drove them to a lonely street outside the penitentiary. There Mexico's most freely elected leaders were shot to death in the face and the car machine-gunned to create the appearance of a rebel ambush and attempt to free them.

Nobody believed the official explanation of their murders, but Lane Wilson declared the Mexican Revolution a closed incident anyway and prepared to enjoy his status as a patron of the new regime, until the election of the reform-minded President Woodrow Wilson in the United States put an abrupt halt to his machinations and ended his tenure in Mexico. Huerta moved to reestablish a Porfirista-like regime gilded with revolutionary rhetoric, but Zapata's land crusade was still out there—as well as Villa and newcomers to the continuing revolution of the north, Venustiano Carranza and Álvaro Obregón. After the carnage of the Ten Tragic Days, Mexico City residents held their noses, hoping that Huerta could accomplish order and that the revolutionaries on the periphery would simply go away. They didn't; the "feast of death" had only just begun.

On the morning of our last day in Zacatecas, we turn our attention to the wonderful hotel in which we have stayed. The maître d' of the restaurant, J. Jesús Delgado Soto, takes us in hand and narrates the story.

The little cul-de-sac side street off the *jardín* out front dates from the 1840s, he tells us. In what is now the lobby facing the street there was a butcher shop, and the rest of the block was an inn, as it is today. The revolution arrived brutally in Zacatecas. Zapata and Villa linked up here and immediately blew up the armory, leaving the federal troops without weapons and the city defenseless. In the ensuing massacre, the revolutionary leaders lost control of their followers. Civilian men, women, and children were killed and the town was sacked. After their victory neither Zapata nor Villa wanted to preside over the mess they had made.

Eventually reconstruction came to Zacatecas and when it did, the old inn was made into a barrio as people who had fled the city started coming back. Jobito was the landlord; he wore a long black cape and a round black military hat and was a terror to his poor tenants who often could not afford to pay their rent. He would stand in the corner of the courtyard, in front of his apartment (the rooms in which I am staying) with his arms folded, waiting for his tenants to appear so he could pounce on them to demand the rent.

When Jobito died, his estate somehow lost the property, perhaps because he loved women and cards and squandered it. Jobito's son was left penniless. He languishes in the streets of Zacatecas today, a homeless beggar. And thus Jobito's ghost haunts his old property until the day when his son finds justice.

Until four years ago the old barrio was an abandoned slum, owned by some elderly women with little interest in it. That's when the current owner bought the place and divided the property between his son and daughter. The son developed his half into the Mesón de Jobito.

Jobito has made his presence felt in a number of ways. One chambermaid lasted only a day because Jobito kept pulling her hair. A woman staying in my suite had to be moved in the middle of the night because Jobito repeatedly turned on the bathtub water. People have seen his shadow in the restaurant and under the little bridge connecting the upper floors above the courtyard. Jesús's little boy saw him on the bridge one day and had nightmares for a week until his parents exorcized him by washing him with a raw egg, reciting the Our Father, and then pouring another egg into a glass under a toothpick cross. When the egg bubbled and took on the likeness of Jobito, the boy was cured.

"People think the way to deal with ghosts is to get angry at them," says Jesús. "But instead you have to be noble to them." He recommends that we show Jobito proper respect if we encounter him, and we will be much more likely to get along.

There is magic in Mexican life, whether we believe in ghosts or not. After our lunch in the restaurant, Jesús shows us the process for making a dessert known as *tuna en crepa,* involving a transformation so wonderful as to cause one to suspend judgment about what these Mexicans are capable of believing in. *Tuna* is the homely cactus, nopal (prickly pear). First the green nopal is mashed until it changes into a bright red sticky pulp called *cardina,* which is aged and then further mashed until it turns brown and sweet. This is *miel de tuna.* It is allowed to drain, and the drippings make a sweet brown sauce. The remainder is pressed in a mold and aged like cheese. This last step transforms it into a semihard candylike substance known as *queso de tuna,* which can be served with goat cheese as an hors d'oeuvre or wrapped up with cheese and the brown sauce in crepes for a dessert, as Jesús now serves to us. It has a taste combining delicate sweetness with the musky breath of old cheese—like hot apple pie with good cheddar, only far more miraculous.

As I am packing to leave, Lourdes stops by my suite and comments that Jobito has not blessed us with his appearance. "Stupid ghost," I say. "He never showed up." Lourdes is aghast. I shouldn't talk that way about ghosts. I turn back to my packing and reach for a cassette that I had just placed on the table beside me. It is not there. Lourdes says, "You did it. You made him angry. Now you have to apologize."

The hell I will. I ransack my bedroom, the little living room of the suite, the bathroom; I unpack and repack my bags. No cassette. Lourdes says we are going to miss our train. "Give it up, Terry, you blew it." So I sit down for a calm moment.

"Jobito, I am sorry," I say. "We have been honored to stay in your lovely house. I will never forget its graciousness." I become aware that I am sitting on something hard. I stand up and look on the cushion of the chair where I have been sitting. There is the cassette.

When we arrive at the station to catch our southbound train out of Zacatecas, we are surprised that there is no crowd waiting, as there usually has been. The ticket window is closed, and a chalkboard beside it has a time scribbled on it—six hours from now. We explore the seemingly deserted place till we find a rail employee nodding at his desk in a back room. "Is the train six hours late?" we ask him.

"Which train are you ticketed for?" he asks.

Confused, we tell him we thought there was only one train, due to stop here in about a half hour.

"There is only one train," he answers. "But is your ticket for today's train or yesterday's train?"

"Today's, of course," we answer.

"The train listed on the chalkboard—that is yesterday's train. It will arrive tonight, but your ticket is not good for that train."

"When will today's train arrive?" we ask. He shrugs. He has no idea. Nothing has been heard from it yet. And so, our hopes dashed again, we trundle off to the bus station to catch a ride to Aguascalientes.

At the bus station we purchase a ticket for the three o'clock bus, but when we arrive at the platform five minutes before departure time, it has already left. There are times when this country enrages me, and this is one of them. Lourdes tries to calm me, "You must remember we are on Latin time. Remember the train way back at Nuevo Laredo? You should be prepared for this kind of thing and not travel with such precise expectations."

And then suddenly an unscheduled bus bound for Aguascalientes pulls in. I don't know whether to feel relieved or more exasperated. Is Jobito still with us? But our tickets are good for the new bus, and we get on and watch another Vicente Fernández movie.

As its name implies, Aguascalientes is a city of hot springs. It is not so charmingly colonial as Zacatecas, but people here tell us that its identity is as a good place to raise a family. It is quiet, inexpensive, and there is plenty of work. In the election it was a PRI stronghold.

In the glorious, blue-sky, clean-air morning we go to the Ojo Hot Springs to take the waters. At the gate outside, there is a conspicuous sign: NO PROSTITUTES OR PERSONS OF DOUBTFUL CHARACTER; NO ALCOHOL; NO ANIMALS; NO HOMOSEXUALS. Inside there are squash and tennis courts, private baths, group hot baths, and full-size pools of warm water. The ticket man tells that people come here from all over—as far away as Veracruz. The waters are good for sore backs, rheumatism, and nervousness. Since he started working here, he has taken the waters every day and says, "It has improved my attitude toward life."

The place is like a water park, with expanses of grassy lawn, concrete walkways and courtyards, water slides, and playground equipment. We dip in several of the pools and find that the larger the body of water, the less hot it is. At the largest there are mothers with their children and more kids taking swimming lessons. Two young mothers tell us that this is a family place. They come here with their kids during the day; father joins them after work. Everyone comes here for picnics on the weekends.

Families and hot water, that's what Aguascalientes is all about they tell us. Even the public water supplying houses is hot; cooling tanks sit outside everyone's home.

Because it's a family city, people here are relieved at the peaceful and stable outcome of the election. The PRI's slogan during the campaign had been "For the welfare of your family." These two women believe it, though they express the usual cynicism about the government. But any other outcome would have been a threat to the tranquillity that they cherish.

In the evening we are directed to a restaurant called the Rincón Maya, run by a Mayan family who brought their recipes from the Yucatán. Here too, families dominate the scene. Huge groups come in with several generations represented, grandchildren sometimes asleep in grandmothers' arms. The elderly owner of the restaurant, José de Jesús de la Torre Barrajas, sits down with us after our supper and says that the restaurant is a family affair. His wife loves to cook and everyone else helps out in other ways. The whole family, including elders and younger married children, all live in apartments off the back.

"My wife is the strong wrist of the family," he says with admiration. "We call her the 'tamer.'" The family business never closes; when he and the wife go on vacation, the children take over. They live and work together and gather around these tables every night after hours.

"There is no other way. Some people think everything is money, but it's not. You need to relax, mixing business and pleasure. You have to live to enjoy the moment." He is happy that he has a family he can share that philosophy with.

I ask him if change threatens family life in Mexico. "We accept modern life," he says. "But it's not ours. For example, we have Halloween, but it's not ours. Ours is the Day of the Dead. We are proud to have some of the most beautiful music in the world. But our TV and radio play rock." He is concerned that the younger generation is being changed by music and drugs, that this might cause the disintegration of the family.

"What can a father do? First you have to give a good example—me, I drink one or two beers, that's it. I work hard: Look at me, I'm big, I work."

He believes if you go to extremes and rule with too harsh a hand, you set up rebellion. "We have to be our children's friends, give them certain freedoms but reproach them when necessary." Concerning punishment, if one of his children makes an error, first it must be called to the child's attention. Then there may be more severe punishment. "What I do, I stop talking to him for a week. That hurts more than a blow. I got this education from my parents."

I ask what I should do if my daughter stays out all night and lies about it.

"Whew," he gasps, and squirms in his chair. Lourdes kicks me under the table. My example is way out of bounds for Latin culture. José sets forth a better example: his son lying about how long he has worked. After investigating to see if the boy worked as much as he claimed, José would discipline him by advising him that he is failing as a man, failing his future. If he lied once, he will lie again and again. "But you have to convince with words. Hitting does no good. Better to make sure that the error has consequences."

He worries about the influence of U.S. culture, that there is a danger of Mexicans becoming materialistic like *norteamericanos.*

"Outside cultural corruption is being imposed on us; we don't want that. Living in cities is not our way. You can observe the real life in small pueblos. We should return to living in small towns."

We ask him for his thoughts about the recent election. "The big story of Mexico," he says, "is that we are proud of our fabulous ancestors, both Spanish and Indian. But it's gone steadily downhill because of rotten politics."

"Then you would have wanted to see a change," I ask, "to see the PRI lose?"

"I didn't say that," he answers. "The PRI may be old and rotten and corrupt. But there is something worse. Look at our history. At least now we will continue to have peace."

6

Feast of Death

Mexico City to Oaxaca

Americans don't like to traffic with death. We spend millions to enable people who have nothing left to live for to postpone dying. We stay clear of our cemeteries and invest them with horrific fantasies. Our dead simply cease to exist if we are atheists, go someplace else if we are believers, or remain the ultimate insoluble mystery if we are agnostics. But there is no joy in our relationship with our dead. We would rather not think about them; if we do, we feel we must mourn.

Not so the Mexicans, who in generation after generation have personally witnessed so much premature death. Mexicans do not mourn their dead; they celebrate them, and they bring them back from time to time to share food and drink. It's partly a persistence of the pre-Columbian belief that the dead, by their deaths, contribute to the fueling of the world, the rains, the crops, the turning of the earth, and the continuance of life. It's also a particularly literal interpretation of the Christian teaching that by his death, Christ guaranteed ours would have no sting. The two alloys of belief, forged in a fire of violence and so much immediate contact with death, define it as the unifying theme of Mexican existence. In it, the land and the sky, the past and the present, the hacendado and the campesino, the sorrow and the joy of life all come together. In death, according to Octavio Paz, the Mexican finds his truest identity.

There are more people than usual riding the Oaxaqueño out of Mexico City this Halloween evening, two months after the national election and two nights before Mexico's Day of the Dead. Almost all are Mexicans; there are just four other foreigners besides us, a couple from Germany and a young backpacking couple, he from Wisconsin, she from British Columbia. An old woman with deep creases in her face arrives in a wheelchair and is carried on board and to her seat by her grandson. Young mothers with very small children, lovers, middle-aged sisters, grandparents, and large families quickly fill up the nine cars of this unusually long train. The fiesta for the Day of the Dead is celebrated all over Mexico, but Oaxaca is a region where the tradition is particularly strong.

This train once had Pullman sleepers for the overnight ride to Oaxaca but no longer, as the paying tourist traffic didn't justify the expense. We won't get beds, but in *primera especial* class we do have good reclining plush seats (with the damnable divider removed by some previous mechanically minded rider).

As the train pulls out of the station, we head for our favorite spot on the open platform but are steered away by the conductor who politely informs us that the division through which we are traveling has had a problem with kids throwing rocks at the trains. Is it political or anything like that? we ask. No, it's just kids without anything better to do, we are told. Surely we have noticed the cracked windows of many of the coaches during our travels. So this is where it happens.

During the slow, halting progress out of the Mexico City yards,

Adelina Zaraut Caso is delighted to find Americans traveling by train to Oaxaca for the fiesta. Clutching her plastic bag of toilet paper throughout our conversation, she is a hale middle-aged peasant woman with a quick smile and a hearty laugh who moved from Oaxaca to Mexico City to take a job caring for a young child when she herself was seven years old. But she has never lost contact with her home in the pueblo of Buenos Aires, just outside of Oaxaca, where her father and grandmother still live. That's where she is going now, to celebrate the Day of the Dead on her vacation time from her current work as a gardener in Mexico City's *zócalo.* Her father lives with six other families on a communal ranch, one of the *ejidos* that are at the heart of the land question throughout Mexico.

Established under Spanish rule during the colonial era, the *ejidos* constituted a workable compromise between the Indians' ancient tradition of nonownership of land and the Spaniards' legalistic sense that land must be possessed by somebody. Before the Spaniards land belonged to the tribe as a whole. It was worked by whoever would or could work it. Produce was distributed according to need and the politics of the pre-Hispanic empires, partly as tribute. Though much blood was shed to determine which tribe had claim to which land, within the tribe there was never any conception of individual ownership.

The Spaniards had to impose some order on this system, especially since they meant to carve out great chunks of land for themselves. They recognized quickly that the Indians would not adapt well to holding individual title to specific plots of land, so they created the *ejidos:* large plots of land, each owned communally by the village or pueblo. Within each *ejido,* the villagers themselves determined the land's use and disposition, with the proviso that there could be no personal ownership, sale, or inheritance. Outside of the *ejidos,* the Spaniards were free to buy and sell and own land in the conventional European way.

Over the centuries of Spanish rule, after independence, and especially during the Porfiriato, two problems with the *ejido* system emerged. First, the Indians didn't always use the land set aside for them. Following ancient custom, they used only what land they needed year by year with no sense that they had to work the land in order to maintain title to it. The result was that great swaths of *ejido* territory often went untilled for years and came to be seen, in non-Indian eyes, as unclaimed. Second, as the criollo and prosperous mestizo population increased, pressure grew to dismantle the *ejidos,* especially those containing unused land, for redistribution to the growing privately owned haciendas. Initially it was primarily unused *ejido* lands that were confiscated. But eventually a pattern of incremental absorption of any *ejido* lands by neighboring haciendas developed, and Indian titles to these properties were allowed to lapse. Thus return of confiscated lands became a central theme of the revolution, particularly for the followers of Emiliano Zapata. Throughout the modern rule of the PRI, land reform has been pursued in bits and pieces with varying degrees of aggressiveness. Today, we would learn, it has become a matter of pure politics.

The government does not currently recognize the title of Buenos Aires to its *ejido* lands, Adelina explains. There are many pueblos facing this problem today. Some get their title rather quickly, others have to wait, and the claims of some are dismissed entirely, with government bulldozers ready to move the inhabitants out. "It's all politics," she says.

But political trouble is the last thing on her mind tonight. Twenty chickens and fifteen turkeys will already have been killed at her father's house. Quarts of *mole negro,* the Oaxacan chocolate-chile sauce, are being cooked as we ride the train. Her family especially likes to bake the "dead bread" in the shape of corpses in coffins with the arms crossed over the chest. The *compadres* who will gather tomorrow are now preparing the big baskets of chicken, chocolate, and bread that they will exchange. Each godfather and godmother will receive these baskets from the mothers of their godchildren. And then they will return the favor. A godfather for several families will feed them all. And there will plenty of mescal, the notably rough Oaxacan version of tequila with the worms in it. All in all, the festival in her town will run for three days.

Adelina is happy to see such crowds on the train headed for Oaxaca but feels there are not enough young people. Her own children have grown up in Mexico City and see no need to return to Oaxaca for the Day of the Dead. She also observes that there are more women on the train than men. Women like to travel and do things like this, she says. Too many men in Mexico City are content to stay home. She shows us an editorial in the *Mexico City News*— "Halloween Sneaks Up on the Day of the Dead." She can't imagine Mexican life with modern and foreign ways usurping the authentic traditions that make this country what it is.

During the evening the train passes through the lights of numerous suburbs and towns between Mexico City and Puebla. Again and again we see the homes of the desperately poor, often constructed out of little more than sticks and cardboard, in the narrow space between the tracks and the road that runs parallel. From the open platform I can smell raw human sewage as we pass by these wrecks of homes, and at one point I see a man squatting to defecate in a hole beside a mattress that must be his bed.

"They are squatters," our porter tells us. They build their shacks on the narrow strips of railroad land and wait till the government intervenes. The lucky ones with a job and a few pesos may find themselves set up in government housing somewhere. The others move on and squat somewhere else, and the cycle repeats itself.

The porter, Luis, has worked on the train since October 16, 1962, the day he realized that there was more to life than sweeping the trains and washing their windows in the Mexico City station. "I suddenly understood that there was a lot going on in the world if you had ambition. Working on the trains could take me places." So he switched from cleaning at twenty-five pesos a day to maintenance at twenty-six pesos a day. He did that for twelve years and then worked with Pullman car supply, doing pillows, towels, and sheets. Now he was earning three hundred pesos every fifteen days with four days off—nearly twenty-eight pesos a day. Finally he got his current job as a porter at thirty-six pesos a day with three days off for every four on the job. He is a man who has it made. And what he has earned, he has earned on his own.

He belongs to the union of FNM but calls it a "white union" because it doesn't really do anything for the workers. "It's for the white people," he says, referring to the co-opting of the labor movement by forces at the top of the social pyramid. It hasn't agitated, for instance, against the government's cutbacks in rail jobs and has allowed the government to neglect the passenger trains. He says he would be proud to serve us on the trains that existed when Salinas first came to power. There was Pullman service with real luxury that was a pleasure for him to provide. For two years Salinas kept his pledge to maintain the passenger trains. These were the years when American outfits began putting together Mexico-by-rail package tours and when the travel guidebooks touted rail travel in Mexico as a salutary experience. But by 1993 policy had changed. Lounge and dining cars disappeared everywhere, and the sleeper was yanked from the Oaxaqueño. Maintenance, cleaning, supply, and personnel accounts were slashed. Now the trains limp along in their sorry state, and old-time rail people like Luis dream of take-overs by Japanese or Canadian private enterprise—or a dramatic change of heart by the new Zedillo administration.

It is a difficult night for sleeping. At each stop more people board so that eventually there are no extra double seats to stretch out in, even if you could remove the divider. Lourdes ends up on a sheet on the floor, and I bend myself into a pretzel on the seats above.

But even without benefit of a good night's sleep, the morning is one of God's very own. For hours the train winds through the deep and narrow Tomellín Canyon, which, unlike the similarly stunning Glenwood Canyon in Colorado, has no highway carved into the opposite wall. Occasionally the gorge widens a bit and there is space for a house or two and a small field of maize. In one of the larger bends we stop at the pueblo of Parién, where there is a joyful bustle of children and dogs and old women selling tamales at trackside. Here too homes hug the tracks, but these are not the dwellings of destitute squatters. The campesino families who live here do pretty well in this little town with its own rail connection to the outside world. Old men, mothers, and children sit on stumps and wave, smiling as we pass. A small boy lovingly brushes his burro while both stare at the train. The homes are built of brick or stucco and adorned with copious flower and vegetable gardens like Doña Carmen's place in Mármol. Paper decorations and Mexican flags mark the entranceways to these rambling microranches. There are no lawns or sidewalks, of course, the homes and gardens firmly rooted right in the dirt. They remind me of a child's playhouse creating a fanciful world out of flowers, reclaimed scrap, and the soil itself. Living in the earth—that's what these people do, and yet, the white pants and blouses of the young men winking at the young women in the market by the station are spotlessly clean.

A concessionaire comes through the car with overly sweetened coffee, and we buy tamales wrapped in banana leaves for breakfast. When the train pulls out of Parién, the porter, Luis, brings out his collection of photos of old steam trains. He is very proud of them, and soon we are joined by another man who collects HO gauge rail models. The collector, Angel Copado González, has several large plastic trash bags stuffed with them, and he too is proud to show us his treasure, particularly his set of hard-to-find FNM passenger cars. He is riding to San Pablo for a model rail exposition, and, like rail fans all over North America, he is soon showing us pictures of himself and his family on previous rail excursions. He belongs to a club that lobbies for restoration of good passenger train service, the Asociación de Trenes de México.

Behind us another old woman is talking about the food she will eat in Oaxaca. "That's what the Day of the Dead is all about— eating," she says. There will be bread and *mole* everywhere. She shares with us her favorite Oaxacan recipe—for fried grasshoppers. They are cooked in oil and then flavored with lime, salt, and salsa and wrapped in a corn tortilla. "You must try it while you're in Oaxaca," she insists.

There is one sour note in this otherwise perfect morning train ride. During the night someone stole the bag of the young backpacker from British Columbia. She had been warned that there might be thieves aboard her second-class car, but since the crew used the word *"rateros"*—snatchers or rats—she didn't understand, despite her knowledge of Spanish. During the night a man got on and sat in the seat in front of her and put his bag under it next to hers. When he got off at the next stop, he took hers with him.

This morning the train crew has not been helpful. They do not want to take depositions or do anything else that might attract official attention. The woman is resigned; she lost her camera and a few other things, but theft is one of the hazards of the backpacker's life.

At the quaint prerevolution station in Oaxaca, a collection of brick and stucco archways surrounding gardenlike interior courtyards, there is a great commotion as family members are reunited and porters scurry to help with baggage. It is sunny and warm here, near ninety, not at all the cool November mountain weather that we expected.

We are staying at the Camino Real, formerly El Presidente, because it has been described simply as the most charming hotel in all Mexico. You hardly know you are approaching one of North America's great five-star hotels as you walk down the walled Calle Cinco de Mayo. To the right a tall archway opens into a chapel; tones of Gregorian chant echo within. The next arch connects through a foyer to an inner courtyard. Here a colorful Day of the Dead altar is set up—a table with candles, skeleton figures, flowers, and a display of the fruits of the earth in both their natural and cooked forms. On the floor in front of the table, copal incense wafts from censers set between more candles. This, it turns out, is the lobby of the hotel; the chapel is the hotel's ballroom, and the entire place is set in what was once a labyrinthine colonial convent. There are several gardenia-draped courtyards, one for dining, one with a swimming pool and a library bar, and one for strolling. Our rooms overlook the strolling courtyard. The heavy stone walls and high roofs with wooden rafters and tiles make air-conditioning unnecessary. Instead windows remain open to the clean Oaxacan air and the sounds of bells, chants, and occasional footsteps on stone. For three days we enjoy the serenity of convent life—without the rigor.

We spend most of this first day here at the hotel, recovering from the train ride, but by sundown we are out on the *zócalo* amid a mixed throng of natives and tourists. There are lots of children—some have Halloween costumes, including Mickey Mouse and Bugs Bunny, and metallic balloons with Bert and Ernie, but others wear Mexican Day of the Dead skulls and black robes. Some carry pumpkin buckets from table to table at the sidewalk cafés, panhandling under the guise of trick-or-treating. The most popular toy seems to be a headband with battery-powered lights inside little skulls mounted on the ends of springs, like insect antennae.

A crowd with a different air and purpose has gathered at the cathedral. Inside a tent here, four people in the fifth day of a hunger strike protest the government's action regarding the *ejido* lands of their village, La Colonia Vicente Guerrero, where six hundred families live. I can see the hunger strikers sprawled on Indian blankets they have spread over the stone floor of the plaza under the tent. Displays of newspaper articles and pictures of bloodied men, women, and children being beaten by police here just three days ago stand beside the tent. Other pictures document what the people of the Colonia have accomplished on their own with these lands: the establishment of a school, their own electricity system, a library, a chapel, and housing.

Around the corner of the cathedral on the big open plaza at the head of the *zócalo,* another crowd watches a street theater performance that is part of the protest. An actress with gaudy makeup, dressed in red, white, and green represents Mexico, carrying a huge stick. With flourishes of bravado and pumped-up pride, she rides on the back of an actor dressed as a poor peasant with a Whole Earth T-shirt and blue jeans with patches. She is saying, "You can ask for whatever you want." The peasant complains that he would like her to get off his back. "Ask for something else," she snaps, eyes flashing. In another skit he is driving a burro and she is driving a car. As she runs over him, she shouts that peasants should work twelve hours a day, and he protests from the ground that he should work only eight.

As a state-sponsored Mexican band on another platform provides feeble competition, the theater troupe begins a third skit, in which the peasant decides to run for president instead of paying his taxes. Mexico tries to woo him back seductively, but when he moves to hug her, she is revolted and pushes him away, finally offering him something else if he will call off his campaign for president. "I'll give you Huatulco [a newly developed resort town on the Pacific]," she says. He says, "You already gave that to the Americans," and there is appreciative laughter throughout the onlooking crowd.

At night there is something frightening about demonstrations on these brightly lit, wide open Mexican plazas. Mnemonic flashes of Tiananmen and the news footage of Colosio's assassination right here in Mexico heighten my unease, and I fear that some night may bring something terrible to this square after the fiesta of the Day of the Dead is finished and the revelers and tourists have gone home.

At the photo display of the beating, we ask several onlookers what they think of all this and the answer is usually a shrug and "It's just a political problem." But one woman becomes animated. She lives in La Colonia de Vicente Guerrero but is not part of the protest—yet. Pointing to a photo of a bleeding woman, she says, "How could they beat her? She only had an egg in her hand. Why did they beat this man? He is eighty years old." The police apparently claimed that the protesters had thrown rocks, but the photos clearly show that the injured ones had only food in their hands. "The governor is prejudiced against people of humble origins," she says, her grievance as old as Mexico itself.

Though the issue here is this particular town and its *ejido,* the protest expands to embrace the whole establishment, as in the street theater skits. This is a phenomenon we have seen before, in San Luis Potosí, where a protest for which I might have less sympathy (street vendors wanting to sell on historic sites) followed the same pattern. First a group is organized, then a letter petitioning for redress is sent to the state governor, then a strike of some sort is called and handbills are printed, a site is selected, and speakers are recruited. All the while the government passively ignores the petition while allowing the expression of "free speech." Then something happens (a provocation according to the government, an inevitable stage in the process according to the protesters) and the protesters are beaten up by police. When it goes this far, the protesters' demands are almost never granted. But by witnessing the process, the activist becomes more radical, the liberal becomes more activist, the passive become more liberal, and the unaware have their consciousness raised. Though it would appear, based on a track record of accomplishing specific aims, that these operations are gestures of futility, revolutionary history the world over is primed with cases of accumulating explosiveness like this that one day blow and rock the earth.

In 1913, after emerging triumphant from the Ten Tragic Days, counterrevolutionary Victoriano Huerta strove to reestablish an order like that of Porfirio Díaz with the opposite methods. Where Díaz had demilitarized the country to maintain his own primacy, Huerta mobilized the largest army Mexico had ever seen—two hundred thousand men strong—to stamp out the rebellions once and for all. But the army was not strong, its ranks filled with unhappy conscripts swept right up off the street and into the military without even a farewell to their families. Meanwhile one state governor refused to recognize his regime. Venustiano Carranza of the state of Coahuila had been an ardent follower of the democrat Madero and now joined forces with Villa in Chihuahua and with Álvaro Obregón in Sonora to forge a solid northern block of revolutionary opposition with the convenient back door to refuge and arms supplies in the United States. Carranza proclaimed that in his territory all federal troops captured in battle would be summarily shot, and quickly Huerta's huge but unhappy army was decimated by desertions and defections to the other side.

The northern countryside was ravished, villages sometimes pillaged by three different armies in the same day. What Huerta had accomplished in raising his massive force was simply the ratcheting up of the scale and scope of violence. And now Woodrow Wilson embarked on an exercise in idealism and arrogance, sending marines to Veracruz to help topple Huerta. He almost succeeded instead at uniting the divided nation against the hated yanquis, but when Huerta turned his forces to face the intruders, Villa used the opportunity to capture and sack Zacatecas. That was the end for Huerta, who left for exile in 1914.

At this point the situation was as follows: In the southern state of Morelos, Emiliano Zapata continued to go his own way, focusing consistently on the issue of land redistribution and distrusting the revolutionaries of the north. Northern rebels Pancho Villa and Álvaro Obregón, their armies poised on trains ready to ride to the capital, were nominally under the command of Venustiano Carranza, now emerged as the strongman of the hour. But Villa in particular pursued his own agenda, with a virulent passion for anticlericalism and an absolute inability to follow orders. The more moderate Carranza distrusted him enough that he held back the coal shipments to Zacatecas that Villa needed to power the trains that would take his army to Mexico City. Instead Obregón took the capital, and shortly thereafter when Carranza arrived triumphant followed by an angry Villa, the revolutionaries were all glowering at each other.

Carranza called for a convention of revolutionary leaders to settle their differences and choose a president, whom he expected to be himself. But secretly Villa and Zapata had joined forces and conspired to garner enough votes to elect their choice for the presidency, a nonentity who would act merely as their puppet. The convention dissolved in disorder, Villa and Zapata marched on the capital from the north and the south, trapping the city between their armies, and Carranza and Obregón retreated to Veracruz.

The inhabitants of Mexico City quaked at the approach of Villa's bandits and Zapata's primitives. But at first the rural invaders were meek, begging door to door for food with their rifles hidden under their serapes, intimidated by the scale and noise of the modern metropolis. After a meeting in which Villa and Zapata agreed only to scourge the nation of Carranza and his middle-class quasi-revolutionaries, Zapata personally returned to Morelos, declaring the capital to be an unfit place for human habitation. With Zapata's departure, the feared debacle descended on the city, as his leaderless troops and Villa's emboldened bandits went on a rampage of murder, theft, rape, and destruction. Carranza and Obregón, their forces replenished, returned and chased out the armies of Villa and Zapata, but urban guerrillas remained behind in the war-torn city, making 1915 a black year for the capital. All sides attempted to extort church moneys to finance their armies, and after Obregón briefly held Mexico City's priests hostage for payment, the panicked clergy abandoned the country en masse. The last remaining bulwarks of order tumbled, and now even ideological bonds were torn as opportunistic Marxist leaders of the trade unions offered their support to Carranza, sending Red Battalions of workers to kill peasant guerrillas in the countryside.

Ignoring Zapata for the time being, Carranza and Obregón directed their armies against Villa in the north, eventually reducing his operations to hit-and-run guerrilla tactics confined to his state of Chihuahua. In 1916 Carranza turned back to Morelos, determined to "depopulate" the state in order to stamp out the Zapatistas. Zapata withdrew to the mountains, and by 1917 Carranza, with Obregón's tentative blessing, was in tenuous control of the nation.

Mexicans of all persuasions were appalled at what the revolutionaries were doing to their country. Something had to come out of all of this horror. And so during the pause in fighting, Carranza convened a congress at Querétaro to draw up a constitution, one that would be moderate and dedicated mainly to legitimizing the bloodshed and his own triumph. But the delegates had other ideas, and the document that emerged was truly radical, thus finally giving the carnage the imprimatur of real revolution. If enforced, it would mark the crashing of power through the last and lowest tiers of the pyramid of Mexican society.

First it completed the secularization of the nation begun during La Reforma by nationalizing all church property, including places of worship; requiring universal, secular elementary education and banning church-run schools entirely; outlawing the monastic orders; registering all priests and ministers; forbidding them from using the pulpit to meddle in political affairs; and barring them from holding office or voting.

In the field of labor, the document guaranteed workers the right to strike and bargain collectively, a maximum eight-hour workday, a day of rest each week, a minimum wage, and double pay overtime. Women were promised equal pay and leave of absence for childbearing. Employers were liable for occupational hazards and unemployment and were required to offer sickness and pension plans. Even in the United States, workers were a long way from accomplishing these ideals in 1917.

Politically the constitution reaffirmed the provisions of La Reforma calling for freedom of speech and of the press, universal suffrage, and the security of opposition parties. But the most profoundly revolutionary sections related to the old issue of land. Article 27 declared that all lands and their development were subject to the public welfare and that the water and subsoil wealth belonged to the nation—only through the granting of concessions could they be exploited. *Ejido* lands were inalienable and all acreage absorbed by the haciendas during the Porfiriato, legally or otherwise, were to be returned. Foreigners could not own land without becoming Mexican citizens and even then they were forbidden to control lands within a buffer zone along foreign boundaries and the coasts. The congress was required to establish maximum-size parcels for individuals and corporations and to enact laws dividing up the great estates that exceeded those limits among the people.

If Carranza had been willing and able to set straight to work implementing the constitution of 1917, perhaps the devastation of the past seven years would not have been so lamentable. This was not just a document for Mexico but one that might have been a blueprint for the third world throughout the twentieth century. Mexico could have been a beacon to the planet, offering a viable alternative to Marxist socialism, and because of this and the fact that it did not actually outlaw private property, some party-line Marxist historians to this day dismiss the Mexican Constitution as just another liberal bourgeois document. It was far more than that, setting forth a plan for revolutionary changes that could have cat-apulted Mexico into a position of leadership among nations throw-ing off the yoke of foreign imperialism and homegrown elitism.

But like a fatally flawed tragic hero, the Mexico of 1917 was fundamentally unable to accomplish its own goals. The constitution established under the reluctant Carranza remains officially in ef-fect, with amendments, today. Most of it, however, has never been applied, standing merely as a statement of ideals to be reached in some far off millennium. And in 1917 it didn't even accomplish Carranza's most limited objectives. The feast of death continued.

Acting on a tip from a hotel employee, we forsake the possibly tourist-tainted evening festivities of Oaxaca center and search for a colectivo cab to take us to the small town of San Agustín for the evening. The colectivos are supposed to be filled with six people before you can get the cheaper rate they offer. Since there doesn't seem to be anyone else heading to San Agustín at this hour, we dicker with one of the drivers, Gregorio Rojas Olivera, to take us out there, wait for us for an hour, and bring us back for forty pesos. Gregorio enjoys talking and takes a liking to these two Americans asking questions about his country. He is proud to say that he owns his own small piece of land and pays taxes on it. But his sympathies are with those who cannot get land. "A small group really governs this country," he says. "Each new leader has to align himself with them and they have no interest in helping the landless." He tells us that there are people living in the Sierra Mija, just fifty kilometers south of prosperous Oaxaca, who have nothing, and no one cares.

Just outside San Agustín, we pick up two teenage girls heading to town for the evening. They offer us a candy made of coconut and nopal—crunchy, rich, and sweet. There are two cemeteries in this town, and as we make our way toward one of them, we pick up a young fellow who says we should go to the other. The people in the one we were going to are "too aggressive"—they might be rude and call us names since we are Americans. We change course and end up at the marshaling center for tonight's parade, where Gregorio knows several of the townspeople.

It's just an open dirt-floored patio between two houses. Here a large crowd has gathered, many of them wearing elaborate costumes, the most spectacular of which are made of hundreds of tiny metal bells. Gregorio's friend greets us and says he must consult with other town leaders about what to do with us. The town supports the festival with its coffers, and the dancing participants have all paid to participate. If we are allowed in there is a question of what we should be asked to pay.

Quickly we are allowed inside the gate, the only nonvillagers, without the payment issue being settled. A brass and percussion band of fellows dressed in field clothes swings into a loud and lively tune and the costumed dancers jump into motion. Most of the dancers are dressed in one of four images: devils (the ones with the bells), spirits of the dead (with wizardlike cone caps and scores of tiny mirrors on their robes), death himself (black robed and carrying a scythe), and old people who are close to death. There are also a few idiosyncratic costumes: one with a rubber mask, a suit, and a briefcase labeled Zedillo, and then the four characters in the drama that will be enacted at the end of the parade: the old hacendado, his wife, his daughter, and her husband.

The dance is wild and violently physical—the participants stomping and whirling in perfectly confused unison, whooping and howling, with the bells of the devils punctuating the thrumming rhythm. They stop when the music stops and mingle and jostle. Occasionally an individual dancer steps out, yells, and does his own funny dance in between songs and the others laugh. Then the music begins again, and with a huge howl the dancers swing into reeling flux. Uncostumed onlookers are rapt and sway and clap with the music. Though a few of the dancers have cigarettes dangling from their masked faces, there is no smell of alcohol yet. That will come later. The inebriation we are witnessing is pure release, made possible by the tradition of the night and the anonymity of the costumes. Earlier in the day, and for most of their existence since the last fiesta, these dancers have been toiling in the fields or the nearby clothing factory. Tonight they let it all go and dance with an intensity possible only for those whose daily lives are hard and whose relationship with death and the earth is close. They dance like demons to bring their dead back to life.

Gregorio's friend approaches us and gestures for us to follow. The leaders have decided what to do with the issue of our presence. We follow four of them to a table on the porch of a house nearby. A man in a white hat, whose home this is, asks us to sit while they all stand. He explains that the dancers pay ninety pesos and the onlookers have paid through their taxes. There is no tradition of charging visitors to witness, and they don't want to lose the purity of their celebration by making it commercial. Thus they can't tell us how much to pay, but there is a consensus that we ought to pay something. We offer fifty pesos since we want to contribute but will not get to wear costumes, dance, and eat and drink later on. The town leaders are relieved by our offer; apparently we had created a real dilemma for them. This town is not used to having visitors in their fiesta marshaling areas (though there will be tour buses from our hotel bringing people out to witness the public drama in the town's plaza later). And the whole question of where to draw the line between allowing tourism and preserving the sanctity of their private village world is a very big deal.

We return to the marshaling area, where the white-hatted town leader gives a little speech. "We want no problems during our celebrations tonight," he announces. He reminds people that there was trouble this night in the city of Villahermosa last year and he wants none of that here. He specifically mentions a man who has shown up drunk tonight and who was not let in. "You have all seen the condition he is in," he says. "This is what we do not want." Knowing glances are exchanged, a potent moment of community censure of one fellow who drank too much too early. White Hat ends his speech by inviting everyone for breakfast at his house at 1:00 A.M.

Now the band cranks up again and the dancers whirl out into the street, where hundreds of onlookers, many with very small children, have gathered to watch the parade to the town square. As the parade winds down the hill, Gregorio takes us into the cemetery, now empty, as everyone is in the streets. The cemetery straddles the highest hilltop of the town, tonight under a moonlit starry sky, and I can see the outlines of mountains in the distance. Up close the flowers on the graves are all black at this hour and the tombstones are just shadows. A nightbird of some sort calls, a light waft of wind rustles the branches of the trees, and that's all. No spirits here. They are all in the town below, where fireworks now arc and boom, where bells toll in joyous cacophony, and where living human voices rise and cheer.

At the square after the parade, the traditional drama performance tells a story that goes like this: The husband of the hacendado's daughter dies prematurely and the disconsolate daughter goes to her father saying, "I need your help. How am I to live?" The hacendado, heretofore always the power of the pueblo, possibly even a bit of a tyrant, goes to his head man and asks him to inventory what he has in the world to help his daughter in her time of need. One by one, the foremen of different parts of the hacendado's domain come forward and inventory the hacienda's wealth, but none of it can assuage his daughter's grief. A doctor attempts to bring the husband back to life but he fails. Finally a resuscitator (a wizardlike priest with powers) comes forward, and with the sympathy and goodwill of the people of the pueblo, the husband is brought back to life for one night, the night of the Day of the Dead. The husband shares the wisdom of the dead with his wife, his father-in-law, and the people of the pueblo. Then all four characters give speeches proclaiming the continuity of life and death, the play ends, and the party for the real-life town begins and goes on all night.

In the play the hacendado is a figure of mixed symbolism. On the one hand, he is the local tyrant, the man under whose hard hand everyone labors. But even though a tyrant, he is the town's own, its father figure, and in his daughter's time of need, he is humanized. When her husband is brought back to life through the goodwill of the people of the village, the conflicts between hacendado and peasant, between father and child, between joy and pain, life and death are bridged for one night. The flower of this tale is the real-life night of revelry and unity of this community.

As Gregorio drives us back to Oaxaca afterward, he talks some more. Though he has seen the festival every year, he expresses a feeling that he has seen it anew tonight, showing it to these American outsiders and hearing our reactions. We want to come back tomorrow, and he wants to explore with us some more. Done deal.

On the morning of the Day of the Dead, we join throngs of people walking to the Panteón General, the main cemetery of Oaxaca. Outside its gates, this looks like market day, but it is not. The dozens of flower and food vendors are here to cater specifically to the needs of people visiting their dead for the day. Inside the gates, the cemetery is a world of its own. The graves, all with more elaborate stones than what is customary in America, are tightly packed amid overhanging trees and a grid of narrow walkways. There is no space for grass; it's all stone and dirt. Preteen boys scurry about with buckets of water for the flowers people bring and to scrub the gravestones clean. They will also paint the lettering black. Families gather at their loved ones' graves and exchange greetings and gossip with those at the neighboring tombs, whom they know from previous times here. People are dressed in a variety of levels of formality. For the most part, it is a social scene, though there are tombs where a solitary daughter or husband, sister or amigo sits silently atop the stone for hours. But there is little mourning; there are few tears. The closest thing to it that we see is a woman saddened because her living sister is dying of cancer and will soon be here. Mostly there is something like the release of the dancers last night. It's a day off from work, of course, and it's a time of relaxation with purpose, like an especially rich Sunday afternoon picnic.

We feel an urge to participate, and since there are a few graves unadorned with flowers and uncelebrated, Lourdes has an idea. She goes out to the vendors and buys some flowers. Then we find an untended grave. Román Muñoz García died at the age of seven, on the day of my own father's death. His stone includes a statue of a child with his hand to his brow in inconsolable grief. The inscription says that he is remembered by his mother, but if she is still alive, she is not yet here.

We hire a boy, who sloshes copious quantities of water on the stone and then scrubs it assiduously with his brush. Lourdes arranges the flowers in the stone cup that is part of all these tombs, and I take pictures. The unremembered boy is remembered. Maybe he will be commemorated again later when his mother arrives and wonders who has already been here. Perhaps she will take it as a miracle or a sign.

For three years Venustiano Carranza governed a turbulent Mexico while the rest of the Western world was embroiled in the First World War in Europe. Even if his vision had been as radical as the constitution handed to him by the delegates to Querétaro, Carranza's government simply lacked the resources to implement it. Instead, it embarked on the same campaign as its forebears—the struggle to bring order to a nation still in turmoil. Zapata and Villa were continuing problems, particularly Zapata, whose rhetoric reminded people how far short of the ideals of the revolution and constitution their new government fell. On April 10, 1919, Zapata was lured to a meeting with a Carrancista general who claimed to want to defect to the Zapatistas. There he was ambushed and shot at point-blank range by an honor guard supposedly presenting arms and offering him a salute. With his death the revolt of the Zapatistas ended. Alone of all the revolutionaries, Zapata never coveted national office or power for himself. Never deviating from his single-minded purpose of redistributing land to the peasants of Morelos and surrounding states, Zapata was the most true of all the revolutionaries. Today he ranks with Hidalgo himself in the pantheon of Mexican heroes.

Villa was another matter. Vainglorious and impetuous, his personal life—distinguished by numerous scandalous affairs with mistresses and vendettas with personal enemies—was a mirror of the tumult in Mexican society as a whole. On any given day it was a good bet that by sundown he would have seduced another woman or killed another man—often accomplishing both several times over. A gift from the government of a twenty-six-thousand-acre hacienda finally prompted him to give up the fight and retire from the field to pursue his private passions. In 1923, after Villa consummated another of his sexual conquests, his car was ambushed and he died in a fusillade of bullets. Whether he was killed at the hands of personal enemies or by a government conspiracy responding to a rumor that he was planning to take up arms again is not known. While Zapata is revered for his revolutionary authenticity, Villa is loved on a different plane. He lived, fought, loved, and killed with unshackled passion. Rarely able to stomach the maneuverings of politics and intrigue, he thrived on the field of action. To Mexicans, Villa was a man.

It was with Zapata dead and Villa retired to his hacienda that Carranza approached the election of 1920, at which under the new law he would have to step down, though he expected to preside over a smooth transfer of power with continuing influence over the affairs of the nation. He could not, however, countenance succession by his strong-minded onetime ally Álvaro Obregón who had come to be associated, despite his moderate origins, with the more radical aspects of the constitution. Thus Carranza had Obregón arrested on trumped-up charges, but in spite of his scheming, supporters sprung Obregón from jail and the army rallied behind him and installed him in power. Carranza attempted to retreat by train to Veracruz, where he planned to build an army to regain power. But sabotage of the tracks forced him and his entourage onto horseback and into hiding in the mountains. There a supposedly loyal military unit offered its protection, and while Carranza slept in a tent, its officers entered and shot him to death. Now Obregón was the man.

Again there was a moment of peace, many contending then and now that Obregón's election to the presidency marked the end of the revolution. At least in terms of rhetoric, Obregón was the first president to vocally embrace the constitution and thus create the appearance of the establishment of a revolutionary order. Under him the first of the government-sponsored labor organizations, the Regional Confederation of Mexican Labor, was established, theoretically to guarantee the labor provisions of the constitution. The National Land Commission cautiously set about implementing some of the tenets of Article 27. But while these efforts were rather modest in scope, the real revolutionary cast of the new Mexico was established by Obregón's secretary of education, José Vasconcelos. With the slogan "Forging the fatherland," Vasconcelos launched a campaign to build schools, subsidize indigenous crafts and culture, and most important, enlist the service of art to promote the ideals of the revolution. It was his program that brought the likes of Diego Rivera and José Clemente Orozco to the task of painting the revolutionary murals that became the modern Mexican nation's great contribution to the world of art.

But Obregón himself, while basking in his image as the man who would finally make the revolution real, chafed at some of the requirements of the constitution, in particular the tenets regarding land redistribution of Article 27. How could Mexico get back on its feet, he wondered, if the constitution required him to dismantle what was most productive in the system? Thus under Obregón, the full implementation of the constitution became an ideal for the future. Progress was made—some land was redistributed, labor reforms were enacted, the franchise was extended—despite the carpings of Marxist oracles, but the main task at hand was to rebuild Mexico's productivity while convincing the people that profound change was being accomplished. Talk revolution, take measured and evolutionary steps toward it, but build prosperity now. That was Obregón's legacy—and it still thrives today.

Obregón honored the nonreelection clause of the constitution, but he set a precedent for twentieth-century Mexican politics by selecting the ruling party's candidate for succession. He chose Plutarco Calles, a man from Sonora with a good record of revolutionary service. Since Calles was believed to be more leftist than Obregón, the choice sparked another three-month rebellion led by Obregón's conservative minister of finance. But once the rebellion was successfully put down, the practice was established. Presidents henceforth would choose their successors.

Not since Villa had the revolution seen a leader so ruthless and anticlerical as the elderly but fearless Calles. Despite the lingering economic realities that impeded implementation of Article 27, Calles redistributed nearly 8 million acres of land (though some historians point out that that figure amounted to less than 3 percent of Mexico's surface). He supported trade unions and allowed a limited number of significant strikes. But his most enduring legacy was his persecution of the church. Unflinchingly he enforced all of the anticlerical provisions of the constitution—and in so doing, touched off another round of Mexican bloodshed.

This time the rebels were conservative Catholics, aided and prodded by Rome, and the war was called the Cristeros Rebellion for their battle cry, "Viva Cristo Rey." Despite its Christian banner, the Cristero Rebellion was one of the goriest chapters of the revolution. The Cristeros targeted young teachers, usually women, working in the state's secular schools, who were taken and butchered in front of their students. Fifty thousand Mexicans died in this episode of blood whose outcome grounded anticlericalism in government policy and in the hearts of many Mexicans more fervently than ever.

When Calles's four-year term ended, Obregón supporters in congress amended the constitution to allow a former president to run for reelection and to extend the term to six years. Calles was silent on Obregón's candidacy, but just after the election, President Obregón was assassinated by a Cristero artist who was painting his portrait. Though the culprit, under torture, reportedly implicated only himself and a fanatic nun, many Mexicans always have suspected that Calles had a hand in the murder. Despite the fact that he had stepped down from the presidency, Calles ruled Mexico from behind the scenes as the *"jefe máximo"* for six more years, personally choosing and then disposing of the three puppet presidents named to serve out Obregón's term. It was a role he clearly relished and one that would not have been available to him had Obregón occupied the presidency a second time.

It was under Calles that the confoundingly contradictory party that rules Mexico today was born, albeit under a different name. Intended as Calles's solution to the problem of orderly succession under the nonreelection clause, today's PRI was originally founded as the Partido Nacional Revolucionario in 1929. By offering its auspices as the orderly route to power and by espousing revolutionary ideals while applying "practical conservative" measures for growth and stability, the PNR was able to enfold under its big tent blocs of the left, center, and right—the army, the bureaucracy, campesino groups, trade unions, and even the church. Its rhetoric declared it the party of continuing revolution. Its practical goal was to establish a state power that would not be challenged, in effect to close down the revolution.

Where should historians pinpoint the end of the revolution? The large-scale violence ceased during Calles's time as *jefe máximo*. However, the ideals of the revolution were far from fulfilled. By that standard the revolution is not over yet, and there are many in Mexico today who ardently hold this view. But Calles was succeeded by a president in 1934 who methodically and honestly worked in an era of peace and stability to make greater leaps toward implementing the constitution than anyone before or since has dared. Chosen by Calles as his fourth successor under the mistaken belief that he would prove an able but malleable puppet, Lázaro Cárdenas removed Calles appointees from office, ignored the *jefe's* attempts to manipulate him, and got away with it. When Calles continued to play his games behind the scenes, Cárdenas had him deported to the United States. What made Cárdenas untouchable were his extensive travels throughout the country—something few other leaders of the capital-obsessed nation ever engaged in—his regular contact with emissaries of the lowliest peasant villages, and his clear commitment to actually realizing the goals of the revolution.

Darker of skin than any president since Juárez, Cárdenas set out to enforce Article 27, establishing the process that inspires those we have met who are struggling to regain their land today. During his tenure, not only were nearly fifty million acres of land redistributed, but it was returned to communal *ejidos* rather than individual ownership. The National Bank of Ejido Credit was set up to assist communities with the financial aspects of establishing their *ejidos*. Marxist critics accurately protest that Cárdenas (a leftist but no Marxist) fell short of accomplishing the full mandate of Article 27. But succeeding governments would never again dare to ignore it.

Besides the land issue, Cárdenas opened up the nation's industry to the full impact of organized labor. Despite pressure from industrialists and foreign powers, he refused to interfere in the record number of strikes that occurred during his tenure. Corporations that did not adhere to constitutional labor requirements were nationalized. And in 1938, when foreign oil companies refused to pay legislated minimum wage scales, Cárdenas nationalized the oil industry in a move that shocked the international power structure and might have led to foreign intervention were it not for events unfolding in Europe at the time.

Perhaps the term of Mexico's greatest president, Lázaro Cárdenas, might stand as a meaningful demarcation for the end of the revolution. Since his time Mexico has not seen another truly threatening civil upheaval until the new Zapatistas in Chiapas in 1994. With the presidency of Lázaro Cárdenas, the feast of death finally ended.

Before noon we find Gregorio at the *colectivo* taxi stand, and he takes us back to San Agustín. The town looks different by daylight. On the outskirts we note the prosperous homes of folks who, according to Gregorio, work for the government. We make our way to the hilltop cemetery that was so empty last night and find the same kind of gathering that we saw at the Panteón General in Oaxaca, embellished with preparations for an outdoor mass.

Here are scores of townspeople, with their bread and flowers, surrounded by the expansive grandeur of the Oaxaca Valley and the mountains beyond. The graves are scattered amid a grove of piñon, *granado,* and *níspero* trees. Gregorio introduces us to the family of the deceased Fidencio Gigón Fernández, who died at the age of eighty-two in 1984. His wife and her daughter and granddaughter are here. With each generation the number of children has dwindled. The widow had fourteen; the granddaughter says, "We had two and then closed the factory." Times have changed. Gregorio jokes that women were better in the old days. Today they have one child and start complaining. The women take his politically incorrect statement with good humor—and comment that women are getting smarter.

Fidencio was a good man, his wife tells us. He was a machinist in the nearby clothing factory who always worked hard, was always there for the children, and put much of his extra time into community work, such as the school board and municipal government. He also worked the land, planting maize, beans, and squash on a plot in the town *ejido* to feed his many children. Today this family no longer works that land; it is available for other families who have many young mouths to feed.

Gregorio introduces us to more people communing with their dead. Some of the men are still drinking beer and have red eyes. We hear stories of earth being turned to receive new dead and containing the unidentified bones of ancestors. One man's brother is buried on top of his father and two other skeletons who must be grandfathers or great-uncles.

As the horns of the same band that accompanied the parade last night are warming up to play for the mass, Gregorio wants to show us a recently studied archaeological site in another town nearby, so we prepare to leave as more folks stream up the ramp to the cemetery. Roosters crow, horses whinny, goats bleat—the sounds of the country life mingle with the receding tones of the mass music as we descend. A mixed scent of flora and dung hangs in the air like a rich incense. In midafternoon the people still come with their chairs, shovels, bread, and the big red rooster-crest flowers, exchanging handshakes all around—"*Sí, sí*" again and again. A prosperous man in a gray pinstripe suit and old-fashioned beaver walks behind a crippled man crawling on his knees. Both are smiling. Girls in fresh, brightly colored dresses grin at the boys in their white shirts with their thumbs in their belts. Now comes the young priest, dressed in country clothes and carrying his vestments. Though we have seen no one praying today, here on this ramp we witness the ancient religious impulse to climb a tower and approach the ineffable. The time is not solemn; it is not even pious. The bones at the top of the hill may be dead, but this day is alive.

In the street below we ask Gregorio to help us find someone who can tell us something about the town's history before we leave. It turns out to be a daunting task. The younger people simply don't seem to know anything about their town's history and the older folks speak only in generalities. One town elder says, "The pueblo was founded long ago for everybody. It opens its arms to those who will come and stand or fall with us." And then he adds something we don't understand that makes some of the onlookers laugh. But a clue to the historical silence begins to emerge when one middle-aged man asks us in response to our question, "Why do you want to know this? I am intelligent and a careful man. Do you want to know this so that you can come and dominate us, so that you can kill us?" And here he makes a machine-gun gesture with his hands. I am reminded of a Pueblo man I met once at Taos who explained that the secret to his people's success at holding their tribe together and preserving their way of life is that "we do not elaborate to outsiders."

Lourdes is disturbed by this incident. It brings up the troubling question of how our work might play a role in the disruption of the culture and the peace of these people in this small town we plan to write about. How can we tell its story without putting the town on the map? Is it possible to find an equilibrium between publicity and privacy—to cast some light on the quiet corners of the world without robbing them of their souls? And the man's machine-gun gesture implies that here in Mexico the implications of outside interest might be mortal as well as cultural.

Gregorio drives us out of San Agustín and a few miles to the even smaller pueblo of San José Mogote. He has listened to our questions about history and ruminates about their significance. Like most Mexicans, he is certainly aware of the broad strokes of his country's story and, through rituals like the Day of the Dead, is probably in better touch with its mythical sense than most Americans are with theirs. But, partly because he apparently can't read, he does not know the details. Why was San Agustín founded? It's a question he never thought to ask before. Now he is going to show us some ruins of the pre-Hispanic past. Maybe we will help him pursue more interesting points of detail.

There is a parking lot in front of a large mound in the pueblo, and a sign next to a path leading to the ruins. An old woman who lives in the village is just as fascinated by our curiosity as is Gregorio. Lourdes reads the sign for them and then translates for me. The woman has lived here all of her life, but she does not read. No one has ever read to her the words on the sign.

And what it says is this: The mound before us is a relatively recently discovered pyramidal structure of ceremonial purpose built as far back as 1600 B.C. That makes it more than a thousand years older than the Zapotecs of the nearby Monte Albán and as old as the Olmecs of the Veracruz coast! The site was occupied from that time until 400 A.D., when it was abandoned. Little is known about the pre-Zapotec people who built it because study of the site has not yet been thoroughly pursued. All that is known so far is that before Monte Albán, it was the biggest ceremonial site in the valley—and that its antiquity raises hosts of questions for archaeologists and anthropologists to pursue.

If ever one needed an example to convince students that archaeology and anthropology are disciplines with vast, as yet undiscovered territory, this site would be it. The mound has about the same size, shape, and geographical orientation as the modern-day cemetery in San Agustín. We climb to the top and look down a steep stairway that has been partly excavated. Though the mound is not all that high and is not located on top of a mountain like Monte Albán, still it is sited so that it commands views of the entire valley in all directions. Some men at the top help Gregorio lift a heavy steel door that the archaeologists have placed over a large stone figure—a dancer, or possibly, because of intimations of another face within its torso, a mother. There are outcroppings of the original stone structure poking up through the accumulated earth of three and a half thousand years and scattered shards of pottery in the dirt—the less significant fragments the archaeologists left behind in their first tentative studies here.

Gregorio is animated during the car ride back to Oaxaca and chatters with Lourdes in a Spanish conversation much of which she does not bother to translate for me. The detail of dates especially seems to provoke wonder and pride. The Zapotecs were before the Spaniards, and these people were apparently before the Zapotecs. He might have seen the date on the sign but never would have thought to consider its significance were it not for our reaction to it. We pay him extra to compensate for the sacrifice of his taxi's exhaust system on the rough stones of the country roads, and when we part, he seems as grateful to us for our adventure together as we are to him.

In the morning life in the *zócalo* has returned to normal. Gone are the balloons and vendors and crowds. Now people bustle about in the workaday mode, and people in the restaurants hunch over coffee and paperwork. A few schoolchildren who have the day off wander about, and several large groups of German and American tourists appear to have just arrived. Lourdes gets her shoes and purse shined by an old man who says he used the holiday to stay home and clean. It's too busy and crazy for an old man to go out on the Day of the Dead. He was happy to drink a little mescal and make a bit of *mole* to eat after finishing his chores. And how much "dead candy" did I eat? he wants to know. And how much chocolate did I drink, and how many legs of turkey did I have, and how many cups of mescal? At the time I think his questions are a simple expression of enthusiasm for the good things that happen on the Day of the Dead. It isn't till much later, near the end of our talk

231

with him, that I realize he is asking these questions in a very different vein.

More important to him than the Day of the Dead is his saint's day, the sixteenth of September (which also happens to be Independence Day). He is named Cipriano, for a man who became a saint because he resisted the temptations of the devil. According to the shoeshine Cipriano, Cipriano the saint was accosted by Satan, who promised to bring him a beautiful girl in three days if he would give up his soul. Apparently Cipriano's first response was acquiescence, because Satan spent the next three days trying to bring him a particularly charming but stubborn young woman. After three days the woman was still saying no (was the wrong character in the shoeshine man's version of the story sainted?), so Satan returned to Cipriano empty-handed. Cipriano said, "Where's my woman?" Satan said, "I can't get her but you are still mine." Cipriano answered that the deal was off, and he would pray to get his girl instead. "And so he became a saint," the shoeshine Cipriano concludes. "Did he ever get his girl?" I want to know. "Who knows what happened?" he answers with a careless shrug, the same shrug Mexicans always offer when they run into the limits of their information. It's a gesture that, in a nation where information is so often imcomplete, is seen all too often.

We ask him about the recent election, and he gives the common response that government today doesn't do what it should for its citizens. "The politicians only manipulate people," he says. Though he can't really remember which leaders of the past were good, he feels they are worse today, but it has always been a problem. "When I was young, I wasn't aware of how bad our government was. Now that I do understand, I am too old to do anything about it." The issue for him is economic. He recalls being able to buy a tortilla as a child for five centavos, and to drink *atole* for one centavo. Today these things can cost a hundred times as much. It's not just that what he earns shining shoes has lagged a bit but that his income has plummeted to make him a hungry man. He tells us that five of his children live in his house, and though one of them is a successful electrician and they all contribute, there is never enough food. I ask how much he earns in a good day, and he replies that there is never a good day.

I express some surprise at this; surely with all the tourists drawn to Oaxaca there should be ample opportunity for shoeshine men to make some money. He laughs with a touch of bitterness. He gets no business from tourists, he says. They all wear tennis shoes. His customers are Mexicans who are regulars. Tourists buy things in Oaxaca, but they don't mingle. Why should they? They are transient; they are here one day on their way to the beach or wherever the next. They wouldn't stop long enough to get their shoes shined even if they didn't wear tennis shoes. He thanks God that today he has already earned ten pesos before we came along. There are times when he doesn't get anything all day.

When he is finished we pay him ten pesos, for the shine plus the talk. He thanks God again and says now he can eat today. It wasn't readily apparent at the start of our conversation that this man is as poor as he now seems to be. And it appears presently that there has been a sardonic edge to his talk all along. When he asked how many cups of this and that I had consumed for the Day of the Dead, he was highlighting the difference between our levels of wealth. At first I had thought him to be a simple man cheerfully responding to the questions of these curious Americans. Now I'm sure he has been in control of the interview from the start, sharply aware of its implications. He is an old man who can do little about what he has learned in his life about politics. But he can raise the consciousness of these visiting Americans.

At the protest by the cathedral, the hunger strikers are starting to stir inside their tent, and we find a spokesman for the Unión Campesina Democrática, whose talk with us quickly draws a crowd. The union is a statewide group, affiliated with a national organization, whose work primarily focuses on the problems of the *ejidos*. As issues pop up with various *ejidos* around the state, they move in and provide support to publicize the cause, to protect the people, and to manage dialogue with the government. Because of the violence that happened here recently, this *ejido* is the biggest issue on the union's plate at the moment.

He narrates for us the story of this episode. The people of La Colonia have lived on the land in question for fourteen years and had been particularly resourceful in providing for themselves many of the services and the infrastructure whose absence is the issue for the union in so many other *ejidos*. So this case was different right from the start. These people weren't asking the government for new services; they just wanted title to the land and the right to stay on it. Under Oaxacan state law, people who have lived on unoccupied land for five years in a peaceful and public way have the right to become communal owners. A former state governor signed the documents promising title, but the current governor refuses to follow through.

The people of La Colonia petitioned him for title to their land. The government responded that the land was needed for a state agricultural project and offered to talk, all before the recent presidential election. When it became clear that the government was not going to cooperate and the bulldozers began moving in, the people of the *ejido* held assemblies and marched, wrote letters, and then finally decided on the hunger strike because it is the strongest form of nonviolent civil resistance. This is when the union came into the action. It is important to understand, we are told, that the issue was independently initiated and carried this far by the people of La Colonia on their own.

There were originally five volunteers who had medical checkups and seemed to be in relatively good health, though the spokesman hastens to point out that there is a chronic anemia among people of this class, for whom complete nutrition is a precarious proposition to begin with. One of the volunteers had to drop out because he got sick, so now there are two men and two women, whose average age is thirty-two. Three of them are from La Colonia, including the two women, who are housewives. The fourth man is from the union, showing solidarity.

When the strike began, the government quickly sent an ambulance that has been sitting here ever since. It contains nothing but bottles of Maalox. Now in their ninth day, the strikers are beginning to deteriorate. A doctor visits them daily and says that the strike should stop—that irreversible damage has already begun. Leaders of the union would also like to see the strike end because it is clear that it is not going to move the government. But the strikers have made an intensely personal decision and are prepared to die.

The union spokesman acknowledges that success in having demands met in cases like this is really rare. But the protest is getting a tremendous response from the public. He points to a government display across the plaza touting new road construction and reminds us that it has had few viewers all week while crowds have gathered here around the posters and photos and street theater. The bottom line is political. After all, it was when the election returns were in showing that once again, the people of this *ejido* had voted overwhelmingly against the government, that the dialogue stopped. "The business about needing the land for an agricultural project is a lie," he says. This is what people mean when they say "It's all politics."

When we return to the *colectivo* taxi stand this morning, Gregorio is not on duty, so we negotiate with another driver to drive us out to Monte Albán. He takes us on the old road that winds up the steep mountain around hairpin curves with towering cliffs to the left and an airy abyss to the right. These Mexican country roads are narrow and have no shoulders or guardrails, and one simply has to tell oneself that this man has driven this road a thousand times and must know what he is doing.

Finally we round a curve and can see where the top of the mountain should be, but it's not there. The Zapotecs removed it nearly twenty-four hundred years ago, building their city on the flat platform left behind. They called themselves the "People of the Clouds," and that's certainly the first impression this place makes. The valley is so far below that any city here must have seemed a world apart.

The first thing we see after we leave the taxi and set out on foot is an abomination: a large stone building under construction to be used as a gift shop and orientation center. The fact that its style is in "authentic imitation" of the stone structures of Monte Albán actually makes it worse. A more temporary-looking wood or even tin building would be less disruptive.

But the new Welcome Center is out of sight when we enter into the grounds of the old city itself past the ancient ball court. Though there are several different levels, with higher platforms at the south and north ends of the city and numerous wide processional stair-ways, the sense upon stepping into this huge open space is of emerging into a single-level, man-made world, almost like arriving on the deck of a half-mile-long aircraft carrier. The great open promenades, in particular the Central Plaza, which were once packed with market vendors and thronged with religious proces-sions, today seem to swallow up the handful of tourists and sight-seers who wander about in little insignificant knots of twos and threes under a high intense sun. The pyramid temples and decks that are such symbols of these ancient places create the same de-fined sense of urban space as do the tall buildings in modern cities, but they are not what most catches my eye. Instead it's the long rows of stone stairways bordering the open avenues—they look almost like bleachers, as if the main function of the city were for its residents to spectate the business of commerce and ceremony.

Several Indian craftsmen wander about selling replicas of Zapotec artifacts found here and now on display at the museum.

The more credulous tourists are sometimes told by the less scrupulous craftsmen that their wares are authentic, originals found in some nook missed by the archaeologists who have crawled over every square inch of this place. Pedro Castellanos presents his pieces to us honestly and with pride in his skill as a craftsman. Characteristically short in stature and bearing the unmistakable fine features of the ancient Zapotecs, he says he is 100 percent authentic, even if his goods are not, and we believe him.

He says he doesn't keep the old traditions himself because he's not interested, except insofar as other people's interest helps him to make a living. "When I was very young," he explains, "I did all of the traditional dances and observances because my father did and because I believed they were magic. But when I learned that they were only traditions, with no magic, I lost interest."

Pedro lives in the pueblo of Arrasola, at the bottom of the mountain, and despite his professed lack of interest in tradition, he has never felt any inclination to move anywhere else. His father works land on the *ejido*, another of those whose people are in the process of getting title. He expects it will happen soon with little hassle. Perhaps due to its proximity to a tourist attraction and national treasure, his village has a good relationship with the government. But Pedro prefers to make his living as a craftsman, rather than by farming. He likes to talk, especially to people like us who come here to visit.

After working for a couple of years with an archaeologist and paying particular attention to lessons about how his ancient ancestors lived, Pedro knows the history of Monte Albán. It was out of this work that he learned how to reproduce so accurately the artifacts of the ancients.

He gives us a disorganized dissertation explaining that the crops were grown on the mountainside, and homes with wooden roofs were tucked into the walls bordering the different levels of the city. The jaguar was an object of worship, and there were pyramids twice as tall as those that remain today. It rained more in the old days, and perhaps flooding drove his people to the top of the mountain, though there was also the issue of defense and a desire to be close to their gods. There were no coins, but gold, jade, obsidian, and ceramics were used as media of exhange. He doesn't believe (contrary to what the historians tell us) that his people ever practiced human sacrifice.

And then his rambling discourse converges to a sharp focus. There were three classes in Zapotec society, he explains. "The poor made their living from agriculture, like my father. There was a middle class of merchants, craftsmen, and people who made things, like me." And there were the warriors, clergy, and nobility at the top. "They lived in the old days just like today," he marvels. "Nothing has really changed in three thousand years."

Pedro has three children and has modest expectations of them. "I want my kids to have a quiet life, to fulfill God's will and get along with everybody," he says. He doesn't want them to live in excess, to get drunk, or to get angry with others. The Zapotecs were a relatively mild and peaceful people, and that is the only tradition he really cares about transmitting to the next generation.

In appreciation we buy several of Pedro's artifacts and wish him well. I begin climbing to the highest point of the city. The rise of the individual steps is high, probably a foot or more, and the Zapotecs were a small people. They had to climb a mountain to get to their city and then exert themselves with big steps to get to its highest platforms. They must have wanted a sense of earning their presence here, just as I do when I prefer to arrive at a place by train, no matter how uncomfortable the ride.

From the top of the north platform I scan the world of Monte Albán. It occurs to me that building a city out of pyramid-shaped structures creates a singular sense of view, affording direct sight lines in almost all directions, near and far. It also minimizes shadows—the place is bathed in sunlight. That's what the architecture of this city effects: a place of open vision and sunlit space, not only of the urban spaces within it but also of the valley below and the ring of cloud-scudded mountains in the distance. The sense of vision ripens as I stand here, along with a sensation of permanence. In its ultimate expression what Monte Albán's siting does is to cancel the boundary between the dirt underfoot and the sun above. Here there is no such division. Land and sky are one. And I think that's why the Zapotecs removed a mountaintop and built their city here. In a threatening world ruled by the predatory jaguar, they built a city whose location helped foil the fear of death. From the dust bloomed their sustenance; in the vault above they felt intimations of their mortality. At Monte Albán they abolished this eternal dissonance of humanity's existence and united the earth with the canopy of heaven.

7

Sand Castles
Cancún to Palenque

From New York, Hamburg, Toronto, Minneapolis, and Stockholm they come, from Missoula, Peoria, and Ithaca. By the thousands they come to Cancún on the silver birds from faraway cold places. It's the sun and the beaches and the aqua-blue water that the tourists are after, of course, but also the side trips to Mayan ruins and the ambience of a truly foreign nation that is hip to international tourism and the amenities of the global village. There is a television ad produced by the Mexican Department of Tourism showing a white-skinned family sculpting pyramids on a perfect white beach. The voice-over says, "If you think you'll like our beaches," then the camera pans back to show the ruins of Tulum towering over the sand where the family is playing, and the voice-over continues, "wait till you see our sand castles."

Seldom has a government program been such a success. Beginning with Acapulco, the Fonatur project has been developing sites for international resort tourism since the fifties. After Acapulco and Mazatlán on the Pacific, Fonatur computers selected Cancún on the Caribbean, then Ixtapa on the Pacific, and the island of Cozumel off the Caribbean coast fifty miles south of Cancún. Now the latest projects are Cabo San Lucas at the southern tip of Baja California and Huatulco on the southern Pacific coast, the place satirized in the guerrilla street theater we saw in Oaxaca. In each case the government provided transportation amenities, ensured clear title to salable lands, guaranteed loans for the pioneer developers, and embarked on a public-private partnership in promotion. "If you build it, they will come," the planners believed, and their faith has been justified to such an extent that resort tourism now accounts for a portion of the national wealth that rivals that of the oil fields.

American and European travel agents love Mexico; the air fares are large enough to generate significant commissions, and all the other costs of a vacation in Mexico are the bargain of the civilized world. Clients return satisfied and warmed and happy to tell their friends to plan a Mexico getaway soon while the good exchange rates and low prices last. Developers, when they have finished stacking rooms on every square inch of places like Cancún, turn their eyes a few kilometers north or south to the vast stretches of pristine beaches beyond the first wave of the investment. Mexican property owners and hoteliers and chefs see their stars rising and catch the wave as it rolls down the coast. There are jobs to be created and from them a growing middle class to be cultured.

A commercial seed of extraordinary virility has been planted in rich soil warmed by the perfect physical, cultural, and economic climate. In less than thirty years, the new invasion, sponsored by the national government of institutional revolution itself, has accomplished what centuries of Spanish colonialism could not—the willing submission of a nation to the seductive advances of foreigners.

Lourdes and I hurry right out of Cancún when we land there after our flight from Miami; what has happened at Cancún is old news, and this place, with its beach row of towering glass-and-steel resort hotels, definitely feels more like Fort Lauderdale than Mexico. We are headed toward the little coastal towns of Puerto Morelos and Playa del Carmen farther south toward Tulum—places where the development drama is still playing out.

Puerto Morelos is a quiet little fishing town that is also the vehicle ferry port for booming Cozumel Island. Arriving at eleven o'clock in the evening, we find freight trucks and RVs already lined up waiting for the morning ferry. The only place open for business is the Puerto Morelos Pizza Shop, run by American expatriates from our own New Hampshire and populated tonight by Americans and their Mexican friends watching a *Naked Gun* movie. There is a little concrete *zócalo* with basketball courts, a beach with fishing boats moored at a dock, three or four *palapas*-roofed restaurants closed at this late hour, a grocery store, a scuba diving shop, and the office of an organization agitating for title to local *ejidos*.

We stay at the Caribbean Reef Club, which despite its name and the fact that it is run by expatriate Americans, is a fine, quiet, beachfront hideaway with excellent Mexican food. The beach is more reef than sand, and the foreigners here are more interested in diving than tanning, spending money, and gathering in large crowds. To the north it's a good walk before we come to the fishing boats of the village, and to the south the palmed beach seems to stretch out forever. At the moment this would be a fine place to hunker down for six months and write a book, but there are economic stirrings in the air. Beachfront properties recently have been bought by outfits that put towers in Cancún and Mazatlán. Bulldozers are pushing sand around, and the road to the Reef Club is muddied by their activity.

We take a few days and drive a rented VW south to Playa del Carmen, Tulum, and Coba. The highway runs arrow-straight through the flat tropical scrub plain. It is not actually lined with billboards, but there are enough of them announcing this or that existing or soon-to-be-opened beachfront hideaway that one has a strong sense there won't be any hideaways much longer. But for now, there are places to camp, wildlife refuges, and intriguing little side roads to archaeological sites not well known.

Playa del Carmen is a little resort town still at a stage that makes it one of this traveler's favorite getaway spots in all the continent. I have gone back there for several vacations since I first discovered the place with Lourdes and have watched the construction of an adobe lighthouse, new small-scale hotels, and the establishment of a Señor Frog's. Fifty kilometers south of Cancún, Playa now attracts Canadians, French, Germans, and Americans (mostly from Minnesota) whose only interest in Cancún is its airport, which makes it so easy to arrive here. The tour books call Playa "the poor man's Cozumel" but aficionados know better. Here you can stay in *palapas* beach cabanas just a few steps from the water; you can carouse till the small hours of the morning at the beachfront Blue Parrot sitting in swinging chairs at the bar while musicians play Mayan love songs; you can worship the sun on white sand beaches where toplessness is the norm; you can stroll the pedestrian market boulevard and poke into shop after shop of glassware, silver, woven goods, and Mayan crafts where the prices are about midway between the outrageousness of Cancún and the bargains of inland towns; you can dine at the open-air *Parrilla* where musicians will play with or without a tip and the waiters will playfully fall in love with the young women in your group. In Playa the Mexican penchant for passionate fun, which is such a rich vein to the tourist industry, thrives without being forced or formulated. The place has been discovered, but it is not yet Cancún. Town leaders hope to prevent its degradation with a construction ordinance limiting new buildings to three stories.

Though the tourism industry in Playa is homegrown and home-owned, we find the place to be as well prepared to assist floundering travelers as the more slick Cancún establishments with their concierges and internationally trained support staffs. After a spontaneous dip in the waves, I discover I have lost the key to our rented VW. "No problem," says the deskman at the casual little Albatross Hotel. "I will call my friend the locksmith." In less than an hour, the locksmith has arrived, opened the locked car, and made us a new key for forty pesos.

South beyond Playa del Carmen, the road goes to Tulum, the ruins of a sixth-century Mayan fortress and ceremonial center overlooking the sea lanes of the coast. It's hot and humid as we tour the old stones, but that just adds to the attraction. Here is where the sand castles ad was made, and so part of the ritual of visitation is to descend the cliff after the tour and plunge into the clear aqua-blue Caribbean waters at its base. Sweating visitors frolic in the waves with or without whatever they wore to the site.

Nearby at Xel-Ha, the Mexican government has carved out a national park surrounding coastal lagoons where freshwater mixes with seawater to nurture an astounding panoply of fish. The place is snorkeler's heaven, and with its clean bathhouse, stone-paved walkways, restaurants, and gardens of hammocks set amid the jungle without disruption of the natural setting, it puts the lie to the old Republican saw that government can never do anything as well as private enterprise. A private operation of a similiar nature at Xcaret just up the road is a crass Disneyesque caricature by comparison.

Inland about a half hour from Tulum and Xel-Ha, lies Coba, one of the most recently discovered and little studied of Mayan ruins. Here the structures are only partly uncovered amid profuse jungle growth, and the ceiba trees, howler monkeys, and tropical birds make it as good a place to study biology as Mayan history. In particular we are fascinated by the leaf-cutter ants, which carry bits of leaves they have carved loose from the trees overhead over long ant-made roads to their earthen nests in spectacular processions of moving greenery. Later, as we walk along the raised Mayan roads built for hauling building stones great distances without pack animals or the wheel, I can't help but think the Mayans might have taken their inspiration from the insect world.

The return trip to Puerto Morelos again convinces us that someday this entire coast will be developed; it is such a natural. We turn off the highway to check out several of the little beach hideaways: La Posada de Capitán Laffite, Kailuum, Las Palapas, Shangri-La. Each fulfills a vision of "the perfect beach paradise"—at least for the moment. It's heartening to know that they still exist at all. It's sobering to imagine what may march down this coast from Cancún.

A fine modern divided highway links Cancún to the ancient Toltec-Mayan capital at Chichén Itzá to the west. It's a hot ride, with only one gas station and convenience store located about three-quarters of the way out on the three-hour trip. The land is flat and featureless tropical scrub—hard to picture the thriving Mayan culture that once existed in these parts. Lourdes thinks the tribe that sited Tulum had to be smarter; there is nothing to inspire the human spirit here. But there is a reason why the Mayans built a capital at Chichén Itzá: water. The presence of deep *cenotes,* water-filled sinkholes in the limestone bedrock, made sacred this spot in the otherwise arid, pool-table landscape.

Some thirty thousand spectators come here annually for the spring equinox to witness the illusion of the shadow serpent crawling up the Temple of Kukulcán, pictured on so many things Mexican from tourism brochures to bottles of tequila. We climb the ninety-two steep steps; at the top we hear German, Japanese, and French as well as Spanish and English. But it's not just foreigners here; we guess that about half of the visitors are Mexicans searching for their cultural roots. An old Mexican woman with crutches struggles breathlessly up the steps on her knees. Younger Mexicans welcome her with outstretched hands when she reaches the top. Their chests swell with pride, and they speak to us visiting foreigners with something almost like condescension, a rare thing in our travels in this country.

Back at the bottom we begin another climb, this time inside the structure to the top of the old temple around which the outer one was built. The dank inner chambers remind us of scenes from Indiana Jones films—moist stone, steep, scalloped steps, and at the platform, a magnificent jade jaguar behind a steel fence marked with signs prohibiting photos. In the blue glare of flashbulbs, we see again the old Mexican story of layer built upon layer. The Toltec king, Quetzalcóatl (Kukulcán to the Maya), rebuilt Chichén Itzá in the eleventh century when the Toltecs conquered the then diminished Mayans and effected the Toltec-Mayan renaissance. His symbol was the plumed serpent, and it is no accident that Toltec builders designed his temple so that on the equinox the sun would create a shadow image of a serpent crawling up the structure and, in effect, devouring the old Mayan jaguar symbol inside. Throughout the ruins, the serpent and jaguar images identify the age of the various structures. But besides the historical tension between the symbols of human power, the most prevalent emblem of Chichén Itzá, Mayan and Toltec, is the Chac Mool—the reclining figure of the god of water upon whom life here depended regardless of the vicissitudes of conquest. Today new icons have supplanted all three as illegal vendors throughout the site vie for *norteamericano* dollars, German marks, and Japanese yen.

From Chichén Itzá we drive that boring superhighway all the way to Mérida, where we will drop off our rented car and get back on a train. After cruising at 120 kilometers per hour for three hours, I slow down a little too late entering the outskirts of Mérida and a motorcycle cop is on us in no time. "You were going too fast," he explains without asking for a driver's license, a registration, or our rental agreement. "You can go before the magistrate at court tomorrow or you can pay one hundred pesos here now."

Lourdes recognizes the pattern of *la mordida*—while I am still fumbling for papers the cop hasn't yet demanded—and asks for directions. She then thanks him with a handshake containing the one-hundred-peso bill. No problem. Then just a few blocks closer to the center of the traffic-clogged city we are stopped again. This might be a stolen rental car, the cop explains with his hand up-turned in the window. Lourdes tells him to get lost and we are once more on our way. The first cop had us dead to rights. The second one was just fishing.

Mérida is a pretty colonial city ruined by the worst traffic we ever see in Mexico. But even here there are tourists. Late that night a group of Germans is sitting in our hotel courtyard drinking beer dispensed by a soda machine and their laughter attracts me. Twenty-eight-year-old Angelica Deulisch and her friends Heinrich and Veronica are on their three-week winter vacation from Garmisch-Partenkirchen, Bavaria. Angelica works as a nurse back home and bolts for someplace warm at the beginning of every winter. The past three years it was the south of France, Greece, and Turkey. This year she chose Mexico for the first time. When I ask her why, she begins to describe the "sand castles" ad I have seen. "That looked pretty good," she says, plus there was the issue of the declining peso.

Traveling backpacker style, she and her friends have already been to Acapulco, Puerto Escondido, Oaxaca, Mexico City, and Villahermosa. Their ultimate destination is Cancún, and despite the fact that she hates Mexican food ("What is it with the chilies and the spicy stuff?"), she is already scheming to return next year. "I've spent less than half of what I would have spent by now in any of the warm places I've gone before and had twice as much fun. There's more color in Mexico, it's earthier and primitive in an attractive way, and yet, everywhere we go it's as if people are expecting us." She speaks excellent English but no Spanish and wonders why I think I need an interpreter. It's easier, she thinks, to get by with English here than in France, Greece, or Turkey. But she wishes there were more Germans around. When I tell her that she will find lots of them on the Yucatán coast near Cancún, she excitedly translates for her friends who do not speak English, and they all launch into a German drinking song.

It was under Lázaro Cárdenas that Mexico emerged from its long isolation in the years of the revolution and reestablished a relationship with the outside world, albeit one only sometimes to that world's liking. In 1936 he set up the Department of Tourism, with the longsighted view that a nation taking a path radically independent of its foreign neighbors might do well to encourage them to come on down and see for themselves what Mexico was all about. With a confidence seldom evinced in Mexico's relations with foreigners, Cárdenas launched an ambitious international advertising campaign trumpeting the country's scenic marvels, its cuisine and folk culture, its colonial architecture, and most important, the treasures of the pre-Hispanic past that archaeologists had begun digging up during the days of Vasconcelos. The Pan-American Highway was built from Laredo to Mexico City, and automobile-loving Americans streamed south with prized dollars and returned home with the sense of a continental bond that would henceforth provide a healthy counterbalance to anti-Mexican feeling in American politics. Passenger travel on the railways was promoted as never before and raised to a level of comfort not seen since. More highways were built, from Mexico City to Guadalajara, a city whose flamboyant identification with all things Americans considered Mexican made it a favorite destination, and to Acapulco, destined to become the first of the great Mexican sun-and-sand resorts.

When Cárdenas's Mexico stood up as the sole Western nation to condemn the fascist rebellion of Franco in the Spanish Civil War, it profited from another influx of talented and educated foreigners as Spanish Republicans sought and received asylum in their former colony.

Despite his leftist sympathies and his early recognition of the evil of fascism, Cárdenas was clear-eyed about the Stalinists in Russia. When Russians fell out of favor with Stalin and sought foreign refuge, Cárdenas offered it. In the most famous case, it was Cárdenas's personal decision to offer a home in exile to Leon Trotsky after half a dozen other nations had been successfully pressured by Stalin to throw him out. With Trotsky's arrival, Mexican intellectuals experienced a healthy revival of socialist dialogue, and Mexico became a hotbed of socialist alternatives to the Stalinist communist model.

Despite the evidence that Cárdenas would walk as independently of Moscow as he did of Washington, there were strong forces in the United States and Britain that reviled him as a communist, especially after the nationalization of the oil industry. But under Franklin D. Roosevelt's Good Neighbor Policy, intervention in affairs south of the border was eschewed. Further, Roosevelt's New Deal Democrats felt some kinship to the progressive Mexican president. And especially after World War II broke out and the United States became an ally of the Soviet Union, relations with Mexico continued to be friendly. The flow of American tourists into Mexico increased dramatically as travel to Europe was no longer an option. Despite Cárdenas's challenge to international money when he nationalized the oil industry, Mexico and the United States drew closer to one another.

Meanwhile at home Cárdenas continued to implement the tenets of the constitution of 1917. The turning point with labor issues came during a strike by workers at a glass factory in Monterrey. In response, employers of the region had banded together to recruit an "antiunion," the COPARMEX, which demonstrated against the strikers and labeled the labor movement and Cárdenas himself as a pack of communists. Cárdenas hopped on a train and went to Monterrey to meet with the dissident businessmen. There he informed them firmly that "if they were tired of the social struggle, they could hand over their factories to the workers or the government." That, rather than lockouts and counterdemonstrations, would be the patriotic thing to do. By this daring confrontation, Cárdenas was able to establish the inviolability of the labor movement. The national labor organization, the CTM, would no longer have to bow to the bullying of employers. Unfortunately, in the years after Cárdenas, it instead became a tool for government manipulation of labor interests and still remains as such today.

Most businessmen adapted and retained control of their factories. In the area of land reform, however, there was a different outcome as Cárdenas actually began to dismantle the hacienda system that had proved to be so entrenched. First in the cotton belt of Coahuila, then in the Yucatán, then Sonora, Nuevo León, Baja California, Sinaloa, Michoacán, and even to a limited extent in reactionary Chiapas, Cárdenas set to work breaking up the haciendas and replacing them with *ejidos*, bound together collectively so as not to lose the advantages of scale enjoyed by the haciendas. Wealthy hacendado families, one after another, saw their fiefdoms carved up and redistributed while they retained control of modest properties so that they could never claim that the government had deprived them of their right to exist. No longer were the hacendados dispossessed of only marginal lands. Now the *ejidos* got the best, including lands irrigated by systems installed with hacendado money but peasant labor.

The case of the Yucatán is illustrative of the process. Here the legacy of the hacienda system was at its ugliest, the great henequen plantations having expanded to occupy virtually all of the peninsula's arable land. For centuries the hacendados of the Yucatán had been the nation's most rapacious, virtually enslaving the peasant population, provoking the nation's earliest outbreaks of indigenous revolt, and so concerned with their own position atop the pyramid that they were willing to give the Yucatán to the United States during the Mexican-American War in return for help repressing the native population.

But by 1937 the bottom had fallen out of the international henequen market, creating a crisis of investment for the hacendados and of employment for the peasantry. State authorities had already redistributed 30 percent of the henequen fields to peasants a few years earlier. Now Cárdenas moved in with his federal surveyors and engineers and set to work subdividing and organizing. By the end of the year, another 40 percent of the original lands had been redistributed to peasant *ejidos.* Hacendados, now reduced to the modest but still respectable role of small independent farmers, kept parcels no larger than three hundred hectares and some of their harvesting machinery, while much of their equipment was given along with the land to its new owners. In one year the hacienda system had virtually disappeared from the Yucatán, scene of its meanest manifestations.

By 1940 Cárdenas had returned 47 percent of the nation's arable land to the *ejidos.* As a result a thing unheard of in Mexico before this time appeared on the scene: a true rural middle class of independent farmers and agricultural workers. Not everything went smoothly. Many *ejidos* were badly cultivated, and the usual problems with collective farming arose. But Mexican peasants were getting their land back and they understood its significance. Hand in hand with its return arose a new pride in Mexican heritage, particularly the pre-Hispanic past. Cárdenas, disturbed at the plight of the Indian, reinstituted the Indianista Program in education, establishing agricultural and trade schools in Indian regions and injecting the history of the pre-Hispanic past into the curriculum everywhere. The nation was now swept with a consciousness of the wrongs done to the Indians during its history and the valuable cultural contribution they made to its identity. The Department of Indian Affairs was established, setting up a variety of federal programs to improve the lot of the indigenous. Cárdenas himself regularly attended the meetings of Indian organizations in the pueblos.

Nearing the end of Cárdenas's presidency, the power of the social pyramid had begun at last to crash through to the lowest tiers. But the programs of the Cárdenas years had been fantastically expensive, and as the 1940 election approached, depression and drought had exacerbated the economic situation to the point where even Cárdenas became alarmed for the future. Knowing his Mexican history, Cárdenas could envision economic conditions ruining all he had worked for. Dissatisfaction was suddenly mounting across the political landscape. Already conservatives had founded the Partido de Acción Nacional (PAN), which threatens to topple the PRI today. Cárdenas determined that the next presidency should be a time to consolidate revolutionary gains rather than to attempt to extend them. Quietly he allowed the emergence of more conservative factions in the party, now reorganized as the Partido Revolucionario Méxicano, or PRM. And he bestowed his blessing on his moderately conservative secretary of defense, Ávila Camacho.

With the help of the usual electoral finagling by the party, Camacho was declared the winner of Mexico's most spirited election yet. But it had been a close call. There are those who believe today that the PAN actually won the election of 1940 and would have entered office with a mandate to turn back the clock. As it was, Camacho presided over the moderation of revolutionary Mexico into the contradictory political entity that it remains under the PRI today. In the meantime, Americans and other foreigners kept coming and bringing their money, and deep dregs of trouble and misery were left stewing at the bottom of the pyramid.

Our train out of Mérida bound for Campeche and Palenque does not leave until evening, so we have the following day for a side trip to the Mayan ruins at Uxmal. This time we take a quiet country road that we think is off the path of tourists. We drive through tiny pueblos where women shuffle along carrying orange, yellow, and blue plastic buckets of *masa* and tortillas on their heads. They smile at us and their children laugh and pose when I poke a camera out the window. Between two of these little villages, the flat dusty land-scape is cultivated as *ejido* plots of oranges, corn, squash, and beans. We spot a small man ambling along carrying a burlap bag over his shoulder and a well-worn machete in his free hand. We stop and Lourdes offers him a ride. He is hesitant at first; he doesn't want to inconvenience us. But then he crawls into the back-seat and offers us his whole bag of oranges as payment for the ride. We accept just one each, and we are on our way.

He wears sandals, patched khaki pants, a T-shirt, and a ban-danna around his deeply lined, weathered forehead. He lives in the pueblo of Muno, ten miles ahead on this road, and makes the walk daily with his burlap bag and machete to tend his hectare of land where he grows corn and oranges. He is Mayan and speaks the Chol dialect, besides Spanish. He is proud of his ancestors and the wonderful things they built and has been to Uxmal but does not like to climb the steep steps of the pyramids there. He is prouder that he owns his own piece of land. I notice that his machete is sharpened to a fine edge, and he says, yes, he sharpens it every day. It is one of his most important possessions.

Assuming that we have gotten away from the tourist routes, I ask if it is rare to see tourists on this road. "Oh no," he says. "They come by all the time, just like you, and they give me a ride, just like you." Lourdes wants to know if there are any other ways that the tourists affect his life. "No," he answers with a shrug suggesting that this is a strange question. "They just pass by like leaves blowing in the wind."

At Uxmal, the Pyramid of the Magician is a steeper climb than any of the ruins we have visited so far, and it's easy to see why the old Mayan man didn't like to climb it. One wrong move and you could easily become a bag of crumbling bones tumbling to the bottom. At the top we step inside a chamber with a characteristic shape we see often here in the Yucatán. All of these interior rooms mimic the profile of the traditional Mayan thatched hut. Even in the Palace of the Governor, those who lived at the pinnacle of society framed their stone dwellings like the homes Mayans inhabited before they learned to build great monumental palaces. A guide shows us holes in the walls where curtains would have hung and overhead rafters would have supported elaborately decorated ceilings. It's very hard to picture today the opulence in which the ancients lived. Now there is just a bare stone outline and the grim piles of bat guano in the corners.

We do not expect luxury as we arrive at the Mérida station to board the train bound for Campeche. This is our first ride on *segunda clase,* but it's just a four-hour early evening run. There are only two cars and they are dark when we board. Apparently the power has not yet been hooked up. One car is an old *segunda clase* car and it is loaded with crying babies. But the other is an old *primera clase* car, so we board this one and flick on Lourdes's flashlight to find seats. There, in the glare of her light—cockroaches, big ones, scurrying right into holes in the old worn fabric. We retreat to the car with the babies. Somehow its plastic seats provoke less fear of the cockroaches.

The train does pull out right on time, but still the lights do not come on. Lourdes shines her flashlight around the car. Overhead we can see where the lightbulbs should be, but there aren't any. There are no lights at all on this train. As the train picks up speed outside of the city, we become nauseated by a terrible smell coming from the latrine. Soon two crewmen are struggling with a rope to permanently close off the latrine door. Never mind toilet paper; there will be no bathrooms this trip.

When Lourdes goes for a walk to take some fresh air at the back platform, a plump but pleasant-looking, gaudily dressed young woman sits next to me and asks with hand signals and broken English if I am married. Even when Lourdes returns, she hangs around in the seat across from us in expectation of something. Lourdes makes conversation with her. Her name is Beatriz and she has just today gone shopping in the town of San Francisco, where the clothing is very inexpensive. She says she bought a million pesos worth of stuff for her clothing business in a town near Villahermosa.

Beatriz emphasizes that she is a single woman living a life of adventure and rides the train because she meets so many interesting people here. We ask incredulously if she means tourists. Not really tourists, she answers, but her last trip was enlivened by a group of Guatemalan men fleeing their country illegally. "Guatemalans have all the experiences," she says. "They are friendly and sometimes very beautiful." She has also met Cubans and the occasional hard-living backpacker from Holland or Germany. If she is bored of the ride by the time she gets to Campeche, she'll get off there looking for excitement. There is an event there that she calls simply "the carnival." It is a social event where the young women make the rules and the guys are only too happy to play along "because this is where they find all the prettiest girls." Her favorite game at the carnival is spin the bottle. "You have to be at least fifteen years old to play. The girl goes to a room for one hour with the guy she got on her spin. If they come out and didn't do anything, they missed their chance."

Since she was thirteen Beatriz has worked and saved and studied business to get to where she is today at eighteen, a successful businesswoman. She has a house and cattle, which are tended by her brother, Virgil. She does most of her business through barter, taking her clothing to pueblos and trading for money, goats, chickens, corn—whatever has value. It has helped that she has a knack for languages so that she can pick up the various Mayan dialects. She is proud to call herself a modern woman.

But it is not always easy. She has been molested by male passengers as she slept at night on the train. Thieves have hit her house because they knew a woman lived there alone. Men have offered to seduce her who were only interested in her money. She shows us a love poem a man recently wrote for her. Loosely translated it reads,

"You have a garden and I have a watering can. If you give me your little flower, I will give you the stalk of my manhood."

"Have I ever been in love?" she asks rhetorically. "No, I just want to have a good time. In this life there is everything. Some people have trouble dealing with a life full of everything. Not me."

Beatriz is the oldest of six children. Her mother is thirty-three and her father is thirty-eight. "He has had lovers and mother has to beat them and drive them away. Twice she broke my father's head, once with a hammer, once with a chair." But they are still together; in fact they are somewhere back in the darkness on this train, and one of the screaming babies is her youngest brother.

As Beatriz has been entertaining us with her stories, the concessionaire has been fiddling interminably, setting up his drinks and snacks in the first pair of seats of the car. He sings a song—"I want to be a fish"—as he works, and apparently it was in response to his request that the crewmen lashed shut the door to the latrine. "People don't buy things to eat and drink when that door is open." He says he needs to get himself so organized because he goes all the way to the end of the line and it can get crazy on this train after a while. At this Lourdes makes a sound half like a laugh and half like a sob. "Did you hear that, Terry?" she says. "It's *going* to get crazy on this train." So far it's been nothing, just cockroaches, no lights, a man who wants to be a fish, a woman named Beatriz with a brother named Virgil whose stories are right out of the carnival fun house. I remind her that Dante did have to descend into hell before he could find heaven. "Maybe," she says. "But I think we're riding the death train."

I try to distract us both from the sense that I have finally dragged my intrepid comrade into a setting she truly hates by encouraging a conversation with the conductor, George. Beatriz appreciates it too, because George is a little drunk and has been leaning over and whispering things in her ear that she doesn't want to hear. George says we would be surprised how many foreign tourists actually ride this *segunda clase* train—Germans, Italians, Chileans, even the occasional crazy gringos like us. "We like tourists to learn about us and our traditions," he says. "And all Mexico benefits from their presence."

At the stop at the pueblo of Hecelchakán, there is some sort of a rally going on beside the station, with speakers on a podium and a large crowd of attentive listeners seated on folding chairs before them. When we ask George if it is political, he laughs and says, "Oh no. This is an AA meeting. You know in Mexico it stands for Active Alcoholics. Because no one ever goes of his own free will and no one ever quits drinking. Family members drag them to the meetings because they think it's the thing to do."

As the train pulls out of the town and into the outskirts, we can see the traditional thatched huts of a Mayan neighborhood. The setting is beautiful under a bright moon—palms, banana trees, bougainvillea in profusion. Some of the huts have a light shining at their doorway, a prideful demonstration, says George, that they have electricity. And all are the shape of the stone chambers in the ruins at Uxmal.

George has been working on this train for twenty-seven years and will seek retirement when he reaches thirty. He has been in three derailments and a crash with a bus at a grade crossing in which all of the people on the bus were killed. He has pulled bodies off the tracks that the train has run over and has stopped knife fights in the darkness on the train. But it will be a harder life when he retires because his income will be cut in half. And most of all he will miss the Sunday runs. I ask why. "Because on Sunday, the pretty young teachers ride the train to Campeche."

The death train runs all night to Palenque, which is where we really want to go. But whenever the distracting conversation has stopped, thoughts of cockroaches and spiders and God knows what else return. George has told us with a laugh that the train is occasionally held up by bandits in the small hours of the night. By

Campeche, at eleven o'clock, we have had enough. George has bought more beer for himself and Beatriz, and he snuggles into the seat beside her as we leave and now she doesn't seem to mind. Somewhere in the darkness of the car a baby cries softly. When we detrain, I imagine I see bats hanging from the ceiling in the vestibule.

It doesn't get much better on our bus to Palenque the following morning. The ride takes all day, the movies are stupid American action films with Spanish dubbing (where is Vicente when we need him?), and something I ate at one of the death train stops has tied my stomach in knots. If I felt better, I might appreciate the changing topography as we finally approach Palenque in the late afternoon. We have left the Yucatán plain and climbed through forested mountains into the tropical rain forest of northern Chiapas. Lourdes is happier and tells me that if I would open my eyes and stop groaning I would see green and orange and magenta of intensities I have never imagined. When I finally do in the late afternoon, we are just pulling into the outskirts of Palenque and what I see is an army encampment with tanks and all the olive accoutrements of a field bivouac. Soldiers stop us and check the bus. Though the rebels' stronghold is south of here, the government is being careful.

We make our way in a *colectivo* taxi out to the resort of Chan Kah, located midway between the town of Palenque and the famous ruins. Here we find heaven. The place is a garden in the rain forest, carved out by subtractive botanical sculpture—the rain forest has provided everything, and the builders of this place have simply culled out all that is not striking to the human eye. There is outrageous color everywhere you look—orchids, bromeliads, and peperomias—but it's not all flowers. Some of it is just greenery with varying degrees of hue and intensity. Trees with huge, fernlike leaves form a canopy overhead, laced with woody vines, and where the ground isn't cloaked with blossoming shrubbery, it is carpeted with moss, spiny palms, and thick-bladed grasses. Toucans, emerald hummingbirds, and blue tanagers perch in the branches, and a euphony of jungle sounds, including occasionally the roar of howler monkeys, makes this one of the most exotic settings in North America. Amid the winding pathways and pools are cabanas designed like the old Mayan huts with ventilation through the ceiling so that they remain cool despite the temperature outside. There is no finer place on the continent to drift off into a dreamy afternoon nap after a hot day of travel.

It turns out that the creators of this place are not Mayan but admirers of their culture from Mexico City who came here with the singular intention of effecting just the illusion we have experienced. After we have settled into our rooms, we meet co-owner Roberto Romano in the *palapas*-roofed lounge for margaritas. He and his three brothers, mother, and father came here from Mexico City in 1971. There was no tourism in Palenque in those days, the ruins were just beginning to be uncovered, and Roberto's father had a thing about jungle places that he thought had a future. "There was something magical here," Roberto says. "There was just the ruins down the road, the jungle, and a few cleared fields here where someone had tried to grow things the jungle doesn't on its own. It was an exercise in ecological foresight. My father knew that someday soon people would want to come here for the ruins and be surprised at the possibility of staying in a jungle paradise."

We ask him about political problems—with the Chiapas rebels, for instance. He says that although their activities are far from here, it does become a problem when Chiapas as a whole gets banned from tourism because of what they do. It has hurt his business here. He is sympathetic with the fact that the Chiapas Mayans do not live well. It's been an ongoing problem and something needs to be done for them. But the instability the Zapatistas have caused is the worst nightmare of people like himself and his family who have found a harmless way to make a good life for themselves. "I don't deny them the land they need; I can give them land here in the jungle around Chan Kah. But there is no communication—no legal framework within which that can happen."

Because of the deep jungle setting, the ruins of Palenque have a totally different feel from the others we have seen. With plenty of water, here it is not Chac, the rain god, who dominates the art, but Tlel, the wind god. His face appears in the T-shaped ventilation openings of the structures. Perhaps in the steamy climate of the tropical rain forest, it was blessed cooling breezes that turned men's thoughts to heaven.

We try to talk to three park service groundskeepers taking a break in the shade. We want to know about the purposes of certain stone brackets we have observed in the interior chambers, the Mayan words for "temple," and the use of some unidentified structures we have seen. The park employees don't answer any of our questions. Of course they all speak Spanish, but as Lourdes asks the question about the Mayan words, they apparently discover for the first time that each of the three speaks a different Mayan dialect: two versions of Tzeltan and Chol. They end up ignoring us and comparing notes among themselves about common Mayan words in the different dialects.

We have better luck with Abela, a Mayan woman who tends to the palace. She shows us that the stone backets were used for hanging plumage, fabrics, furs, and curtains. She explains how the Mayans made down mattresses for their stone slab beds and that little or none of the hard stone we see today in these interiors would have been exposed when they were inhabited. It would have all been rich color and texture from a panoply of softening biological materials.

Abela also tells us that since the days of the archaeologists a few years ago, Palenque hosts tourists from different countries on what almost seems like a clockwork schedule, though she has noticed that the numbers have declined recently. Mexicans come here in

December, Germans in January. In February it's the French and in March, the Scandinavians and Canadians. Most of the tourists who come here time their trips to this tropical paradise for months when it is cold in their own country. It's only the Americans whose time here makes no sense. They come in June and July when it's warm at home and it's hot and rainy here, but that's when their children get out of school. She concludes that in America children must be more important than weather.

It is easier to picture the life of this city than at other ruins we have visited. Classic and pre-Toltec like Coba, Palenque was laid out not so much with grandeur, power, and ceremony in mind, but comfort, grace, and community. In the palace the order and domestic purpose of the chambers and courtyards are more apparent than elsewhere. It is clear where people slept, where they ate, and where they sought relaxation in cool shade on verandas exposed to any breezes that might waft up the hill from the plain below. The public spaces are more intimate and social than those at Chichén Itzá. The structures do not stand so much in grandiose isolation but rather relate to one another the way that planners tell us our modern city structures should. You descend the steps of one building and immediately face the prospect of entering another. There is an organic order that is apparent and all of it encompassed in the context of the shade of the ever-encroaching jungle. But the ruins also testify to danger that lurked in that jungle. They are dominated as much by tall watchtowers as by religious pyramids, and more than any setting I have ever seen, this place evokes the words of Bob Dylan's song, "All Along the Watchtower," especially the ominous menace of the lines: "Outside in the distance, a wild cat did growl. Two riders were approaching, the wind began to howl."

When we ride back into town, we slow to get a good look at the military encampment. Besides the tanks, sod block machine-gun emplacements, and olive tenting, we also see uniformed men at ease playing volleyball and soccer. Lourdes asks the checkpoint guard if he has seen any rebels and he says, "I don't know." Then she asks if he believes there really are any rebels and he says, "I don't know; they say they're real." Does anyone ever get denied passage at this checkpoint, Lourdes wants to know. "No, everybody gets through." And what if we covered our faces? The soldier laughs and waves us on. He is so young he has not yet shaved.

But the rebels are real, as we discover when we take a ride out to the waterfalls of Misol-Ita and Agua Azul. As we wind over the mountain road, the taxi driver slows twice for places where the pavement has been trenched and refilled. "The Zapatistas," he says. He also shows us huge tree trunks with which the Zapatistas have blocked the road from time to time. At Misol-Ita we meet a young backpacking Dutch couple who have worked their way north from Guatemala. It was scary near the Guatemalan border, they tell us. The sky was filled with helicopters, and the guards at army check-points were not friendly like the fellow we met. Just today they had tried to get to Agua Azul, the other waterfall we had hoped to visit, and were turned back by an army patrol because something nasty had gone down there last night.

I ask if they would come here again, knowing what they now know about the instability. They answer that they might be a little more careful about the specific regions they backpacked through, but otherwise Mexico is the place. No other place they have tried is so cheap and so beautiful—not New Zealand, not India, not China.

Back in the town of Palenque that evening, we talk to the friendly owner of a small restaurant that caters to locals on the main street. In a refrain that is already becoming familiar, plump, middle-aged, balding Alonso begins by saying there really are no problems with the Zapatistas in the town for now, but as we have seen, their graffiti are scrawled on walls everywhere, and the insta-bility is driving the archaeologists and tourists away. When the EZLN first announced its campaign back in January, businesses closed and some people left. "There was a saying, 'The world is ending; I'm going to Mérida.' And then the tourism office of Mérida picked it up and used the phrase in their advertising. Now Tabasco is doing the same thing, using the fear of the Zapatistas to lure our tourists away."

Though he caters to locals, Alonso has no illusions about how important tourism is to Palenque. And now it may be even a matter of life and death. "Why do you think Marcos has not come to Palenque?" he asks rhetorically, referring to the enigmatic leader of the EZLN. "If something happens to a tourist, his embassy will speak for him, there will be a big fuss, the government will send more troops, and Marcos will have more trouble selling his ideas to the foreigners. Marcos doesn't come to Palenque because there are too many Americans, Russians, British, French, Germans—all the people he wants to impress. The zone of the ruins protects us from trouble. But you go three kilometers out of town and they are out there."

Alonso thinks the military presence is just psychological. "If someone says he wants to fight with you, you pull your gun out first so that you don't have to use it. That's what the tanks and machine guns are all about. They mean nothing. It's the tourists that matter." Without the presence of so many people from the outside world, he fears this could become another Guatemala.

In fact, one of the reasons for the current trouble is the spillover from the conflict in that country. He suspects that armed Guatemalan refugees helped to radicalize the Lacendonians (the main Mayan tribe of the EZLN). "It's the problem of Central America landing on our doorstep. The Nicaraguan flees to Guatemala, the Guatemalan flees to Mexico. But where is the Mexican to go? They don't let you into the United States, and in Guatemala they shoot you."

He is not sympathetic toward the Zapatista demands for the replacement of the PRI regime in Chiapas with a populist, socialist, indigenous government committed to a program of revolutionary land redistribution. He believes that land reform may have already gone too far. We are surprised to see this same attitude among other working- and small-merchant-class people. A Mayan taxi driver says, "We lived in a paradise till the Zapatistas ruined it." A night watchman at Chan Kah says that though he is 100 percent Mexican, it is true that too many Mexicans want something without working for it. Another cab driver with dark features says that too many of the indigenous people are "soft—they lie around and don't make their *ejido* lands productive."

In the morning I sleep in at Chan Kah with the pleasing sounds of the rain forest's awakening melding with dreams of ease in a jungle palace. The death train isn't due till nine to take us on toward Mexico City, and it's sure to be hours late. There is no knock on the door from Lourdes to urge me to get up so we don't miss the train.

When we finally do arrive at the train station, it is empty but for a wreck of a man who writhes on the floor in the final phases of some form of alcoholic or chemical toxicity. He is filthy and smells like death itself. He howls numbly and stares wildly, seeing nothing. His brain is just gone.

And so is the train, having passed through here right on time an hour ago. Lourdes is relieved. I am upset. As we are lingering outside the station mumbling, "No brain, no train, no Zapatistas," a man in a white cowboy hat leaning against a fence says he can tell us why we haven't seen any Zapatistas. It's because in this region they only become Zapatistas at night. By daylight they are just ordinary campesinos pursuing their normal lives. But he can take us to a place they frequent if we want. He can even arrange for us to have a good Zapatista lunch.

Gilbert is a whirlwind, and soon he has us in his car and headed out of town on a winding road where we see more of the tree trunks the rebels have cut down to block the road. He talks without taking a breath, expounding that he is a small rancher, but his pride is his work with the local rescue squad. As we roll along a bluff above a river, he points out spots where he has pulled accident victims out of the water. Some of them were alive; some were not. He has plans to start a junkyard—potentially a very profitable business, he thinks, because at the moment there is none. Junk either rusts in arroyos or is trucked somewhere else for recycling. His home is in the town of Salto de Agua a few kilometers from Palenque. It has a population of forty-two thousand, a small town by Mexican standards. The Zapatistas are a presence here simply because 80 percent of the people in this region are indigenous. They don't do much except block the roads and spook the government troops who never actually see them. They haven't invaded any ranches in the area because they want to keep this as a friendly region.

We pass a truck with a half dozen dark faces in back. "They are Zapatistas," Gilbert says. And the truck was stolen by rebels from the municipal government. "But if we asked them, they would just say they are campesinos on their way to work and the man driving the truck borrowed it from a friend." Actually we could not talk to them, even if they would let us. All of the Zapatistas around here are Mayans who speak the Chol dialect; they do not speak Spanish. It is just one of the ways they are alienated from Mexican society to begin with.

Despite the issue of the truck, Gilbert insists that the local Zapatistas are not bandits. "There are people in some parts of Chiapas who take advantage of what is going on and use the mask to be bandits. Those people are not honest. Whether you agree with them or not, the Zapatistas around here are honest." And apparently they are not very skillful revolutionaries either. Gilbert shows us a bridge they tried to blow up that is still very much intact. "They didn't have real explosives."

Soon we turn off the main highway above the river and rumble down a gravel road into the little valley. Where the road ends, an open *palapas* structure with picnic tables in its shade stands just a few feet from the water. We park the car in a small open field, there are no other cars or people around, and Gilbert leads us to a tiny kitchen at the back of the building where he speaks to two older women and a boy. Soon the boy marches off toward the riverbank and we follow. He climbs out on a limb over the water and pulls on a rope. At the end of the rope, a trap emerges dripping from the water containing half a dozen large langostinos (also known as langoustines)—freshwater lobsters not much smaller than Maine one-and-a-quarter-pounders. The river also feeds the locals with its fish and its turtles. "And occasionally the river's crocodiles feed *on* the locals," Gilbert says with a laugh.

We are at the heart of the community of Paso Narajo, population five hundred, Gilbert tells us when we sit down at a picnic table, and the langostinos fry out in the kitchen. It is a Chol community and hotbed of Zapatista sentiment and activity. Rebel groups come and sit at these very tables after dark and get the same lunch we are about to have.

Ambitious fellows like Gilbert had hoped to see tourism come here, and a better highway was in the process of being built, but the trouble with the Zapatistas has put all of that on hold. Gilbert, despite his ambitions, is sympathetic. "The Zapatistas represent people who have nothing. I can wait until something is done for them."

The women from the kitchen bring us plates of steaming langostinos, corn on the cob, and tortillas. They have fried the langostinos with garlic and chilies. Gilbert clarifies that the Zapatistas do not always eat this well, but in places like this, rich with natural foods and sympathetic people willing to feed them, why not?

Lourdes speaks to the heavy, dark woman whose kitchen this is and finds out that she was born here. Until recently the only way to town was by horse; there was no road. Her family has a little ranch, and her husband has made it his special cause to help out the indigenous, with food, loans, farm supplies. That's why the rebels will never touch his ranch or his family. And they come here to eat.

We never do meet any Zapatistas by the river that day. As Gilbert drives us back to Palenque to catch our bus to Villahermosa, from where we will fly to Michoacán, he explains that visitors to the towns outside of Palenque are rare. Our presence is probably already the subject of local gossip. Less than fifty years ago, the only way to get here was by boat on the river.

He insists he is not alone in his fantasy about tourism enriching the area. Ever since the ruins were discovered at Palenque, people knew that they had something to offer the outside world—a paradise of the past. "But history is still unfolding here in a troubled story. And we have problems to deal with before we should think of inviting guests to our home."

8

The Migration of the Butterflies
Mexico City to Playa Azul and back

Riding the train from Mexico City to Patzcuaro in Michoacán state, I drift in a half-asleep reverie as the car rattles
and rolls and the tracks *clicketa-clacketa* underneath. The feeling of
the Copper Canyon *tesquinada* and the vision of the pair of horses
running under the full moon has come again. I am thinking of
ghosts, and women, and why I make these journeys. Lourdes sleeps
in the seat beside me. Our collaboration began with a casual conversation in a grocery store over bags of breakfast cereal and cat
food. Now it occurs to me, in fact, that for only the second time in
my life, a woman has become a best friend. This journey has
changed me. That's one reason why we travel addicts do this.

It started for me with ghosts. My father's untimely death and his
nightly visitations to my bedside nearly ten years ago sent me on
the first of these North American odysseys, riding the American
rails until finally making peace with him and my heritage on a
mountaintop in Montana. A quest for the secret to "born-again"
marriages accompanied the second, exploring Canada at a time

when Quebecois aspirations for separation held mirrors to my life wherever I went. A search for a new place to live propelled the third, as if place alone were the antidote to restlessness—as Americans have always believed. Now wrestling with the implications of divorce, I wonder what I am after this time—what I seek for myself besides this quest for the soul of another part of the continent. Each of these sojourns has been transforming, and always I have found something I didn't know I was looking for. Now once again it's getting close—somewhere just out there a little farther down the tracks.

Patzcuaro, in the west central state of Michoacán, is the other place, besides Zacatecas, that Mexicans will tell you to visit if you liked San Miguel de Allende but wish to see such a colonial town without the heavy gringo overlay. It is surrounded by the country of the Tarascans (more accurately known as Purépechans), the strong tribe to the west that was never conquered by the Aztecs and has anchored the firm pre-Hispanic identity of the state of Michoacán for centuries. Michoacán has also been a crossroads of Mexican history, and through it runs a rail route built in modern times to expedite the movement of materials to and from coastal Lázaro Cárdenas, a city built by the government specifically to generate jobs.

We feel the difference between Patzcuaro and so many other places we have visited as soon as we set foot on the cobblestones of the *zócalo* in front of our hotel. The square is lined with the gracious two-story mansions of the colonial era, now become hotels, restaurants, and shops. There is something dusty about the place, as if the compulsion to scrub everything clean were somehow lacking here, even in the town's showcase plaza. A patina of age tints the memory's image of the physical streetscape in halftones, like old black-and-white photos. But the human apparitions flash with reds and coppers and turquoises, whether it be the flamboyant serapes of the native Purépechan women or the foods and crafts sold by vendors under red tarpaulins on the walks in front of the old gray buildings. Obvious *norteamericano* tourists are conspicuously absent, though there are dusty pale-faced backpackers with colorful bandannas who seem to fit right in.

We are staying in the Hotel Los Escudos, a seventeenth-century mansion once the home of a local heroine of the independence movement, Gertrudis Bocanegra. Like other old places we have stayed, the hotel is structured around open flowered courtyards with the rooms on balconies above. But here we find something new: working fireplaces in the rooms. Patzcuaro's elevation is more than eight thousand feet and it gets cold here. The night watchman will bring wood and build a fire when needed.

This first evening we are entertained in the lobby of the hotel by "The Dance of the Old Men." There are twelve of them, wearing masks, carrying canes, shuffling, and clapping with an exaggerated stoop that makes Lourdes wonder if behind the masks they might be young men imitating old men. We are reminded of Octavio Paz's contention that Mexicans always wear a mask—rarely do they show to the world, least of all a pair of nosy *norteamericano* writers, their true selves. It is a lesson in humility that we take to heart as we approach the final legs of our journey.

A woman with long dark hair and black eyes whose family owns the hotel sits with us and tells us a little about the place. Blanca Estela Báez came here when she was only fifteen days old and has lived here in the house of her father ever since. Today she manages the hotel, and it is her life. "So many people from so many places pass through a hotel," she believes, "that it becomes a place where you can be rooted and still have wings." And she is especially proud that she is a woman doing this job in a place draped with the history of a female hero.

Gertrudis Bocanegra was born in this house in 1765, a woman of Spanish descent who developed a bond with the Indians and mestizos her people had exploited for centuries. When the war for independence broke out, she offered her home as a place for Hidalgo's followers to hide weapons. She was at first arrested and imprisoned several times for her outspoken beliefs, and when the soldiers of the government discovered what she had been covertly doing to back up those beliefs, they killed her husband and son. "Still she didn't relent," Blanca Estela says with fire in her eyes. "So then they came one day and dragged her right out through this front door and murdered her right on the stones in front of her house. There is a dried-up tree out there at the edge of the plaza that marks the spot."

The air turns cold that night, so I decide to avail myself of the night watchman's fire-building services. He comes to my room carrying a bundle of scrap wood, all stooped and slow like the old dancers and dressed in dirty work clothes. He bends down painfully by the fireplace and meticulously constructs a little wooden tepee from the scrap. He has no paper kindling, but with one match and a good deal of blowing breath, he has a fire going in no time. I send him off to make a fire for Lourdes and later ask her how old she thinks he is. "Thirty-five or sixty-five," she says. "Who can tell?"

At breakfast Blanca Estela has arranged for us to talk to a man who is considered the philosopher of Patzcuaro. Rogelio is a heavy, slow-speaking man wearing thick wire-rimmed glasses and is clearly used to having a captive audience before him. When the waitress brings coffee and toast with honey he intones, "Do you realize how long it took this coffee to grow on some faraway mountainside, to bear fruit, to be prepared and come to our table? Do you remember the job that the bees in some distant valley have done to bring us this honey? That is the way with us all. We are nourished by things that come from labors done afar. I have spoken."

He then explains in a matter-of-fact voice that he has stated this little paean in honor of Lourdes and myself, travelers from lands far away. The Purépechans were wanderers who found this place aeons ago. "Like you and me, they were fleeing something," he says with a wink in my direction. "These people were noted for their aggressiveness, and they were not always welcomed in the places they came to. Unless you build something, you will be sent home." And again he gives me a wink.

He goes on to tell us how the Purépechans fished from the lake and, as the climate dried, cultivated what had once been swamps. They were never conquered by the Aztecs. And even the conquest by the Spanish and the church continues to be a tenuous one. "They say we live here at the tail of the dragon. Exploiters have come and gone, come and gone, but there is something here bigger than the intentions they bring. When they go away far from here they find themselves changed. And then they know. We have done something to them here. In the end, who has conquered whom?"

From behind his mask, he has flashed me this warning. While seeming to be egocentrically talking about his philosophy, he is actually talking about his audience. "From the moment that you begin doing what you want to do," he goes on, "you remember that the mind lives and dies by how well you love yourself." Like all living things we have an instinct for self-preservation. But as humans we also have social, sexual, and material needs that go beyond that. "Let's find people like ourselves, let's make sex into love, then let's gather material things to protect those we love." But all three of these emotional dimensions are prisons until we can love ourselves well, he argues. Only then can we love in a larger sense. He ends by turning to me directly and asking, "Is that why you come to Mexico, señor? To better learn to love? If not, go home, señor."

Rogelio's mask has been ambiguous but patent. Less so are those of Arturo and Vatche, young painters we meet at a sidewalk café on the zócalo later that day who become our companions for the duration of our stop here in Patzcuaro. Arturo is a handsome, angular, blue-jeaned man with a strong jaw and intense gestures. When we meet him he is drinking black coffee from a huge mug and casually doing sketches of faces and trees. But his regular work is murals into which he paints the faces of real people and of himself. His art has had phases—Egyptian, impressionist, modernist—that have corresponded to the various places he has lived and worked. Now he's doing romantic, almost Gothic work in Patzcuaro and likes being here amid the stones of the old world. It's a nice turn from his last phase, which was commercial and Daliesque. He painted classic rock stars such as Hendrix and the Beatles on the outside walls of bars throughout the country. The sketches he is doing now are practice for his current project, a large painting of the *zócalo* right here before us. "It's people in a painting that makes it work for me," he tells us. Even in a landscape he will find a way to imprint it with humanity, perhaps a tiny fisherman on the river in the distance.

Arturo has always been a wanderer. For twelve years he was a musician up by the U.S. border and then he studied glass-blowing in Massachusetts. He also dabbled in architecture and engineering. Life for Arturo has been a continuing metamorphosis. Is painting murals his final butterfly phase? He thinks so, but he knows he has felt that way before.

His friend, Vatche Khan, is an Armenian immigrant to Mexico, whose original two-week visit here has turned into twelve years. He is swarthy and speaks with a conspiratorially muted tone, telling us that although he once painted in the United States and in Wales, Mexico has become his true home: "In Mexico, I learned how to be spiritual, not by seeking, but by letting go." Vatche and Arturo invite us to join them for live music at El Viejo Gaucho that evening, and then maybe we will go to Vatche's house.

Later in the day while Lourdes visits the market, I stop back by the café to see if Arturo and Vatche are still there. They aren't but in their place are three friendly, attractive women who are here for a day's getaway from their homes in Morelia. Pilar, Gloria, and

Lupita are teachers and Lupita speaks good English. They are flirtatious and, by Latin standards, outrageously liberated. With Lupita translating, they take turns introducing themselves.

Pilar, tall, dark, and sexy, has no children, wants no children, and plans to be a millionaire someday. "Maybe I'm afraid of being responsible," she says. It's not really that she covets money but that she would like to live out her own life compensating for what Mexican women have not had for six centuries. She says she is not afraid of being alone and believes that there are more women like her in Mexico than anyone knows, "but society has not changed enough yet, so many of them can't show their true selves."

Gloria, fair and freckled with blond-red hair, calls herself a bohemian. She is divorced with three adolescent sons. "Already I don't fit this society," she says. What's more, she is not shy about saying that she has no intention of getting remarried but does like to couple.

Lupita is married with three teenage daughters who haven't yet dated any of Gloria's sons. Her husband manages a restaurant and is a friend to many women just as she is a friend to many men. When I suggest that the three of them seem very atypical of this country, she says I am wrong. "We are part of the modern, educated, professional middle class that you Americans are always so surprised to find in Mexico. You wouldn't be surprised to meet women like us in your country. It's 1995, even here in Michoacán."

When they learn that I have been traveling Mexico for the past year they are full of questions for me about their own country, particularly about what I have seen in Chiapas. "You can't believe the media," Lupita explains. "You only get the truth from people who have been where the news is." When I relate my experiences in Palenque, Lupita says, "If we lived in Chiapas, we would be more afraid of the army than the rebels. In Morelia we worry more about the police than we do about thieves." Pilar's house has been robbed, and everyone in her neighborhood is sure the culprits were policemen.

I ask them how the economic crisis has affected them personally. They roll their eyes and Lupita says, "We have had to change our whole way of living. It's us middle-class people who are hit hardest by this." She used to go out and have a hamburger once a week. Now it is once a month. She used to take two-week vacations to the beach at Zihuatenejo. Now she has to settle for a day of coffee in Patzcuaro. "It's not just that we can afford less, but we have to take second jobs just to stay where we were." She has seen friends lose their cars, their houses to the banks. That's the peril—actually losing something you had gotten used to having.

She believes the rich will, of course, continue to get richer, and the poor had nothing to lose in the first place: "They ate beans before and they will eat beans now." It's those who have experienced rising expectations who will have the hardest time. Some will hang on by their fingernails. Some will be radicalized and join the cause of the indigenous rebels. Some will quit and go north of the border.

Lourdes and I meet Arturo and Vatche that evening. At the cozy El Viejo Gaucho Bar, it's open mike night, so he and I take the stage after a couple of margaritas, with Lourdes and Vatche as our groupies. Somehow people are clapping when we finish, and when we join Vatche and Lourdes, Arturo says we are making a happening. Vatche says a happening is not complete without storytelling, so he tells us about a haunted house he once lived in because he wanted to do a painting of it. A man lived there with his ten-year-old son who would wake at night feeling hands on his body. The man brought in a priest one evening who offered incense and prayers to exorcise the ghost, but in the morning he found his cat torn to pieces on the front step. So the man took his son and went away on a vacation.

When he returned, the house had been vandalized and violent phrases threatening to kill him and all his family were scribbled on the walls in lipstick. Friends urged him to move away permanently, so he bolted up the doors and left in haste without even taking his dogs with him. Now Vatche leans toward me with his conspiratorial whisper. "The man came by the house a year later to check on things. The doors were all hanging open, and his three dogs were all slaughtered on the front step."

"What's the point of the story?" we ask, confused.

"When I lived there and was painting the place, nothing happened. Nothing. But that other man could not live there in peace. It made no difference for him whether he stayed or left; the trouble was glued to him. He had no escape."

Vatche invites us all to come to his house for a drink with the promise that it is not haunted. We pile into Vatche's VW van and he drives us through narrow, dark cobbled streets to an adobe vine-covered house with a tiled roof on a little rise at the east end of town. It is quiet here now, past midnight, except for some distant barking dogs. Inside, Vatche's place is three large, airy rooms, their corners cluttered with the tools and materials of the artist, the walls hung with his and his friends' paintings. We sit in wooden rocking chairs around a heavy oak coffee table while Vatche starts a fire in the fireplace. He then brings us juice glasses of straight mescal and we sit and talk.

For a while Arturo and Vatche wear the enigmatic mask, almost vying with each other to see who can make the most inscrutable statement. "Huitzilopochtli and Quezalcóatl are opposite forces," says Vatche. "What about the dust on the mirror?" says Arturo. "If there is no mirror, there is no dust." But as they drink, their conversation becomes more lucid and direct.

Vatche thinks that the true story of modern Mexico, in fact of the modern world at large, is the rise of the indigenous—the rule of the red. He sees a historical connection between what is happening in Chiapas and what is happening in, say, Algeria or the Caucasus states of Russia. "It's the beginning of the end of the old order. The land will revert from those with power and money to those who have always lived on it."

I ask how this squares with the other historical trend I have witnessed today in my conversation with the three women from Morelia—the rise of a new middle class that will not tolerate the fundamentalist repressions of traditional peoples when they gain power. Vatche just shrugs. "God, I didn't create the world. How can I know these things? But you may be right. That may be who will be the ultimate adversary."

Arturo thinks there will be lots more conflict. "Some people want money, some want land, some just want power. Those are the things that people fight for."

I ask him if there is anything that would make him fight, and he thinks for a moment before answering. "Land maybe. I would fight for my place on the planet if I couldn't get it just by moving on." But so far in his life, he has always been able to find his place by packing his bags. So he sees no real reason to contemplate fighting. For a generation now, that's how Mexicans have been dealing with hardship.

For thirty years after Cárdenas, Mexico turned and marched down a different path than the one he had opened. Land redistribution did continue, but usually at a snail's pace compared to what had been accomplished under Cárdenas. Labor organizations grew in size and power, but they were manipulated "for the good of the nation" from the top by the party, usually on terms favorable to industrialists. Constitutional bars to foreign domination of the Mexican economy were tinkered with to allow investment that was deemed constructive to the economy. Occasionally certain presidents would wallow in revolutionary rhetoric, but policy was consistently aimed at stability and economic growth.

That was the clarion call of the post-Cárdenas era. A new concord was established between politics and business to build a massive urban industrial and consumer edifice. In sum, the record of those years looked to the world like a huge success, until events of 1968 ripped away the mask of achievement and revealed the ugly face behind it. What the post-Cárdenas regime really forged turned out to be something more like the Porfiriato than the consolidation of the nation's revolutionary ideals.

For the elite (now often former revolutionaries who cashed in their chits of service to the nation) and the rapidly growing middle class, these were golden years, as Mexico's economy expanded by leaps and bounds and commentators frequently cited "the Mexican miracle" as proof of what could be accomplished in third world nations. International bankers fell all over themselves to help finance the bonanza, often with no questions asked about how loans would be spent. Presidents obligingly stepped down after their six-year terms and usually avoided meddling with the policies of their chosen successors. Civil upheaval became a thing of the past. Mexico enjoyed its role as an independent voice in the third world movement, frequently departing from the line out of Washington concerning issues from Castro's Cuba to recognition of Red China. Capitalism flourished here as Mexico had become an orderly, modern, Western nation.

But the boom was radically unbalanced, and large segments of the nation's geography and demography did not share in it. The cities boomed at the expense of the countryside. The affluent surged into consumerist comfort while the poor struggled harder to make ends meet. Exponential population growth, largely the result of improved health services established during the Cárdenas years, re-created the conditions that had enabled the building of the great pre-Hispanic monuments—a huge surplus of labor. Wages could be kept low because of the horde of available, landless rural laborers. And Indians especially were left out of the order entirely, becoming invisible in the calculus of the system. One view holds that during these years the pyramid was rebuilt around a different scheme of strata. Another holds that the pyramid was replaced by a simple two-tiered society of haves and have-nots. Whatever the case, since Mexicans all knew there was prosperity to be had out there somewhere, they set about moving to find it and share in it. Thus began a massive migration from the countryside into the cities, particularly the capital. Simultaneously, and partly as a result of the exigencies of World War II, a second migration began, headed northward across the border.

Despite Cárdenas's programs for redistributing land, rural folk fared especially badly after his departure from office. Many *ejidos* simply could not support growing families, farming became increasingly mechanized, and prolonged drought made bad harvests a regular occurrence. As a result, between 1940 and 1960 there was a 74 percent increase in the rural landless. Meanwhile the proliferation of newspapers, radio, and films presented to these dispossessed a vision of glittering urban prosperity so that for the first time, the rural poor were able to actually see what they were missing. Small wonder that they packed up in droves and abandoned their ancestral homes to chase a dream in the cities that all too often turned out to be another kind of nightmare. Four million headed for Mexico City alone. Those who were lucky would find low-paying jobs and long hours that at first seemed like an improvement over the impoverishment of the countryside. But working seven days a week at a dollar a day, even the fortunate eventually discovered they had to work second jobs or sell lottery tickets to feed their families.

Their new homes would be crowded tenements abandoned by the middle class in the rougher parts of the inner city. As many as a dozen family members would jam into a one-room dwelling rich with the smells, sounds, and privation of too many people living too closely together. Those with jobs would climb over their kin sleeping on mats on the hard floor to go to work before the sun was up and return mean and often drunk after it had set. Violence and sexual abuse were common. Coffee, beans, chilies, and tortillas constituted the "forced diet" that Mexicans saw as the emblem of the poverty they all wished to escape. Marriage became impractical, with most couples living in "free unions." Men saw no advantage to it when they knew they would have nothing for their children to inherit. Women accepted the situation as their only means of escaping the claustrophobic confines of the one-room dwellings of their parents.

The new life became a hard caricature of the dream the migrants came to the city to pursue. Meanwhile they had to harbor pained memories of what they had lost—the fabric of life in their ancestral places; the weddings; the inheritances, no matter how pitiful; the cycles of planting and harvest; and contact with the land itself. They retreated behind the stoic Mexican mask and endured, or else, if they retained any of the initiative that prompted their first migration, embarked on another to the north or on a series of quests for a life that rarely got any better.

During World War II, in order to alleviate the manpower shortage in the United States, Washington and Mexico City established the bracero program, sending millions of unemployed Mexican laborers north of the border under work contracts. After the war, rising economic expectations in the United States led to a shortage of American manpower willing to do the kind of work the Mexicans had been doing at the wages they had been doing it. Thus the program remained in effect until 1964 and established the pattern of migration across the border that so bedevils relations between the two countries today. Those who had gone north to work sent back paychecks the likes of which their families had never seen before and letters describing a land of opportunity. The two migrations, to the cities and to the United States, so drained the land of its inhabitants that they further exacerbated the decline of the rural economy. Those who were left behind became a subclass, permanently locked out of the nation's prosperity.

With the traditions of their ancestral places so disrupted, the migrant poor turned en masse to another form of festival occasion, the religious pilgrimage. As a Catholic country, Mexico had long had a tradition of pilgrimage, but during the fifties the practice became a mania for people with a sense of being trapped. A pilgrimage to Chalma, for instance, to honor its black Christ, offered escape from the burden of daily existence and a chance to revive the sense of festival so important in the rural life of distant memory. In these journeys the essential Mexican passion could be expressed in a circumstance that would not turn it into the violence and meanness of the ghettos. Pilgrims experienced such a welling up of release that they turned it into intense displays of religious fervor, often crawling on bloody knees the final few miles to the shrine.

The greatest of all these excursions was, of course, the pilgrimage to the Basilica of the Virgin of Guadalupe, which took place each December 12. Millions of the poor would make the passage every year seeking, in addition to the flight from the hard reality of their lives, direct contact with this most tangible icon of their lost Mexican identity. Priests offered mass and sacraments at the basilica, but it was the middle class who attended those. The poor crowded around the statue of the Virgin for their chance to touch her themselves. It was the one place in their lives where there stood no barrier between them and their dreams.

When we climb on board the train leaving Patzcuaro, we are laden with treasures. I have found handmade copper pots and big wooden spoons for cooking. Lourdes has embroidered mats with scenes of weddings, the Day of the Dead, the Day of the Bulls, the Dance of the Fishermen, and some large Talavera pots. We also have little watercolor paintings of Arturo's, each a landscape with a tiny splash of human color somewhere.

The passengers on the train are all Mexican except for a man and a woman from Minnesota whom Lourdes befriends during her first walk through the cars. He is Tim Francisco, a photographer who has published a book of his photos from a time when he lived with and got to know the Purépechans. He tells us that our purchases are representative of a piece of Purépechan history. When the Jesuits came to convert them, they taught a different craft to each of the fifteen villages. The making of copper pots, embroidery, wood carving, and pottery were four of these crafts.

His friend, Kim Christensen, is just trying her travel wings. She has made a life of nourishing people with food. Starting with sandwiches delivered on her bicycle, she now runs a business called Film Food that caters to the film and entertainment industry in Minneapolis. She likes traveling by train. "You feel the torque of travel when you ride a train," she says. And Mexico experienced this way is a particularly good, vigorous, textured ride. That is the theme of her conversation, the sense of torque so often missing in modern American "virtual" experience—whether it's through television, video games, shopping malls, or fat- (and taste-) free food.

The theme makes me wonder whether we Americans may have our own masks, just as impenetrable as those of Mexicans. We hide our weakness, our failings at dealing directly with sensory experience, through our technology and all the facades of virtual experience. When a red sun sets a foreign horizon afire and we might succumb to a searing passion in our hearts, instead we pull out our cameras—or in my case my laptop computer. I think of Rogelio's question, "Why do you come to Mexico, señor? What are you really looking for?"

The woman from Minnesota rides with me for several more hours, and we exchange stories. I talk about my travels; she speaks of her life's mission to bring color, flavor, and nourishment into the cold, gray world of Minnesota. By the time she and her friend detrain, we have exchanged addresses, and I have spoken of my father's ghost and the dream of the *tesquinada.*

This rugged country south of Patzcuaro is the land of the butterflies, destination of the millions of monarchs we *norteamericanos* see heading south every autumn. Somehow they navigate the thousands of miles, every whip of the wings earning them only an inch of that distance they must fly. How do they know? How do they find their way to that one valley in this country where they mate and fulfill their journey's purpose? It's fitting that it is in this region that Lourdes and I find stories of Mexican restlessness, of a passion for moving on that we thought was a purely American patrimony—and that here my own purpose in making this journey seems rounding to an answer.

We roll past the looming volcano, Paricutín, and passengers around us break into telling the famous story, familiar even to American schoolchildren, of its sudden appearance as a small hole spouting steam in the middle of a farmer's cornfield. Eventually the cornfield, the farm, and then an area the size of an American county were buried under the massive mound that become a nine-thousand-foot peak in less than a year. It is still very much alive, we are told, just recently burying a church that the local faithful had built on its slopes.

With the volcano behind us, the talk turns to more stories of Mexicans in motion—of trips on the train to see relatives, or to partake in a festival, to visit a lover somewhere far away, but most often to find work and a better life. A man shows Lourdes an article in a magazine comparing the northbound flight of the monarchs to the migration of Mexicans headed that way so that they can feed their families.

When the train slows for the tiny pueblo of El Rosario, my attention is hooked by a particularly emblematic peasant home near the tracks. The walls are of cardboard, sticks, tar paper, and dried reeds; the roof, a piece of crumpled tin scrap that does not cover the dwelling entirely. Inside I can see a dirt floor, beds of newspaper piles, a couple of stools, and a table with a stack of paint cans for one of its legs. There is no glass in the windows and no door at the entrance. The house has no electricity, and rows of buckets outside testify to the lack of running water. The latrine is a hole in the ground surrounded by a dirty sheet strung on a wire between several trees.

There are chickens out front, so this family would not appear to be starving. A little garden of beans and squash and some stunted corn is the most meticulously tended piece of the property. The woman of the house bends on her knees, scrubbing laundry on a rock, and three young children play with shards of glass, sticks, and cardboard in the dirt near her. There is no sign of a car, or telephone lines, not even any bicycles. The yard is cluttered with collected cans, crates, and broken boards. This home is built of and furnished by what very poor people have thrown away. I do not see a man around. In my imagination I picture him toiling in a vegetable field in California for the few dollars it takes to keep this home alive. If he ever returns, it will be testimony that he has a very strong heart. I fantasize about his homecoming: the friends gathering round, the teary laughter, the breaking out of festive food and drink however meager—and for a moment, I envy him.

As the train descends from the mountains down into the canyon of Tepalcatepec, we meet two young men out on the open platform who are teachers in Sinaloa. Every fifteen days they have to ride this train to Lázaro Cárdenas to get paid. "We must pay out of our pocket for tickets to get our paychecks," they complain. But it's not all so bad. They have family there and they use the weekend to go to the beach. They concur with the women from Morelia that it is hard to make it as a teacher these days. Though the job does offer security, it does not pay enough, and they have second jobs tending avocados and fruit to make ends meet.

Actually neither ever intended to be a teacher. Juan was trained as an agricultural engineer and Julio is a veterinarian. Each did the five years of teaching preparation after discovering that work in their chosen fields was simply unavailable.

When we ask about the specific ways they have been affected by the economic crisis, they gesture to their threadbare shirts and trousers. Clothing is too expensive to buy, so they wear things longer. It wasn't so long ago that teachers could count on being well dressed all the time. Not any more.

The other killer is the price of basic food—meat, rice, even corn and milk. A liter of milk has gone from two to three pesos in just a month. "I ate better when I was picking apples in Washington state than I do now as a professional," says Julio. "And it is going to get worse. Zedillo must take further austerity measures to get your president to give him the loan he needs."

"Does anyone have confidence in the new government?" we ask.

"You can never trust the government," Juan responds quickly. "They are all demagogues." Our two friends are insistent that everything that the government has done so far has been wrongheaded. "Too many things have been privatized. That just helps a few of the rich. It's the same with foreign investment and NAFTA and even tourism. They promised that these things would make new jobs, but we haven't seen any."

They believe that the people voted the wrong way in the recent election. Maybe Cárdenas would have been better. Certainly his father was the model, showing a rare time when the government helped rather than hurt the people. And the city named for him, where this train is headed, is an example of what should be happening. Planned and financed in the seventies by the government in partnership with private enterprise, Lázaro Cárdenas was built specifically to create a new center of employment and economic vitality. First they brought the railroad there, and then the highway, and then the cement and steel-wire plants. It really made a difference:

there were jobs created that didn't exist before. "But no one thinks that way anymore," Juan laments.

"What will happen when economic conditions get to a point that is insupportable?" we ask.

"Some may take up arms if they have nothing," Julio says. "But many will just try to move on. Some will leave the pueblos for the big cities. Some will leave the country for the United States."

I ask if there isn't any way that educated professionals can stand their ground and somehow change the direction of the country. "That's what we do as teachers," Juan answers. "We educate the children so that they can have a different point of view. The basis for improving the country over the long term is education. It's the only way to have a more idealistic country."

"What about more immediate action, like getting involved directly in politics?" I ask. The question really throws them. It just isn't an option in a country that has no tradition of ad hoc citizen participation in government. They stumble for an answer and mumble about how corruption is the greatest evil. Most people who go into government do it only to take advantage, or if they don't start out that way, they end up that way. There are just too many opportunities to lose your soul on the inside of government.

Perhaps it has always been in the Mexican nature to wear the masks we have seen, but it was the actions of government between 1940 and a single shocking event in 1968 that sowed the cynicism, the mistrust, and the fatalism that now seem so prevalent. Ávila Camacho, who succeeded Cárdenas as president, inaugurated the new era with the same strategy Porfiro Díaz had used a century earlier: by removing the church and the military as potential sources of opposition. Concerning the church, he accomplished the goal with the public utterance of two simple words, "I believe." With this open declaration of Catholic faith by a president, he ended the anticlericalism of the revolutionary era and earned for himself and the party a new allegiance from the church. Meanwhile he took advantage of a period of tranquility in the military to disenfranchise it as an official wing of the party. Henceforth the party and all presidents after himself would be thoroughly civilian.

His successor, Miguel Alemán, took this military policy a step further, drastically reducing the size of the armed forces to the point where they occupied one of the smallest budgetary percentages of all Latin American countries. Commanders were rotated regularly and units kept on short rations of munitions. Quickly the military lost its attraction as the avenue to power, and the ambitious chose other careers less threatening to the established order.

It was Alemán who in 1946 reorganized the party into the PRI that still exists today. It was composed of three separate wings representing agrarian campesinos, labor, and the "popular sector," which was basically the white-collar middle class. Theoretically this structure guaranteed a voice to all and provided the party with the legitimacy of a broad base. In practice it tended to divide and play off the sectors, one against the other. PRI functionaries were particularly careful to prevent alliances between the labor and campesino groups, and the popular sector could always be counted on to counter their influence. Furthermore, the three sectors tended not to have equal weight in the party, with the popular sector having the most and the campesinos the least. Add to that hierarchy the coterie of lawyers pulling the strings at the top under the supreme hand of the president and his government, and it appears the PRI itself was a five- or six-tiered pyramid in the traditional Mexican pattern.

But not quite. The presidents sitting at the top learned over the years that their power was not absolute, and there were certain parts in the charade of PRI democracy that they were obliged to play. Most notable was the need for the president to covertly consult with the powerful moguls of industry and finance, now intimately tied to the top of the PRI pyramid in an era when Mexico was betting the entire ranch on economic growth. Yet the illusion of authority had to be maintained, so that when measures turned out to be unpopular or unsuccessful, it was always the president himself and not the system or the powers behind it that took the blame. Presidents learned to brook opposition within the party, which could involve swallowing candidates for office not at all to their liking, as long as these adversaries adhered to the PRI rule of keeping the squabble behind PRI doors.

Presidents discovered that though they could get elected on a slogan of promising to combat the corruption that was now erupting into a national way of life under the PRI formula, in office they would find it to be the very grease to the nation's political machinery. During the economic boom, there was just too much opportunity for politicians to acquire wealth, and the short-term limits within which they had to operate under the antireelection clause created an ethic of "get it while you can." Officials didn't have to actually dip their hands into the public till. It was easier to accept bribes from developers and industrialists and cleaner simply to invest in areas where they knew something was in the works. Nonetheless, the public was far from fooled and called for a cleanup. Thus began the pattern of the incoming president's launching a limited investigation of abuses in his predecessor's government, but one that fell short of establishing a precedent he would not want to face when he left office. Only one president of the era, Alemán's immediate successor, Adolfo Ruiz Cortines, is believed to have left office without enriching himself.

Finally the PRI saw a danger in the lack of opposition it faced in elections, as people developed a political fatalism and began staying away from the polls. By 1963 it had become necessary for the PRI to create an opposition in order to assure its own legitimacy. Legislation was adopted allowing proportional representation by seating one opposition deputy for each .5 percent of his party's vote if the total was above 2.5 percent. But leaving nothing to chance, the PRI actually helped to establish several parties of the left to further splinter any leftist alternative to PRI rule.

Cortines the clean was followed by López Mateos the duplicitous. In an attempt to recapture a cachet of revolutionary spirit, he declared himself to represent "the extreme left under the constitution." But Mexicans remember Adolfo López Mateos as the author of the infamous *"disolución social"* laws, under which agitators of any sort could be jailed despite constitutional guarantees of the right to free speech and assembly. When national railroad workers went on strike under the leadership of former communist Demetrio Vallejo in 1959, the legislation was used to jail him, whereupon he received a sentence longer than those given to murderers. On the international scene, López Mateos may be better remembered by Americans for his opposition to Washington's policies regarding Castro's Cuba.

Still, under these presidents, the Mexican miracle charged ahead until Gustavo Díaz Ordaz, president from 1964 to 1970, just about blew up the whole pyramid that was Mexico. Under him the regime began to believe its own rhetoric. The poor in the cities dissolved against the backdrop of skyscrapers and flourishing consumerism. The campesinos were quiet. The Indians were invisible. Mexico had shown the world how, under its third way, order and progressivism, capitalism and social welfare could go hand in hand. When Mexico City won the honors to host the 1968 Olympics, the first ever to be held in a developing nation, Díaz Ordaz saw the event as an opportunity to showcase to the world what the new era had accomplished. Few noted at the time the parallels between his lavish expenditures for the event and the celebration of the centennial by Porfirio Díaz in 1910. Nothing could be allowed to disrupt this culminating spectacle of the miracle of Mexico.

But student unrest was sweeping Mexican universities, just as it was in the rest of the Western world during these years. Like the young middle-class generation of 1910, the new generation had a darker view of the Mexico they would inherit. They saw the corruption of public office, the subversion of democracy, the co-opting of workers and peasants, the lies in the media, and the implications of the laws of *disolución social*. Further, they were all too aware of the vulnerability of the power structure during this time when the politicos wanted so dearly to project a positive image to the world. If the Olympics would give the PRI a stage to tell its story, so too would they offer student protesters access to the television screens where the whole world would be watching.

The trouble began with simple street fights between students at rival schools in Mexico City. When the mayor took the unprecedented step of sending out riot police to handle the routine situation, a melee broke out and hundreds of students, now united against a common enemy, were teargassed and clubbed to the ground in a scene similar to what Americans would see at their 1968 Democratic convention.

Student demonstrations, which had already become a common and usually peaceful sight before this, now took an ugly turn in response to the unleashing of the riot police. The smashing of windows, hurling of Molotov cocktails, and overturning of buses became a regular feature of what had been a tradition of nonviolent protest. In its counterresponse, the government broke into Mexican Communist Party headquarters, where they claimed to find evidence of communist instigation of the latest round of student protests. Students called for general strikes at all universities. The government answered their challenge by closing down the schools and sending in regular soldiers to assault the students they found on campus. In one particularly controversial incident, a bazooka was reportedly used to blast open the doors of the National Preparatory School.

Díaz Ordaz spoke out, claiming that his hand was outstretched in a gesture of conciliation. But no offer was made to meet with students, and so the outstretched hand became a subject for ridicule and vilification of the president. On August 13, 150,000 marched on the *zócalo* carrying signs and chanting slogans personally denigrating a sitting president as no one had ever dared before. Onlookers were shocked and aghast. On August 27, 500,000 entered the *zócalo* and chanted in front of the National Palace, "Come out, you loudmouth."

With the Olympics approaching, the inner circles of power were now reeling from the unprecedented antipresidential rhetoric, and the huge numbers the students were able to mobilize. The official line was hardening, as Díaz Ordaz made clear in his state of the union message to congress. The army moved in to formally occupy the national university, and more than a thousand students were arrested. In September the demonstrations continued, though now in a more orderly fashion. Student leaders paid heed to the new hard line, and the largest march of the month, 250,000 strong, walked in silence to the *zócalo*, where they stood quietly holding their signs and placards and then withdrew in a respectful, orderly manner.

On the night of October 2, 1968, there was no massive march in Mexico City. But the Olympics were just ten days away and the government had made a fateful decision. A small group of 7,000 had gathered in the Plaza of the Three Cultures to listen to tame speeches. The crowd contained many parents and younger children from the families of the students. A planned march was called off due to the small turnout, and people were beginning to go home. Then at 6:00 P.M. a helicopter dropped flares, and government troops on the periphery opened fire. As army vehicles blocked escape routes at both ends of the plaza, the panicked crowd fled back and forth, cut down as they ran. Some attempted to surrender and were shot with their hands in the air. Others dropped to the ground only to have their bodies riddled with bullets. Parents and children, as well as students, were massacred indiscriminately as the gunfire continued for nearly an hour. When it was over, military vehicles removed most of the dead before ambulances were allowed on the scene. Their bodies were never seen again.

The government claimed in the aftermath that only 49 died in what came to be known as the Tlatelolco Massacre. But times had changed. Foreign journalists had witnessed the carnage and supported student claims that as many as 500 were killed. The Olympics went off without further incident, but an era ended in the Plaza of the Three Cultures that night. As Octavio Paz wrote, "a swash of blood dispelled the official optimism and caused every citizen to doubt the meaning of [Mexico's] progress." The ugly horror beneath the pyramid of power had been revealed, the image of the government's paternal benevolence smashed. Nothing had changed since the days of the Aztecs, Octavio Paz concluded, and now when the government-manipulated media printed only the official version of events, people knew better. Most would never believe the government or the media again. Mexicans, even the masses of the prosperous middle class, retreated behind their masks once and for all.

As we have talked on the open platform, the train has descended from the high, dry Sierra Madre into the canyon of the Río Balsas. Though not quite as spectacular as the Copper Canyon run, this is still an eye-popping ride down the canyon rim. After we pass the power-generating station at Infiernillo (Little Hell), the river below slows and widens into what looks almost like a fjord. Soon we are seeing coconut trees, mangos, and bananas, and the air is becoming heavier with heat and humidity until finally we break out at the bottom of the canyon into the coastal tropics. Those who are still on the train begin to stir and check their baggage. Most are going to Lázaro Cárdenas for work, but a few are headed, like us, to the beach. The conductor tells us that in better times, this train would be packed with people heading on beach vacations at this season.

When we detrain we can see that, despite its role as a model for job creation, Lázaro Cárdenas itself is a busy, grimy, industrial center and port—not very pretty. But we catch a cab that will take us the fifteen kilometers north to Playa Azul, a beach resort frequented almost entirely by middle-class and working Mexicans. The driver tells us that the steel-wire plant doesn't pay very well, but there is steady work with good benefits and you can get by. The rail yard and port offer better-paying jobs, but people wait for years for new job openings there.

On the way to Playa Azul we pass a dead horse at the side of the road. Its head is split open—the brains putrefying on the pavement. It is covered with flies and its stench is nauseating. "It's been here awhile," shrugs the cab driver—a car accident. Someone will cart it away when it gets really foul. There aren't many tourists these days, so things like this go untended longer.

Playa Azul is a perfect stretch of Pacific beach backed by quiet lagoons and lined with inexpensive little hotels and open-air eateries. Hundreds of folding chairs face the ocean. Our hotel has a fine pool, Ping-Pong tables, and a water-slide complex out back. Its restaurant serves wonderful octopus, conch, and shrimp. But only a handful of the rooms are occupied. It's places like this that my teacher friends would have frequented in better days. The chairs at the beach sit empty all weekend. A few Canadian tourists we meet marvel at the wonder of having this place almost all to themselves.

My publisher has caught up with me here, and some pages from a previous book that need editing are waiting for me at the hotel desk. I sit by the pool or under a *palapa* at the beach for the weekend, reworking some of my travels for *A Good Place to Live* while Lourdes warms her soul under the sun. For me it's a time when wires get crossed—reading what I have written about 1990s Americans seeking alternatives to the nests they have soiled in so many parts of the United States in the midst of this Mexican odyssey with its own themes of turmoil, change, disillusionment, and restlessness. I find the phrase I have used to describe Mexico—"a place where humanity is not stifled"—wanting to creep into the text for the American "good place" book.

What do I mean by that phrase? I wonder all weekend as the Pacific breakers crash against the deserted beach. At the start I think I was referring to Mexicans' penchant for outbursts of unbridled joy, sadness, passion, and lust for living the moment. But the historical fact of idealism and dreams dashed by a massacre in a public square clashes with my perhaps naive adulation of how Mexicans live. I've learned now about the masks, and how you have to look behind them to see Mexicans' real humanity.

By the end of the weekend on the empty beach, I think I have my quandary partly resolved. Something does lurk behind the Mexican disguise that we Americans might emulate—I knew what it was when I talked to the woman from Minnesota on the train. She would describe it as the ability to feel the torque of experience. We Americans put so much faith in our comfortable institutions, our social constructs, our jobs, our politics, our communications, our goods and services, our material possessions—all of the mechanics of living in an "advanced" society—that we lose contact with the ground under our feet, never mind the vault overhead, or the heart inside. Mexicans have no such distractions—their institutions and social constructs failing them so profoundly again and again. There is a Mexican saying that only he who has fully experienced loss, disillusionment, and tragedy can really love.

It's tempting to stay longer in this Pacific paradise. But the date of Mexico's greatest pilgrimage and festival is December 12, two days from now. So after a weekend on this perfect beach we head back to Lázaro Cárdenas to catch a plane to Mexico City. On the way we pass the dead horse, still festering. The cab driver says someone is coming to move it in the mañana.

Our flight from Lázaro Cárdenas glides in over Mexico City late in the evening. Down below us, stretched to the limits of the horizon with a glow beyond in all directions, rolls an ocean of undulat-

294

ing light. Again the sheer size of what may be the world's largest city takes our breath away. At more than 20 million inhabitants and growing so fast the census takers can't keep up, Mexico City gobbles up more than half of the nation's entire investment in internal infrastructure. We search for more metaphors besides the obvious living net of electrical surging. Lourdes sees sprawling lava flows from some huge unseen volcano. I see windswept prairies, their grasses afire.

After landing and hopping a cab to the María Cristina, we see that we have become part of the reason for the apparent motion of the city lights as seen from the air. Tonight the streets are thronged with pilgrims journeying to the basilica to commemorate the national miracle.

In groups ranging from a dozen to a hundred, they parade carrying their religious *estandartes* and the glass-encased shrines of their local parishes. Most are on foot, though some ride bicycles. They are all ages—decrepit old women with canes and sprightly youngsters dashing about with the fervor of the holiday spirit. Mothers carry wrapped babies in their arms, and some of the men bang drums and bells while others ride herd on the older kids. Over the taxi radio we hear announcers giving a moment-to-moment account of the movements of the celebration, just as I have heard before when arriving in New Orleans on the evening of Mardi Gras. With that precedent in mind, I expect to see drinking, but I don't. As on the Night of the Dead in Oaxaca, the intoxication here comes from a sheer sense of release from the daily grind of hard life. Tonight there is also a bonding of national kinship. The Day of the Virgin, more than Independence Day or Cinco de Mayo, is Mexico's Fourth of July.

In the morning we ask directions to the Basilica of the Virgin. A man sends us down a westerly street where he says we will find a bus that goes right to the site. But after several blocks there is no bus, and we ask a woman for more directions. Maddeningly she turns and points in the direction from which we have just come. "Take a poll," says Lourdes. After two more queries we finally get the right bus, and soon we are disembarking amid a huge crowd a block from the plaza.

The streets adjacent to the plaza are packed with vendors as if this were a giant market day, again prompting visual echoes of the Day of the Dead. But today the street action is nothing compared to what we find at the plaza itself. We climb a stone staircase and enter through a flower-bedecked arcade emblazoned with crosses and Mary figures as well as pre-Hispanic symbols. The plaza is a vast space, as big as the *zócalo* itself. Above it towers the terraced hilltop and the old shrine, the actual site of the miracle. To the left squats the big, modernistic basilica, looking as much like an American sports arena as a church. But the real action is on the plaza itself.

There are thousands of people here and they are of three kinds. Least significant are the meandering nonparticipant visitors like ourselves. The second-largest group are the pilgrims with their Catholic shrines and banners, collapsing in sprawling circles of shawls, water jugs, snack food, and pillows to rest. But the plaza is dominated by tribes of indigenous dancers and musicians. As the faithful kneel and pray to the strains of organ music and chanters inside the Catholic basilica, the plaza outside thrums with the sounds and color of pre-Hispanic culture and religion. There seems at first to be a sense of competition between the two rites, though it may be only we outsiders who see it that way. When Lourdes asks a few revelers about it, they tell us that the two rites go together, that this is Mexico's day and that both are a part of the "deep Mexico."

From Morelos, a group of Purépechans dance with traditional red-feathered headpieces and rattling ankle bracelets of *ayocote* shells as their musicians play on guitars and drums. When the strolling, rifle-toting security soldiers come by, they are asked to

join in and they do. They even know how to do the Purépechans'
barefoot dance. A group of male dancers from Oaxaca undulates in
green plumage to the beat of big goat-skin drums while women
wend through the formation carrying dishes of burning incense.
From Veracruz, a troupe performs a dramatic dance in which half
are dressed and made up as white-faced Spanish conquistadores
while the rest play Aztecs. In a mock battle the conquistadores
flourish their swords while the Aztecs evade the blows, circling and
taunting their attackers. Periodically the Aztecs all fall down in
positions of death upon the stones, and then they rise and swirl
once again in defiance of the soldiers' swords.

The dancers from Zacatecas came here by train, they tell us, and
sure enough, it was ten hours late. Their leader, wearing a
skateboard T-shirt and baseball cap along with his Indian feathers
and ankle rattles, says that his group comes here to do the Indian
dances because of a promise they have made as Catholics to the
Virgin Mary. "We promise at Confirmation to make the trip every
year. The dance we do is the dance of our pueblo." He knows
nothing of its symbolic or religious significance. "We just do it because that's what we were taught."

We encounter another odd hybrid of indigenous and Catholic
traditions in the form of a group of ragged pilgrims from Santa
Cruz. Wearing sackcloth and leaning against their knapsacks, they
sing in Spanish, then in their Indian dialect: "From the sky she
came triumphant, she came to give us peace, from the sleep she
woke me up, peace for the Indian republic."

Bicycles decorated with flowers and pictures of the Virgin weave
throughout the commotion. Near the base of the old shrine another
tired-looking group is more interested in dozing than singing at the
moment. A plaque just above them reads, "I am always the Virgin
Mary, mother of the true God, author of life, creator of all in
heaven and earth. I ardently desire that a temple be erected here,

and as your loving mother I will show clemency and compassion to all who love me and look for me."

A mother in the group who is nursing a baby tells us that they started from a village near the city of Puebla at 11:00 P.M. two days ago and arrived yesterday at 5:00 P.M. and have been here on the plaza ever since. Some of the group rode bicycles while others walked. "We have slept only four hours in the past two days," she says. "But no, we are not tired. We would do it again next week. This is the finest week of the year." This group of thirty is from the pueblo of San Juan Tuxco, population thirty-eight hundred. They have their own *ejido* lands, and the men tend corn, beans, and green vegetables while the women toil in a sewing workshop.

As we talk to the woman with the child, her compatriots stir from their napping and begin to gather around us, nodding assent to the things she tells us. We have seen this pattern so often. Mexicans seem happy to let one of their group assume the role of spokesperson, and they invariably nod assent to what is being said. It makes me wonder what would happen if the spokesperson deliberately said outrageous things. Would they all still nod in agreement?

"Why is the pilgrimage so important?" we ask. "This is the day our Virgin appeared," she answers. "I am telling the truth; we who live around Puebla are more spiritual than those in many parts of Mexico. We know this in our hearts but the pilgrimage is how we show it to God, to the Virgin, and to the world. She is our Virgin; this is our Mexican miracle; we do this because we know who we are."

Several of her companions have now joined in a tight knot about Lourdes and me with my notebook, and are interested in telling us about the experience of the pilgrimage. It was nice at first, they all agree—the sense of communal adventure as they set out from their pueblo in the dark of the late evening with torches firing the way. "But the time comes when you get tired, especially late that night, and people get crabby. You have to be patient so that everyone stays together."

They travel with a rule of always slowing down for and helping those who are most tired. When they come to a hill, the younger men will charge ahead and look to have refreshments ready for the rest of the group when it arrives at the summit. But sometimes this gets to be competitive, and the men then expect to get extra attention and appreciation. Then there are times when the young women will accept a ride in some fellow's car up the hill. This always makes the men very unhappy, and if they are around when such a proposition is tendered, they will physically forbid it.

The only case of someone getting separated from the group and possibly lost occurred when one of the young men and his girlfriend stopped off in a field, perhaps to make love. As the woman tells us this story in low tones, everybody in the group knows what she is talking about and they snicker and whisper. The couple in question are curled up together under a blanket on the stones, sound asleep. Perhaps to divert everyone from embarrassing the two kids, a young man poses a question to the group for our benefit, "Is this devotion or diversion? Is it a sacrifice of trouble or a vacation?" There seems to be little agreement on an answer. The group splits several ways—some say diversion, some say devotion, some say both, and a couple say it's just tradition. As Lourdes and I have listened to the stories of too little rain, stunted corn, never having enough money, children getting sick, and a workday that never ends, we conclude that diversion, à la Woody Allen ("I believe in the power of diversion; how else would we cope with this vale of tears?"), has to be part of the true mix. Here we have a plaza full of people who have deprived themselves of sleep and comfort for two days, and all of those we talk to express a sense of release. We hear over and over again that life is measured from one pilgrimage to the next. The event is a punctuation mark, an exclamation to the hard lives these people lead. This doesn't seem to be a matter

of unpleasant religious duty or sacrifice. No, this is more like
Christmas, and indeed, here in Mexico, this day is the beginning of
the Christmas season.

After talking to the pilgrims, we attend mass inside the basilica.
The interior is designed to resemble a honeycomb, since the witness of the miracle was a beekeeper. And as the pilgrims come and
go, many of them walking in with their *estandartes* and standing for
only a few minutes before leaving, the place has a feeling like a
great beehive. Even down front, in the heart of the faithful, there is
buzzing movement as believers file up to take Communion.
Through the open entranceway, the drums of the native performers
out on the plaza punctuate the swells of the organ inside.

The climb up the hundreds of steps to the top of the hill where
sits the old basilica and the site of the miracle is another passage
through the curious combinations of Mexicana. Young newlyweds
pose for formal photographs at turns in the stairway for a blessing
of their marriage. Out of carts that look like those of hot dog vendors, we are offered fragrant tacos and steaming pork sausages.
Hawkers of ballpark-caliber souvenirs wave their banners in our
faces in competition with purveyors of holy trinkets. Lovers nuzzle
beside elderly pilgrim nuns in religious rapture. At the top, the
grotto of the miracle is disappointing, just a plaque on a rock wall
and an old chapel no longer open to the public. But the panorama
below is the miracle here: a shifting swarm of thousands of people
in a cloud of incense born aloft by the booming of Aztec drums. If
we see contradictions and conflicts here, the crowds below us see
only Mexico's day, with all of the country's complexity and fecundity.

It's another tableau that belies the *norteamericano* stereotype
that characterizes Mexicans as a provincial people unaccustomed to
movement beyond their pueblo. On the contrary, Mexicans' continuing search for a better life somewhere, on this earth or beyond
it—or at least beyond toil and hardship—has made them as restless

as us rootless Americans. Their lives, their history has been a pattern of spiritual pilgrimage and corporal migration.

In a flowered corner of the grotto, a handsome dark young Mexican man in a threadbare but spotlessly clean white shirt kneels before a similarly beautiful young woman wearing a faded purple dress. He takes her hands in his and gazes up at her, beseeching. She smiles, blushing in rapture, and says, *"Sí, sí, sí, mi amor."* Then he stands and they embrace, laughing away tears of joy and passion. *"Sí, sí, sí,"* she continues breathlessly, now kissing him heavily on the mouth, oblivious to my entranced stare.

I remember the broken historical promises, the dashed economic expectations, the poor trackside peasant homes, the lure of the cities, the alternative to the north, the horror of the dead horse. Who should be surprised that so many Mexicans choose flight on butterfly wings? But this young pilgrim couple have shown me here in this public place their appetite for the torque of the moment and the universal wonder of love. I find myself thinking again of the woman from Minnesota—the softness of her laugh, the swing of her hair as she let it down during our conversation, the angle of her knee under her skirt. Perhaps we are all butterflies, driven to find ourselves despite ourselves, despite trouble in our lives, despite the disillusionment of age, experience, and history.

9

Faces to the Sun
Tapachula to Tuxtla Gutiérrez

Chiapas. Nearly every story we have heard describing the condition of modern Mexico has contained some reference to what is going on here. In our brief incursion into the northern part of the state at Palenque, we were more interested in tourism and the Mayan past. Now we are returning to its southern region to have a look at the present in this remote place whose name evokes so much anxiety throughout Mexico today.

We fly into the city of Tapachula from where we will ride a train to the Guatemalan border before turning around and working our way back north by train and bus to the capital at Tuxtla Gutiérrez. The U.S. State Department has issued warnings about travel in Chiapas. Tourists and foreign journalists have on a few occasions been caught up in the political turmoil. We come armed with letters in Spanish (though maybe they ought to be in Chol or Lacendon) from our publisher, airline schedules listing the quickest ways out, and a wired intensity and watchfulness that we haven't traveled with before.

Tapachula is hot and humid even in the weeks before Christmas. The streets of this city are narrow and crowded, the buildings are low-rise, few over two stories. It is neither colonial nor the ticky-tacky modern that we have seen in other places, especially near the U.S. border. It is third world tropical.

Most of it is not terribly pleasant. As the center of commerce and agriculture for the southern region of the state and the first city on the route of everything coming out of Guatemala, its roadways are noisy and fumy from the continual disorderly procession of trucks and buses. And these days the streets have the added un-pleasantness of army vehicles, which roar by every few minutes, sirens wailing and heavily armed soldiers skulking in the back.

But as is so often the case in Mexico, the *zócalo* is an island of tranquil civility. Planted with large ficus trees pruned square so that they cast perfect shade over the benches and fountains, Tapachula's *zócalo* hosts more people during the workaday hours of the late morning. Men and women dressed in casual business clothes swinging briefcases pass barefoot campesinos in caps and T-shirts carrying burlap satchels. There are also young men and women dressed fashionably, as if it were the early evening hours. The men sport open cotton shirts with gold chains, black pants, and Reeboks; the women wear low-cut bodysuits or colorful blouses with tight jeans and have flowers and bows prettily done in their hair. Varying levels of wealth are clearly evident here, and it seems that everyone whose path passes by the *zócalo* stops off here for a half hour of shade and talk and seeing and being seen.

The shoeshine guys are not doing any business but don't seem too concerned as they chat among themselves. From across the street the strains of recorded mariachi music drift from speakers above Jugos Hawaii. Fruit juice bars are as common as drugstores here, with clothing stores—Reebok, Puritan, Canada—close be-hind. Someone enjoys prosperity in Chiapas.

When the army trucks roll through, people pause and follow

their passage, then turn to each other and utter furtive comments. Lourdes and I sit for juice at a café across the street from the *zócalo* and find that it is easy to get people to talk. A fellow who has a small coffee ranch says that yes, people here are worried. The Zapatistas are up there in the mountains and the government has increased air surveillance in recent weeks. The radio is telling people that troops are being mobilized and, of course, they see them in the streets every day. When we say we will soon be traveling to Tuxtla Gutiérrez, he says there have been warnings about traveling over the mountains. Bandits unaffiliated with the rebels have used the insurrection to become bolder in holding up buses.

Eduardo reassures us that everyone—government, citizens, even the Zapatistas themselves—is particularly concerned about trouble involving foreign travelers. Any assault on travelers by anyone is viewed as a likely provocation to the escalation in conflict that everyone seems to want to avoid in this setting where the sensitivity to international opinion is so strong on both sides. His description of the situation is consistent with what we read in the newspapers and hear from other citizens in the next couple of days.

The sense is that up until just recently, in December of 1994, there had been a precarious balance for peace. Both the government and the rebel EZLN are painfully aware of the great desire for peace of Mexicans at all class levels and realize that whoever violates that peace will suffer the blows of adverse public opinion. Thus the government has taken the unprecedented step of offering to negotiate with a small movement that dared threaten to carry revolution all the way to Mexico City. This is even more extraordinary in light of Mexico's historical inclination to shed blood.

On the other side, the Zapatistas find themselves in an absolutely untenable situation with a revolution declared, a worldwide audience for their movement, and a newly installed PRI state governor who they passionately believe was elected by the old corrupt means. They have declared that he must be removed and a PRD candidate installed. The man in the middle, Robelledo Rincón, has resigned from the PRI, but that won't be enough. The EZLN is now considering setting a deadline for hostilities to resume if their demands for his replacement by a people's government are not met.

Eduardo believes, as do a surprising number of people we talk to, that despite the legitimacy of their cause, the Zapatistas have blown it. Everyone seems to agree with the truth of their basic tenet—that the promises of land reform and the rights of the indigenous peoples that were central to the revolution have never been realized. Everyone seems to agree that it is a crime when, in a country of radically rising wealth, 20 percent of the people still have nothing. And almost everyone seems to agree that the PRI is corrupt and morally bankrupt.

But there is a sense that somewhere along the way, the EZLN became "political" just like everything else. We ask a lot of questions to find out what that means, and the best we can decipher is this: In Mexico "political" describes a situation when political means are used for the advantage of one group over another, rather than for a consistent philosophy or program that is blind to who may benefit. In this case there is a widespread feeling that the EZLN has allowed itself to become a vehicle for the rehabilitation of the electorally unpopular leftist PRD. In this view the EZLN has become simply one more faction working for the advantage of certain politicos over others.

Eduardo says, "The war is not for the Zapatista leaders or their PRD sympathizers. It should be for the people." He believes that for too much of their history the Mexican people have suffered the violence of contending leaderships. "So everyone is on good behavior for the moment because neither side wants to alienate public support." The fear, however, is that behind the mask of willingness to negotiate, both sides have already staked out concrete positions that will inevitably clash in cataclysmic violence.

Tapachula is one of the places that would be hit first and hardest by such a calamity. If the rebels broke out of their mountain redoubts, they would first take San Cristóbal, as they have already shown they can do, then would march west to the capital, Tuxtla Gutiérrez, and finally south, to this town with its roads and rail lines into Guatemala. Even without an assault, Tapachula's thriving peacetime economy is already suffering, and it would be ruined by hostilities advancing this way.

Eduardo fears the new year. The new PRI government will be installed, which may provoke the EZLN to strike. It will also be the anniversary of the EZLN's first attack on the government, which may prompt the government to launch a counterattack.

Another man in work clothes, just finishing his *comida*, has overheard our conversation and wants to give us his slant on things, so we slide over to his table and buy him a drink. He is an engineer working for a construction company and believes he has witnessed firsthand that the government is trying to do good things for Chiapas. He cites several specific projects: a bridge into Guatemala that he helped to build, an arts theater, and 580 low-income housing units here in Tapachula. But Chiapas has a dangerous mix that can render the best government efforts futile. First there is the fact that so much of the wealth here is not local; people from the north or from foreign countries control too much of it. There are too many indigenous people with too little prosperity and for whom nothing has ever been done. Then there is the influx of radicalized illegal aliens from Guatemala. And there is the heat, which makes people's tempers short. "Dig a half meter into the ground and you can grab the devil's tail," he says.

A third fellow at the table next to us, whose family owns five hundred acres of cotton, has a different view. He thinks the government has failed Chiapas because it has not educated and helped the poor indigenous to raise themselves up from their squalor to the point where they can carry on with a sense of personal responsibility. Instead the law offers a sop to their aspirations by simply allowing them title to fallow lands. "They waste the land they get legitimately, and then they go on to take and waste lands that are cultivated and legally owned. Then when you try to get them off the land you have put your sweat and heart into, they tell you that you are an oppressor.

"The poor get land and money from the government, but no help at all to change their ways to become productive citizens. So they drink up the money and squander the land. Then it all comes out of my hide—my taxes, my land. And when this all leads to revolution, they have nothing to lose since they had nothing in the first place. But I will lose what I have put my life into."

The threat of violent catastrophe notwithstanding, he believes the situation is already a disaster. No one will invest because of the unrest. "Anything that you plant in this miracle soil and climate produces. But now, because of politics, we have the insane situation that we cannot profit from our land."

Voicing his disagreement with the engineer, the cotton farmer goes on to say the government is not helping at all in ways that matter. If war can be avoided, it will be up to small property owners like himself to band together to finance public improvements that benefit everyone—roads, schools, irrigation. The government will never focus on these things because it ultimately works only for the benefit of the very rich, and here in Chiapas, the simple truth is that the very rich see no advantage in such projects. Forty-five percent of the communities of Chiapas have no electrical power or water. Adequate health, education, communications, and means of production are even rarer. Whatever progress has been made in other parts of Mexico, Chiapas is the last to benefit. No one has any faith in the government. And people don't like to say so, but deep down they believe it's all going to blow.

. . .

Following the Tlatelolco Massacre of 1968, there was a brief panic that things might be about to blow then. Small guerrilla groups began to appear in various parts of the country, and the ruling elite were seriously concerned about the implications of the student revolt. If students were to link up with disaffected workers or campesinos, there could be a revolution. Something had to be done.

Luis Echeverría Álvarez entered the presidential office in 1970 with a mandate for change. He quickly declared himself the new Cárdenas, promising to return the nation to the path of social reform. He took modest steps in that direction and initiated a struggle between his administration and the lords of industry and foreign finance that earned him their permanent enmity. Under him, the state, functioning on behalf of the people and the sovereignty of the nation, would become master of Mexico's destiny as it never had been before.

But his real agenda was to diffuse the trouble where it had originated—in the universities. Despite the initial hostility of students and intellectuals, he worked tirelessly to woo them and, to a large measure, eventually succeeded. First he adopted their rhetoric, to the extent that American politicians in Washington wondered whether he was a communist. He championed the causes of Castro in Cuba, Salvador Allende in Chile, and revolutionaries in Nicaragua. More important, he released the protesters jailed in 1968 and began offering them jobs in government. During his tenure the federal bureaucracy ballooned as Echeverría made room in government for intellectuals of all sorts. Simultaneously increasing the budget for education, he expanded the University of Mexico to 350,000 students. Salaries of professors were boosted and a shower of benefits conferred on the university community.

Echeverría went on to address intellectuals' greatest frustration from time immemorial—the difficulty of getting their message out to the public. Besides putting many on the government payroll, he offered intellectuals free access to the halls of power and its printing presses. It became fashionable for politicians from the president on down to be followed by a noisy coterie of intellectuals who, if rarely heeded, were surely heard. Censorship was shelved and intellectuals enjoyed the right to publicly criticize just about anything but the president himself. Ex-presidents were another matter, and it was under Echeverría that the Mexican practice of excoriating the previous officeholder reached shrill levels (Echeverría himself became a victim of the process after his departure from office).

What Echeverría had accomplished was the co-opting and compromising of the intellectual community. Intellectuals began to be indistinguishable from the politicians—with whom they felt much more comfortable than they did with labor or campesino leaders on the one side and businessmen on the other. Like the politicians, intellectuals were full of rhetoric but short on action, never once rallying to the banner of actual revolt. Instead they measured their integrity by the scale of how long they could hold out before selling out.

There were those who did revolt. Small Zapatista-style guerrilla groups emerged from time to time and were quickly and quietly dealt with by the government, which was not queasy about the use of torture or assassination. More than four hundred people were "disappeared" during the years of Echeverría and his successor. It was not a very well-kept secret, but it wasn't talked about.

Meanwhile Echeverría expanded the power of the state over industry. Corporate taxes were increased to finance public spending on housing, education, and agriculture. State-owned corporations came increasingly to dominate the economy, and the government absorbed a large segment of the money banks had to loan. Inflation took off and the peso had to be devalued. The business community became increasingly restive, especially after the assassination of a Monterrey industrialist by a rebel group. From the viewpoint of private business, Echeverría was reacting inappropriately to the 1968 massacre and taking the country down the road to ruin.

As the end of Echeverría's term approached, national nerves again became frayed. Rather than lie low to prepare a smooth transition for the next president, Echeverría ratcheted up his rhetoric against the private sector, distracting attention from his chosen successor, José López Portillo y Pacheco. When the car of Portillo's sister was attacked, rumors flew that it was a failed assassination attempt, intended for Portillo himself and planned by Echeverría, who was preparing a coup to remain in office. Simultaneously an uprising by peasants in Sonora provoked a weak response from the president. Instead of stifling the rebels, Echeverría rewarded them by expropriating and redistributing 250,000 acres of farmland. And finally somebody began bombing Mexico City office buildings by night. After all that the PRI had done to guarantee a stable political climate and smooth transitions of power, it had come to this. Confidence even in what the regime did best was shaken.

But then, despite all the upheaval, Portillo was quietly inaugurated as Echeverría sat respectfully in attendance. Like clockwork, the new president declared a break with the previous policy, Echeverría was discredited by all sectors of the body politic, and Portillo was hailed as the man who would save the nation from Echeverría's folly. Small wonder that ordinary Mexicans were left bewildered. Was it all a charade staged by the PRI? Had there been a backstage coup by anti-Echeverría forces within the party?

Eschewing inflammatory rhetoric, Portillo began backpedaling toward austerity measures. But we will never know what sort of program would have ultimately emerged, since his term was marked by a spectacular new economic factor: the discovery of huge oil deposits in the Gulf. Here out of the blue was the panacea for Mexico's troubles. Oil could make the economic pie big enough to provide for everybody, and Portillo threw everything the government had to offer into the new recipe.

From 1978 to 1981 Mexico indulged in an orgy of industrial growth, development of infrastructure, and foreign borrowing under the illusion that oil would eventually pay for everything. When the bottom fell out of the oil market in 1981, the economic house of cards that was Mexico collapsed. In six years Portillo had put the nation in hock to foreigners for $60 billion. The peso crashed to one one-hundredth of a dollar. Capital fled the country and Portillo, in a desperate attempt to find a scapegoat and save his legacy, nationalized the banks. He left office in 1982, thoroughly discredited, with the nation in bankruptcy. Mexicans noted that their leaders had failed them once again.

They also noted the escalation of corruption that had occurred during the Twelve Tragic Years, as the combined terms of Echeverría and Portillo came to be called. Ordinary Mexicans believed that the real cause of Mexico's troubles was that their leaders literally stole the nation's prosperity. It was during these years that the big drug operators, soon to become such a concern to the United States, moved into Mexico with the complicity of political leaders and police throughout the country. High-profile cases like that of Mexico City police chief Arturo Durazo highlighted what people had come to believe was business as usual.

Durazo was a thug, plain and simple. When he took office he cleaned house—of honest cops. Those that did not deliver his share of their take were fired. He turned the Mexico City police force into nothing less than a crime syndicate that made him fabulously rich and powerful. Brutality, torture, and extortion were the norm, and citizens came to fear the police more than they did common criminals. Durazo openly conducted himself like a mafia crime boss, always accompanied by a gang of bodyguards and boasting of such exploits as the pleasure he had taken in personally torturing Fidel Castro and Che Guevara with electrodes when he brought them in for interrogation during one of their forays into Mexico in the 1950s.

The public was appalled at the doings of the Portillo era, so the next presidential candidate, Miguel de la Madrid, campaigned, of course, on a platform of anticorruption. Once he took office, Durazo and the crooked boss of Pemex, the national petroleum company, were indicted, but the cases moved forward ever so slowly. People believed that de la Madrid intended to showcase these two trials for the duration of his term so that he could delay indefinitely prosecution of the widespread corruption now endemic in the system.

To revive the economy, de la Madrid embarked on an ambitious austerity program dictated largely by the World Bank, to which Mexico owed so much. He made attempts to decentralize industry away from the increasingly unmanageable capital, with little success. But Mexico's economic situation began slowly to revive. Through the cutting of social programs, it was paid for largely by those of the lower middle class and at the bottom of the pyramid who depended most on the government activism established during the Cárdenas and Echeverría eras. The story is widely repeated today that Lázaro Cárdenas himself, now an old man, visited the Yaqui lands in Sonora that he had once given to the indigenous. Times had changed. The Yaquis were landless once again, and their rural countryside was more destitute that ever. Cárdenas looked on what had become of his legacy, and wept.

As dusk gathers each evening on the *zócalo* of Tapachula, the air is filled with the sounds and flurry of thousands of birds flying in from all directions and alighting on electrical wires, tree branches, statues, and every other architectural perch. Of several species and sizes, they gather in bunches of their own kind until virtually every horizontal line of the tableau is softened by the feathery sheath of their close-packed little bodies. As they fly in they are raucous and noisy, the air filled with nonmusical screeches, but after about an hour of this, they settle and remain silently fixed on their perches until the sun rises in the morning.

We "take a poll" about the phenomenon, and most people just take it for granted—in the evening the birds come in from the countryside. Why not? But we get enough agreement from a consistent minority that we think we have found the truth. There are terrible predators out in the coastal flats—nighthawks in the air and wildcats on the ground—that at night make the countryside a dangerous place for small birds. Over the centuries they have learned to flock to the haunts of humankind for sanctuary during the dark hours. The *zócalo* of every southern coastal town, with its trees, greenery, and open access to lots of man-made horizontal perches, is a natural haven.

The headlines in the morning newspaper announce that the PRD, speaking perhaps without endorsement from the EZLN, has declared that there will be no peace until Robledo resigns. His renouncing of PRI membership is just a ruse. Editorials declare that the chances of new confrontation are increasing every day. We have learned enough about the co-opting of Mexican newspapers to wonder whether the PRD story is true or is just a government plant to discredit the EZLN.

One thing is clear as we stroll Tapachula this morning. There are even more soldiers out than before—a half dozen or more at every intersection. Nonetheless, commercial life goes on as it did that first day.

In the late morning we board the second-class train that runs from Tapachula to Cuidad Hidalgo at the Guatemalan border. Riding this daytime train is not as bad as the death train we took in the Yucatán. But in the bathroom, in the space where there should be toilet paper, there is a huge spider, maybe two inches in diameter, eating a large squirming cockroach.

It's a short run, full of people whose livelihood brings them on this little journey. A peasant-merchant who owns a small store in his pueblo of Hermanos is carrying a sack filled with batteries and fruit from Tapachula. He has had his store, along with a small piece of good farmland, for twenty-two years and rides this train for supplies several times a week. There is a highway, but he is not rich enough to own an automobile.

He got his land, carved out of an *ejido,* when the government was encouraging the production of cotton and giving away *ejido* lands to those who would commit to growing it. As we have heard before, the lands of this region are fabulous for that crop. But he no longer grows cotton. Food is more important. His land is also excellent for growing corn.

Lourdes talks to a colorful family riding in the seats behind us. The mother wears a crimson dress, the father sports a blue shirt and blue jeans, the teen daughter wears a green smock, and the infant is wrapped in a baby-aspirin-orange blanket. Besides us, they are the best-dressed people on the train, and they have been to Tapachula to shop. They can afford to do this once a month. As we pass a large banana plantation fenced with barbed wire and signs warning PRIVATE PROPERTY, KEEP OUT! they tell us that their pueblo, Veinte de Noviembre (Twentieth of November), is a good place to live because there are only real Mexicans there—no Guatemalans. It's the first of several conversations we have with Mexicans in southern Chiapas that shows the universality of human prejudice.

Nowhere is Mexico the garden of Eden so much as it is in Chiapas. As we ride, we pass stands of coconuts, bananas, papaya, oranges, avocados—many of them growing wild outside of cultivated orchards. A profusion of tropical flowers beyond the ability of anyone on this train to name them bursts like fireworks at every turn of the tracks. Besides the orchards, the cultivated land is rich with corn, cotton, rice, sugarcane, and oil-producing African palms. The lands along this route are a mixture of *ejidos,* big haciendas, and small land holdings that, except for the hostile signs on the barbed wire of the haciendas, seem to reside in peaceful coexistence. Even the drought has been less severe here in this rain forest climate than it has been in other parts of Mexico, and the trackside hovels of the poor look better than they do elsewhere, usually made out of cane and thatched with palms rather than cardboard and rusty tin.

There is a caboose attached to the rear of this little train of two coaches and five boxcars, and Lourdes and I precariously step over the open gap at the back of the rear passenger car to talk to the conductor riding there. The caboose is old and dusty, with a wooden floor, rusty lockers, a desk carved with initials and numbers, and benches with cushions losing their stuffing. Several bicycles lean against the wall, and someone has set up a little shrine to the Virgin of Guadalupe with her portrait, some red and green bunting, and flashing Christmas tree lights.

The conductor is a jolly fat man who says that the only problem in his life in Chiapas is the thieves who occasionally rob his train. They aren't political or even conscious enough, he says, to be connected to the rebels. They are just ignorant peasants who rob when they get hungry. When he catches them, the constables beat them up and throw them in jail for a few days before letting them go to rob when they get hungry again.

It usually happens near the end of the line at the border and it is not violent. The thieves simply get on at one stop, look for an opportunity to take someone's satchels, and then get off at the next. People on the train are terribly casual, sleeping and wandering out to the vestibules. They should know better but they don't, and then when they are robbed, they make life miserable for the poor conductor.

So here are Lourdes and I, two cars away from our stuff—my laptop computer, her camera. We invite the conductor to come sit with us back at our seats to talk some more and he obliges.

As we walk back to our car, the conductor tells us that he can spot Guatemalans by their attire. "Their women travel with shame-fully dirty clothes," he says. "They have no pride. The men wear old sweaters, even when it's hot—and ratty tennis shoes." And again here is this parallel to the prejudice one might hear in say, Texas.

Back at our seats our bags are unmolested and the conductor leans over us as we settle back in. The train is an essential govern-ment social service, he believes. Fares don't match its cost, but it is the only way for many in these little pueblos along the coast to get to Tapachula. They don't have cars and many simply won't ride buses. Maybe they don't think the bus offers enough space for the things they have to carry.

But roads are essential too. He believes that roads, electricity, and telephone lines will help bring the land reform Chiapas needs. Maybe that's why the rich here have never pushed for those ameni-ties as they have elsewhere in Mexico.

When we slow for the end of the line at Hidalgo, our friendly conductor bows formally to Lourdes and tells us that he has much work to do to prepare for his return trip, when he will bring tank cars of natural gas back to Tapachula from Guatemala. Out on the platform, we are the only people in sight whose skin is lighter than ochre. Taxi service here is human-powered tricycle carts, and quickly one of these fellows assumes that we want to cross the border and offers to take us over. "I'm taking an American writer across the border," he says. "I'm going to be famous."

As it was way back at Laredo, the border here is a river, and we cross it on a traffic-clogged bridge. We have no business in Guate-mala; we just want to set foot on that side of this border to com-plete a symmetry that began back at the Río Grande seven months ago.

Traffic on the bridge is all headed, but not moving, one way, toward Guatemala. Our bicycle guy tells us that it's part of a sys-tem. Every four hours the direction of traffic flow reverses. The drivers of tanker trucks and big refrigerated rigs don't seem too concerned about the fact that they are not moving. Some of them nap in hammocks slung beneath the underframe of their rigs. One casually smokes a cigarette just a foot or so underneath his cargo of fifty thousand gallons of gasoline.

Out in the muddy river, dozens of Guatemalan families are doing their wash or just cooling off. There is a Mayan pueblo just the other side of the bridge. Our cart driver says that there is a big problem here with Guatemalan illegals. They cross this border seeking a better life for themselves or at least the chance to earn pesos, which have a very favorable exchange rate with the quetzals of Guatemala. Many support their families back home this way. I urge Lourdes to delicately suggest that this is similar to what happens at the other border to the north. The cart driver, says yes, perhaps that is true, but there is an important difference here. These Guatemalans are oppressed people, some with a violent revolutionary tendency. They come and swell the ranks of the Zapatistas and make them more crazy.

Stepping over the border is anticlimactic. The immigration officer in the little paneled booth on the Guatemalan side is perplexed by these two gringos who want to turn right around and walk back. He scratches his sweaty head as he ponders whether or not we should fill out immigration papers. The sling of his automatic rifle seems glued to his shoulder, its black barrel wet with the perspiration from his sunburned neck. Illegal immigration is a serious issue, he says (though no one would illegally immigrate this direction), and he wants us "reporters" to see that he is conscientious about his job. Finally he shrugs and gestures us back toward the border. If we're going to do this weird thing, then do it quickly and get off his watch.

A day later we are back on the train headed north from Tapachula to Tonalá, gateway to the little Chiapas resort town of Puerto Arista. The route parallels the coastline about midway between the shore and the sharply rising mountains where the

Zapatistas are ensconced. This train has never been molested, we are told by the conductor.

Though the tropical jungle here is not quite so lush as it was south of Tapachula, still Lourdes observes that she has never seen so many mango trees. Most of them are in huge orchards, but they spill out in disorderly patches across the uncultivated land. "Spit out a seed here and a tree will grow," one man tells us.

Besides fruit, the next most prolific sight along this route is the antigovernment graffiti—"Robelledo, get out," "PRI = killers," "Viva EZLN." At the stop for the pueblo of Huixtla, passengers mumble that this is a Zapatista town. At first it looks no different from any of the others, but then armed government soldiers in civilian clothes and carrying guns board the train and check baggage. Outside the train drunks sleep in hammocks and children sell sweet milk as they always would. Eventually the government soldiers leave without incident and the train rolls on.

We arrive at Tonalá after the sun has set. Its brightly lit *zócalo* is jumping with people, but we are headed out to the locals' beach resort, Puerto Arista. It's a dark cab ride on a straight-arrow road until we smell the ocean, turn right, and cruise down a totally empty beachfront street. We can see the shapes of small darkened hotels to our left and occasionally a light and a little knot of drinking men in front of a store or a work site. At our hotel a sleepy desk boy checks us in. He does not know where we might find food or drink—it's after ten. We can have any rooms we want. We are the only guests tonight.

We are hungry, so we strike out on foot down the dark street. Under an open-air *palapas* roof we see lights and tables. The family who lives here does serve food during the daylight hours, but the taciturn ageless woman in a stained white dress consents to fix us something now. She brings us beer, scrambled eggs, fried ham, beans, and a jar of vile-looking red *picante*. Puerto Arista is pretty quiet these days, she tells us. People aren't as comfortable traveling as they used to be before the trouble with the Zapatistas. Her husband sleeps in a hammock beside us through our whole mealtime.

In the morning there are still no other guests at our hotel, and we have the entire beach to ourselves but for some young local fishing fellows. As at Playa Azul, the beach is lined with now empty folding chairs before a string of little restaurants, most of them closed. But Lourdes has gotten up ahead of me and found a friendly spot for breakfast, La Puesta del Sol. The beachfront open-air *palapas* restaurant is run by a family that is this morning busily constructing an elaborate Christmas crèche scene on a table in the center of the dining area. Berta, the mother, takes time out to make us some shrimp and eggs with Mexicana sauce. Then she returns to directing operations while the three children arrange figures and Papa sculpts background landscaping materials to represent water and mountains. Puerto Arista may be too quiet for good business right now, and the Zapatistas may have everyone's nerves on edge, but the traditions of Christmas will not be neglected. On the sixteenth, the townspeople will conduct the *posada,* taking handmade figures of Mary and Joseph from house to house asking for and receiving food and shelter. On the twenty-fourth the figures will be taken to church. The miniature world of the crèche must be completed before that evening.

After breakfast we talk to a group of fishermen milling about their boat down on the beach. There are eight in this group of three interrelated families ranging in age from twelve to fifty-two. Like most of the fishermen on this coast, they are illegal—they don't yet have their permit. "It takes one thousand pesos to get a permit," one of the twenty-something fellows explains, "So everyone fishes illegally till they earn enough for the permit."

Today they have an additional frustration. Someone took the propeller from their boat, so they cannot fish. They think whoever stole it did so out of jealousy, since they have been the envy of many for their success in fishing for the *lisa,* a fish prized for its sweetness and firmness.

They will have to earn twenty-two hundred pesos to buy a new propeller, but without one they have not the means to earn that kind of money. Instead they will swim out to other boats to sell refreshments, which they will tug along on a little raft behind them. They might earn fifty pesos today doing that and don't care to even attempt the math to figure out how long it will be before they are in business again, let alone legal so they don't have to worry about the authorities taking their propellers and everything else.

When we ask about trouble from the Zapatistas, one of the older men with a grizzled Hemingway beard begs us to "tell the truth about the truth." He gestures toward the empty beach, "You see trouble here? No señor. You see vacationers here? No señor, because lying journalists have told people to stay away, that there is conflict here. Every vacationer is proud to come here; it is tranquil and beautiful."

Puerto Arista is like a ghost town. So Lourdes and I abandon our improbable scheme of learning about Chiapas from the comfort of a resort beach and relocate back to Tonalá. Its *zócalo* is screaming with the little birds seeking nighttime shelter when we arrive near sunset.

Though smaller, Tonalá has much the same feel of robust commerce as Tapachula. At a café adjacent to the *zócalo,* we meet a dignified, white-mustached man who wants to play chess. Jorge is clearly a landowner of some stature, though he playfully introduces himself as the poorest man in Tonalá.

While he beats me at chess, we discuss our mutual interest in trains. He says he has worked to reestablish good Pullman service on the Chiapas route: "It's a civilizing influence and God knows we need that." He thinks that since the train is often the only communication into some of the smaller pueblos, it was good for everyone when the well-off rode the same train as the poor, albeit in different sections. Now only the poor ride the trains.

He has an interesting explanation for why train service has fallen so badly in all parts of Mexico. "It's because of the corruption that is possible under the policy of allowing people to pay for tickets after they board the train," he says. For years corrupt conductors have pocketed the money from passengers who purchase their tickets on board. Thus the managers think there are fewer passengers and less money coming in than there really are. "So they believe there is little demand, and they have little money to run things. They draw the obvious conclusions and take appropriate actions. The train people themselves have ruined the service and sabotaged their own jobs."

He pointedly adds that that's also how it is with the Zapatistas, but he wants to save the rest of that conversation until he has told me a little about Tonalá. "We have the rich sea and even richer land here," he begins. So the economy is based mainly on beef, fruit, coffee, and fish. Mexico's best of all four products comes from Chiapas, he believes, and the reward is that Chiapas is a rich zone. There is a lot of money here. But there are problems.

"Too much of our wealth is owned by people who don't live here; that's a valid complaint. And it is true that our pesos have not been used well to give people in the remote zones services and a chance at a decent life." But the Zapatistas are like the corrupt conductors of the trains. "If they continue their actions, the train that brings the good life to Chiapas will stop coming." Already investment and commerce have suffered sharply from fears about the rebellion.

Jorge has no sympathy for the Zapatistas. "These people hiding behind ski masks have no shame, no civil valor. If they did, they would fight with their faces to the sun. It's all politics. They want Robelledo out of Chiapas; they want the PRI out of Chiapas. That's not asking for schools, water, power, infrastructure, and welfare for the children."

"Maybe they don't believe they can get those things until the PRI is out of Chiapas," I venture.

"Bullshit. They are bandits; the poor people of the pueblos will tell you that. Maybe I'm drastic in my opinion, but I think, when the illness is big, the cure must be bigger. The problem is that the whole world is watching. Just give the army a week and look somewhere else during that time."

Jorge realizes he has said too much and quietly focuses now on obliterating the remains of my weak defense on the chessboard. Meanwhile his son, a handsome fellow in a white hat, has joined us and takes our discussion of Chiapas in a new direction. "Places in Mexico are not really planned," he says. "People just show up. Fifteen to twenty people congregate in one remote space, and you have a pueblo that will need services, and it seems like a social inequity." He thinks that's okay and that society should find ways to provide those services when needed. The problem is when this little group starts to make claims on the nearby land, land that someone else has worked to cultivate. "Give them services; raise my taxes to pay for it, fine. But don't tell me I have to give them the land I have put my life into." Besides the injustice of it, he argues that it's not good for Mexico to see its bountiful lands in the hands of the unorganized campesinos. "Let's face it, the average *indio* is ignorant, a little lazy; he works only in the morning. The lands that fall into his hands will be forever less productive."

He hastens to point out that this should be a temporary situation. "The ultimate solution for Chiapas is education. Teach those campesinos how to farm efficiently and the whole equation changes. Then they will not waste the land. And then they will not need so much of it that they have to take so much of mine because they will use what they get more efficiently."

And here he and his father agree that they part company with the PRI and the government. For many years it has been more convenient for the rest of Mexico to just take the riches out of Chiapas and leave a serious social problem festering. "There has been less investment in social infrastructure here by the government than in any other state in the country. Mexico robs Chiapas as the colonials robbed Mexico. And do not forget that Chiapas was originally part of Guatemala—Texas all over again."

It was bound to happen sooner or later. Lourdes and I decide to take different routes to our next destination, Arriaga. I've spent most of seven months in Mexico now; I should be able to survive despite my absolute tone deafness with the language. She takes the bus. I, of course, take the train from Tonalá.

The first advantage of this arrangement is an opportunity for me to confirm the goodness of human nature. When I ask the taxi driver what it will cost to get to the train station I think I hear him say fifty pesos. Hmm. Train station must be far away. But after a short dusty ride of a few blocks we are there. Hmm. Well I agreed to the price. So be it. I offer him a one-hundred-peso bill, and he gestures that he can't change that. So he takes me to get change at a grocery store about as far from the train station as the hotel where I started. When the transaction with the cashier is completed and I hold forth a fifty, he shakes his head and draws out fifteen pesos from the wad in my hand. Fifteen pesos, not fifty. I shake his hand. He seems to understand my gratitude at his honesty. This will be a good day.

The train station has a nice, airy platform and a little restaurant serving *comida corrida*. The people waiting for this second-class train seem better dressed than those we've met on similar trains in other parts of the country. There is a friendly agent in the ticket office who explains to me with gestures and Spanglish that I have about a half hour till the train arrives. It is on time today.

During the wait I wander across the street, where a particularly virulent batch of antigovernment graffiti seems freshly scrawled on walls all down the block. The writing is colorful and stylized—almost like the creative gang graffiti we see in cities back in the States. I begin taking pictures of it—Lourdes can translate what it says for me later when the photos are developed.

Suddenly I feel a heavy hand seize my shoulder from behind. I turn and there stand three beefy men in civilian clothes pointing shotguns at my belly. They speak sternly and gesture for me to back off the open street and up against the wall I have just been photographing. One of them whips out a plastic credential identifying him, I assume, as an officer of the army, while another holds out his hand for my papers. As I fumble for my passport and the Spanish letter from my publisher, the third man repeats what I take to mean "Who are you and who sent you?" gesturing all the while to the graffiti and my camera, which he finally takes from me.

On seeing my American passport, they lower the guns to my knees and seem perplexed about what to do next. I shudder to think what their plans for me might have been. Still they gesture and ask, now in broken English, "Why take pictures of this?" waving their hands all the while at the graffiti. Finally I get one of them to read the letter from the publisher. The letter refers to the presence of Lourdes as well as myself and when they have finished reading it they ask, "¿Dónde está la doctora?" wondering why she is not here. The only Spanish phrase I can think of pops out, "En la playa—at the beach," and as I say it I make a sunbathing gesture. At this they suddenly melt, laugh, and hand me back my papers and my camera. With a pat on the shoulder they apologize and end with a final plaintive "Why you want to take these pictures?" Because the translator is not here, I fumble to explain, adding that I don't know what it says. Later my translator can tell me what the writing means. This makes them laugh again and shake their heads. Stupid gringo doesn't even know what he is in the midst of.

During the episode the train has arrived, but I needn't fear that it would leave without me. It must stand in the station while these same officers search for contraband. On board now, I see them come through the cars poking into people's stuff. The campesinos, the old women in particular, seem terrified of the men with the guns. On their second pass through the car they hoist several passengers' satchels on their shoulders and carry them off the train. The owners of the satchels, all women, stand in the aisles wringing their hands with grief and fear. Outside the car I see the soldiers stack their bundles with a pile of others under a tree where more soldiers mill about. The goods are not returned, and as the train pulls out of the station, the passengers' fear turns to anger. "The army is all thieves," I hear one woman say. Two of them sit and cry resignedly over what they have lost.

De la Madrid was succeeded in 1988 by Carlos Salinas de Gortari—the names and the rhetoric keep changing, the parade remains the same. But there was something new this time. Salinas, according to most Mexicans and much of the international press, lost the election. The PRI had to steal it back for him.

Within the ranks of the PRI an ambitious and unpredictable politician with a fabulous name had arisen. Cuauhtémoc Cárdenas, son of the great president, could count on the mere pronunciation of his evocative name to build a following. When de la Madrid picked Salinas as his successor, Cárdenas and a band of Priista dissidents broke with the PRI to advance his candidacy for president. Their new party, the National Democratic Front (FDN), formed a coalition with the old Mexican Socialist Party to offer Mexico's first strong leftist alternative to the PRI. The FDN rallied the support of the disenfranchised and disillusioned and put together a serious challenge to the PRI largely on the strength of that wonderful name but also because the dissidents Cárdenas took with him from the PRI were experienced politicos who knew the ropes.

For decades the PRI had been perfecting its election machine, and it had never missed a stroke. First there was the token nature of the opposition. The left was carefully splintered into the Authentic Party of the Mexican Revolution (PARM), the Popular Socialist Party (PPS), the Socialist Party of Workers (PST), the Mexican Socialist Party (PSM), the Mexican Communist Party (PCM), and others of even less significance. Most of the time these parties just barely scraped together the 2.5 percent of the vote needed to keep them on the ballot and earn them a few seats in congress. When there wasn't a sufficient number of these parties putting forth candidates and dividing one another's power, the PRI invented new ones and bankrolled them. On the right the PAN could be counted on to offer a spirited conservative alternative, but one that had rarely been a threat because the PRI itself, despite its revolutionary slogans, housed the heart of the conservative element under its big tent. And after Echeverría, the difference between the positions of PRI and PAN candidates became increasingly hard to discern.

The second mechanism in the PRI machine was its ability to reach deep into the masses through three specific branches of interest: the campesinos, labor, and the popular sector. Each was run something like the machine that kept Mayor Richard Daley in power in Chicago for so long, with patronage and the firm hand of caciques guaranteed to get out the PRI vote. Election day was a festival for PRI voters, as masses were bused at government expense to the polls, provided with food and drink, and entertained by mariachis and Priistas handing out fistfuls of pesos. As many as a fifth of the names on voter lists were of the deceased or underaged, leading to the joke that the PRI was so popular that even the dead and the children voted for them.

Finally, when things did go badly, ballot boxes containing an unfavorable count could disappear and the arithmetic of tabulation could count every PRI vote as two. In the most extreme situations, local victories by opposition candidates could be voided due to suspicion of irregularities or fraud on their part!

In 1988 Cuauhtémoc Cárdenas campaigned as a populist promising to reinstate the constitution and reestablish the program of social justice engineered by his father. He defined his platform in terms he had learned as a Priista, aiming a piece of it at each of the three traditional PRI sectors. Instead of the austerity programs favored by the PRI, Cárdenas would postpone the national debt and even cancel a part of it so that the huge drain of pesos into debt service could go back to rural schools, public health, and benefits, including land redistribution, to campesinos. Labor would be promised wage increases and truly autonomous unions. The middle class could count on honest elections, a crackdown on corruption, and government support of Mexican-owned and -operated industry. He would tell Washington to back off from Mexican and Central American affairs entirely. His campaign caught fire.

On election day the PRI machine mobilized all of its forces. Poll watchers from the opposition were harassed, voters in high-opposition regions were turned away due to "ballot shortages," ballot boxes were stuffed, and others were burned. And yet when election tallies began to come in, they were initially unfavorable to Salinas. When the trend started to appear firm, the national computerized tabulation system suddenly and mysteriously "crashed." The Electoral Commission, staffed in that election by Priistas, announced that the results would be delayed as it worked to find other ways to count the ballots. When the tally was finally announced, twenty-five thousand out of fifty-five thousand precincts were missing. After all of these irregularities, the Electoral Commission could only declare Salinas the winner with 50.36 percent of the vote, the smallest majority ever!

Many in Mexico believe that the stolen 1988 election was another watershed like the student massacre twenty years earlier. During Salinas's tenure, the PRI allowed the PAN to begin to win regional elections. But the same generosity was not extended to Cárdenas's party, now renamed the Party of Democratic Revolution (PRD). When the PRD won in Michoacán, the results were invalidated. In the two years following 1988, fifty-six members of the PRD were killed in political violence. In this bitter atmosphere, Cárdenas moved further left, abandoning, in what would prove to be a fatal move, the portions of his platform aimed at the middle class. Salinas and the PRI moved further to the right. Mexican politics were becoming polarized as never before.

Later in his term Salinas began to covet the presidency of the International Monetary Fund. To enhance his credentials he furiously embarked on grandiose new schemes financed by the IMF to revive the Mexican miracle. He declared nonexistent the problems of the poor, or in more sober moments, argued that there were limits to the extent to which government could diminish poverty. Those at the bottom of the pyramid became, under Salinas, invisible.

As the election of 1994 approached, another bubble of progressivism popped up in the froth of the PRI. Eager to demonstrate his progressive and democratic standing in his campaign for world leadership, Salinas bestowed his blessing on Luis Donaldo Colosio, who began campaigning on a relatively radical platform that had distinct echoes of the Cárdenas campaign of 1988. When Colosio was assassinated in Baja California in the spring of 1994, Mexicans everywhere had no doubt that he had moved too far too fast for the powers behind the presidency at the top of the pyramid. Perhaps to ensure that no further such embarrassments happened, Salinas named Ernesto Zedillo, a quiet, soft-spoken financial moderate, to take his place.

Meanwhile the Zapatistas in Chiapas had issued their challenge to the system, their leader, subcomandante Marcos, promising to march all the way to Mexico City before they were finished. Instead of pursuing the eradication policies of the past, this time the government said, "Let's talk." Mexicans reeled at the confusing picture of a government that they believed had just gunned down one of its own for advocating reform now sitting down to negotiate with avowed revolutionists. The PRI was losing its grip.

But Zedillo did win the election that Lourdes and I witnessed, probably genuinely. And the PRD and Cárdenas were thoroughly repudiated, most likely because of his move to the far left and his support for the Zapatistas. What did emerge out of the election was a clear surge for the PAN. Mexico now marched right in step with the new zeitgeist favoring conservative politics from Paris to Washington to Japan. And when Salinas's vaunted economic wonder crashed just before Zedillo's inauguration and then the new government took the unprecedented step of launching a prosecution against family members of the departed president in the case of the assassination of Colosio, it appeared to the many Mexicans we talked to that the PRI was on the ropes at last. The PAN would win in the next election, they told us, if Mexicans could just hold on, if the army would stay out of it, if the Zapatistas didn't spark a revolution first.

The *segunda clase* train in Chiapas is much better than the death train. It does not smell and there are lights in the fixtures. There are no pigs and chickens, though one man does have a bucket of fish and several carry bundles of produce. These people are families who work hard and simply cannot afford other means of transport. Some of the women wear very fresh prettily colored dresses and adornments in their hair. The men wear clean T-shirts, black jeans, and boots.

The ride to Arriaga is short—thus the reason Lourdes and I thought I could go it alone for this stretch. The countryside is more of what I have seen between Tapachula and Tonalá, though as we have moved north, the climate has seemed to become drier—things are less deeply green.

Restoring my equilibrium after the scrape with the men toting shotguns, this ride provokes contemplation. There will be plenty of time later on for reflection with Lourdes about what we have learned of Mexico. Now, by myself, I take stock of more personal dimensions to this latest in my series of four meanderings across the continent. Something began in the Copper Canyon, where I couldn't escape the sociologically inaccurate view that the Tarahumara were dying because they could not close the cover on the chapters of their past. It's clear to me now that I saw them that way only as a personal metaphor, because it was in the midst of their land and their story that in my own *tesquinada* I learned the right way to say good-bye to a woman I had lived with for twenty-four years, to tender peace to the daughters of that marriage, and to thus gently close the book of a personal past.

The image of the two horses I saw running under a full moon has returned again and again during these travels, and I think I am beginning to understand its significance as I watch a young man cradle his girlfriend's head in his lap while she sleeps on the train to Arriega. He gazes down at her, strokes her long black hair, and then looks out the window with a smile on his face.

When I saw that my marriage would end, I thought I might never love again. And maybe I wouldn't have, if I hadn't come to Mexico. It's not just travel-industry hype to say that the estranged foreigner can find himself reborn in this country. And now I believe that Mexico will become the place where I will renew my love with my daughters, and that somehow I will return here as a lover of a woman.

As the train slows into the Arriaga station, we pass a funeral march. A plain pine box casket rides on a flatbed truck led by a little knot of black-clad women wailing and crying. The flatbed is followed by a mariachi band playing sprightly music that seems to be out of keeping with the solemnity of the event. Following the band are maybe twenty or thirty men, dressed in black suits, who look extremely hot and uncomfortable. Trailing the spectacle, small children and dogs skip about the street, objects of disapproving glances from the men in the last rows of the procession.

Just before the station, the train passes a military encampment, with machine guns set up behind sand-bag emplacements, and when we stop, plainclothes soldiers carrying guns board. I detrain inconspicuously, keeping my camera tucked in my bag.

I meet up with Lourdes at the bus station. She is upset at my misadventure and feels guilty that she wasn't there to help me out. But soon we are on board one of those excellent air-conditioned Mercedes-Benz first-class buses enjoying the spectacular ride over the mountains to the capital of Chiapas, Tuxtla Gutiérrez, where we have an air reservation to fly us out of Chiapas one day ahead of the deadline Marcos has just today set for hostilities to resume if negotiations aren't settled.

The road winds up a deep canyon, with thousand-foot drops just beyond the pavement and the blue Pacific back behind us. At the top of the cordillera, it is hot and piney. We see several campesinos with burros carrying huge bundles of piñon wood for cooking fires. There are little ranches and an occasional cow but mostly dense forest—the western edge of the Zapatistas' abode. This bus has been held up during its night runs, but there is never any trouble during the daylight, says our driver. And indeed the ride is uneventful—just a display of rugged mountain scenery and placid little tableaus of people getting on with the business of mountain living.

Tuxtla Gutiérrez is a booming city compared to anywhere else we have been in Chiapas. It has the cosmopolitan feel of cities farther to the north, though it is hotter, and the *zócalo* foliage seems like the remnants of jungle. "Oh yes, Tuxtla is cosmopolitan. There are two airports here," says one of three men who ask us to join their table at the open-air Trattoria San Marco, just off the *zócalo*. They are an interesting group: one has long hair and the tough-eyed look of a drug dealer, the second has his head shaved like a skinhead, and the third sports a magnificently bushy salt-and-pepper mustache. They are intellectuals, in their robust thirties, and do not offer their names since they intend to tell us things they would not like to see attributed to them under the current political climate—call them señores Longhair, Skinhead, and Mustache.

When we relate what others have already told us about the situation in Chiapas, señor Mustache says we have been missing the point. The issue is not services, nor is it really land. It is hunger and the fact that the hungry people in Chiapas are from a culture that is not Mexican. It is Mayan, not Nuahtl, and has nothing to do with the historic word "Mexico." "The landowners will tell you the issue is services because that's something they think can be given to the people with no loss to the elite. The rebels will say the issue is land because when they take it they have something to show for their efforts. But you don't know Chiapas unless you have seen that the people are starving in a land of plenty. And they are people who are not part of the 'Mexican family' so that's why they are left to starve."

Skinhead says he knows these people well. He used to import them as labor to the ranches of Culiacán. He would take whole families, husband, wife, and children over the age of thirteen, to harvest tomatoes, cucumbers, and chilies. He also has seen first-hand why the rest of Mexico so often rejects them. He had to end his business because Culiacán ranchers complained that his workers didn't speak Spanish and didn't work hard enough. "Maybe they work at a different pace from Mexicans elsewhere, but they will do work that no one else will do. Hungry people will do anything to feed themselves and their families."

Tuxtla has seen a rise in crime and prostitution as desperate people from the countryside have been drawn by its false promises of work. "If we really had a government that cared about creating jobs for people, there would be no hunger. It is a crime that there is hunger in such a land of abundance, and why? Because of greed.

He who prospers has not yet transcended his desire to have more than his share."

Señor Longhair interjects that it is also a question of racism, and he lists the various indigenous Mayan groups that are the objects of prejudice: the Tzotzil, the Chol, the Tzeltan, the Tojolabal, the Mame, the Lacendon, the Zoque, the Mixe, and Oxacay. It is a catalog of the deprived, he says, and the solidarity that could be created by their exclusion makes them a potentially dangerous foe to the establishment.

But señor Skinhead does not agree with this last point. "The rebellion that is going on now is just a flash fire," he says. "We have seen this happen over and over again in our history. It is part of a myth of redemption that actually helps to preserve the status quo." Every few decades, he believes, there is some rebellious outbreak in some part of the country that offers a false hope for change. "Twenty-five years ago there was a surge like this in Guerrero. It's a political mythology. The least informed then will go with whatever is the latest passing movement. If you really want justice by the year 2010, he who claims justice will have to fight tons of iron. None of this talking and negotiating. None of this easy false hope that comes along every twenty-five, every hundred years."

Surprisingly all three of our radical lunch comrades have a very dim view of the Zapatistas and their leader Marcos. Señor Skinhead goes on to argue that Marcos is just a mercenary in the service of political causes. "Since last January Marcos has said his fight is with the national army. Who's in the national army? People like me, who have been drafted. Since then I haven't given him any credit. I can remember before, when I was twenty-five years old and I believed the myth of redemption. Brave souls would face down the errors of the government, and the country would rediscover its revolutionary soul. But this guy is such a coward he hides his face. So on December eighth I shaved my head because it's more honest for a citizen to shave his head than for them to wear their masks. When they turn their faces to the sun and are prepared to die facing the iron that cannot be redeemed, then I will grow my hair." Skinhead is perhaps the only Mexican we have talked with who advocates what everyone fears so much—total confrontation—the real revolutionary thing.

As we ride in the taxi to catch our plane at the airport, Lourdes translates for me the lead article in the newspaper, "Uno más uno." The government and the EZLN are talking, but there are eleven rebel demands that cannot be met, topped by the removal of Robelledo and the installation of a non-PRI state government. Sources on the rebel side say that hostilities *may* begin in forty-eight hours if progress is not made. Sources on the government side say that hostilities *will* begin in forty-eight hours if no progress is made. It's an interesting distinction that prods us to read between the lines as Mexicans do. Apparently the government is more intent on creating a sense of impending disaster than are the rebels and their PRD allies.

A side article explains that in the meantime the governments of Mexico and Guatemala have been discussing how to prevent a linkup between the EZLN and the URNG, the revolutionary army of Guatemala. There are rumors that trouble has already begun at a ranch in Las Margaritas. "It's getting hot here, isn't it," Lourdes says to our cab driver.

"Maybe," he answers. But he concurs that it seems to be part of the government's strategy to create an air of imminent crisis. We ask him about the curious fact that of all the people we have talked to—intellectuals and ordinary people as well as landowner types—none seem to show support for the Zapatistas, despite agreeing with many of their aims. "It's because of the masks," he says. "People don't think it's the Mexican way when your aims are noble and honest. Bandits wear masks."

When we arrive at the airport, we discover that we have made a horrendous mistake. There is no flight to Mexico City from this airport—Tuxtla has two and the flight departs from the other one.

We speed off to the other airport, arriving ten minutes after the scheduled departure of our plane. There is a 727 whining out on the tarmac behind the terminal and starting to move. Lourdes bounds out of the taxi and disappears into the terminal. I follow and see several airport officials running out toward the tarmac. Soon Lourdes returns with one of them and gestures for me to follow quickly. Along with another man who has arrived late for the flight, we clamber past the baggage counter and out to the tarmac where the rear steps to the plane have been lowered. We climb on board, collapsing in our seats, and soon we are off, Tuxtla shrinking in the landscape below us.

When Lourdes has caught her breath I ask, "How did you do that?"

She is modest and says it was nothing, just a matter of speaking to the right official. "I just kept asking, 'Who's in charge?' and when the airport manager arrived I said, 'It's not your fault, and it's not my fault. But there will be less problems if you get us on that plane.'" The underlings had all said no and tried to have her arrested as she stood in front of the 727. The man in charge said yes.

Throughout our time in Chiapas we were aware that Marcos and the leadership of the EZLN had previously been notorious in their desire to communicate with visiting journalists. But in the weeks we traveled the region, things were too tense to make any contacts—Marcos was not in a communicating mode, and those who could have put us in touch with representatives of the EZLN were particularly fearful. But we left word wherever we went of our desire to know more.

Three months after this journey, Lourdes received Marcos's Communiqué Number One on the Internet at her office at Keene State College—the first of a series of letters sent to foreign journalists over the next few months. Talks had broken down, a government offensive had been launched into the Zapatista strongholds, and Marcos was being hunted in the mountains. Here is what he wrote.

A Letter from Marcos—3/17/95

There exists on this planet called "Earth" and in the continent called "America" a country whose shape appears to have had a big bite taken out of its east side, and which threw out an arm deep into the Pacific Ocean so that the hurricanes don't blow it from its history. This country is known to both natives and foreigners by the name of Mexico. Its history is a long battle between its desire to be itself and the foreign desires to have it exist under another flag. This country is ours. We, our blood in the voices of our oldest grandparents, we walked this land when it was not yet known by this name.

We were born between blood and gunpowder, between blood and gunpowder we were raised. Every so often the powerful from other lands came to rob us of tomorrow. For this reason it is written in a war song that unites us: "If a foreigner ever dares to profane with his foot your dream, think, oh beloved motherland, that heaven gave you a soldier in each son." For this reason we fought yesterday. With flags and different languages the foreigner came to conquer us. He came and went. We continued being Mexicans because we weren't happy with any other name or with walking under any other flag that does not have the eagle devouring a snake, on a white background between red and green.

We, the first inhabitants of these lands, the indigenous, we were left forgotten in a corner, and the rest began to grow and become stronger. We had only our history with which to defend ourselves, and we seized it in order not to die. Later this part of the country became a joke because a single country, the country of money, put itself in the middle of all of the flags. And they said, "Globalization," and then we knew that this was what this absurd order was to be called—an order in which money is the only country that is served and borders are erased, not out of brotherhood, but because of the impoverishment that fattens the powerful without nationality.

The lie became the universal coin, and in our country, a dream, based on the nightmare of the majority, of wealth and prosperity knitted for the few. Corruption and falsehoods were the principal products that our motherland exported to other countries. Being poor, dressed in the wealth of scarcities, and because there were so many lies and they were so broad, we ended up thinking they were the truth. We prepared for the international forums, and poverty was declared, by the will of the government, as an invention that had vanished in the face of the development that the economic statistics shouted.

But we, the indigenous Mexicans, became even more forgotten, and now our history wasn't enough to keep us from dying just like that, forgotten and humiliated. Dying does not hurt. What hurts is to be forgotten. We discovered then that we did not exist anymore, that those who govern had forgotten about us in their euphoria of statistics and rates of growth. A country that forgets itself is a sad country; a country that forgets its past cannot have a future.

And so, we took up arms and we went into the cities where we were considered animals. We went and we told the powerful, "We are here!" and to all of the country we shouted, "We are here!" and to all of the world we yelled, "We are here!" And they saw how things were because, in order for them to see us, we covered our faces; so that they would call us by name, we denied our given names. We wagered the present to have a future, and to live . . . we died.

And then the planes came and the bombs and the bullets

and the death, and we went back to our mountains and even there death pursued us. And many people from many parts said, "Talk," and the powerful said, "Let's talk," and we said, "Okay, let's talk." And we talked and we told them what we wanted and they did not understand very well, and we repeated that we wanted democracy, liberty, and justice, and they made a face like they didn't understand, and they reviewed the points of their macroeconomic plans and all their neoliberal points, and they could not find the words anywhere. "We don't understand" they said to us, and they offered us a prettier corner in the history museum, and death with an extended time line, and a chain of gold in order to tie up our dignity.

And we, so that we ourselves could understand what we asked, began to create in our own lands what we wanted. We organized based on the agreement of the majority, and we demonstrated what it was like to live with democracy, with liberty, and with justice.

We were doing this, making our own mistakes, learning, when the tanks and the helicopters and the planes and the many thousands of soldiers arrived, and they said that they came to defend the national sovereignty. We told them that national sovereignty could not be defended by trampling the rebel dignity of the Chiapas indigenous. And they did not listen because the noise of their war machines made them deaf and they came in the name of the government, where betrayal is the ladder by which one comes to power. The legality of the government came mounted on bayonets, and our legality was based on consensus and reason. We wanted to convince and the government wanted to conquer, and we said that no law that had to resort to arms to be fulfilled could be called a law, so that he who orders the fulfillment of a law by the force of weapons is a dictator even if he says that the majority elected

338

him. And we were run out of our lands. With the war tanks came the law of the government, and behind the war tanks came again prostitution, drinking, theft, drugs, destruction, death, corruption, sickness, poverty.

And people from the government came and saw all this and said they had restored law in the Chiapas lands. They came with bulletproof vests to step out of their tanks, and they were there only a few minutes, with just enough time to make their pronouncements in front of the chickens and roosters and pigs and dogs and cows and horses and a cat that had gotten lost. That's how the government did it, and reporters from the rest of the world saw it and verified for you that it was true. This is the legality and national sovereignty that rules in our land now. The government also waged war against the rest of the Mexicans, but elsewhere, instead of planes and tanks, they launched an economic program that will kill them just as dead, just more slowly.

And now I remember that I am writing on Saint Patrick's Day, and when Mexico was fighting in the last century against the empire of the bars and crooked stars, there was a group of soldiers from different nationalities who fought on the side of the Mexicans and this group was called the Saint Patrick's Battalion. For this reason the compañeros *said to me: "Go on, take this opportunity to write to the brothers from other countries and thank them because they stopped the war." And I believe that this is their way of getting to go dancing—they keep me busy writing so that I don't yell at them, because the government plane is wandering around there and all these* compañeros *want to do is dance, dance, dance to the marimba even with danger all around them.*

And so I am writing to you in the name of all my compañeros *and* compañeras, *because just as with the Saint Patrick's Battalion, we now see clearly that there are foreigners who love Mexico more than some natives who are now in the government and will tomorrow be in some jail or in exile— natives whose heart belongs to foreign flags that are not theirs and whose thinking is not of their equals. And we learned that there were marches and songs and movies about peace in Chiapas, the part of Mexico where we live and die. And we learned that "NO TO WAR!" was said in Spain and in France and in Italy and in Germany and in Russia and in England and in Japan and in Korea and in Canada and in the United States, Argentina, Uruguay, Chile, Brazil, and other places where it was thought but not said. So we have learned that there are good people in the world who live closer to Mexico than those who live in the house of the government.*

We want to say to you, to everyone, thank you. And that if we had a flower, we would give it to each of you, and since we don't have enough flowers, we can offer this so that each person can say in their older years when they talk with the young children of their countries, "I struggled for Mexico back at the end of the twentieth century, and from over here I was with them, and I only know that they wanted what all human beings want—for it not to be forgotten that they are human beings and for it to be remembered what democracy, liberty, and justice are. Maybe I did not know their faces but I did know their hearts, and they were the same as ours."

And when Mexico is free (which is not to say happy or perfect) then a piece of you all and these letters will represent dignity, and then the flower will be for everyone or it will not exist at all. Now it occurs to me that with this letter, a paper flower could be made and worn in the lapel or hair, and you could go dancing with this adornment. Now I must go because the surveillance plane comes again and I have to put out the candle, but not the hope. Not even dead will I give up the hope.

Good-bye . . . Health and a promised flower: a green stem, a white bloom, red leaves, and don't worry about the serpent. This that flaps its wings is an eagle that subdues it. You will see.

Like yesterday's train, the political regime of today's Mexico always arrives too late, and when it does, it is not the train that people want to ride. But it keeps coming simply because it has been the only train on the tracks; it owns the tracks; it has been the sole conveyance for so long that people fear the turmoil of changing trains. But in Chiapas the Zapatistas of the left are ready to rip up the tracks, and elsewhere the PANistas of the right seem poised to lay new ones, promising trains that run on time. Everyone waits in fear and hope of what approaches under a smoke cloud on the horizon. Is it tomorrow's train? Or a whirlwind of fire? Beneath the serpent and the eagle, the eternal cactus imperceptibly sways beside the tracks in the hot Mexican breeze.

Epilogue
The Return of Quetzalcóatl

After reading headlines at home in the United States about the installation and the promises of the new Zedillo government, the devaluation of the peso, President Clinton's economic bailout of the Mexican economy, the de facto exile of Salinas now under suspicion for complicity in the murder of Colosio, the victories of the PAN in state elections, and the letter from Marcos, Lourdes and I returned to see for ourselves what was happening at the center of Mexico in the late spring of 1995. We didn't ride trains at all this time; like Mexicans abandoning the PRI, we felt that yesterday's vehicle had taken us as far as it could.

It is hotter in Mexico City and more polluted than it has ever been on our previous visits. The political banners from last summer's elections are finally gone, and prices for taxi rides, rooms, and meals have finally been adjusted to reflect the devaluation of the peso. Our taxi driver taking us from the airport to the María Cristina says that Zedillo hasn't got a prayer of changing the pattern of

342

the presidency: "His hands are tied." Meanwhile people will pull their belts tighter and wait out the six years until the PAN wins in the next elections. They have already won in Jalisco (Guadalajara) and are expected to win in Guanajuato, Baja California, and maybe even Yucatán in a few weeks.

We make our first excursion of this journey to the posh streets of the Zona Rosa. No sign of economic crisis here. At the fashionable Angus sidewalk restaurant, the scantily clad waitresses are just as voluptuous as ever, and the yuppie businessmen who frequent the place flash just as much money as before. At the table next to us, two middle-aged men dressed in dark suits discuss their yachts and investing in marinas. A younger fellow with a briefcase and a *New York Times* under his arm strolls the place eyeing the waitresses. A foursome descends the stairs from the reserved rooms inside lit with the afterglow of buying and selling the world. There are cellular phones all around us, and out on the sidewalk I notice a surreptitious drug deal go down between two impeccably dressed men who approach each other and make a smooth transfer of one briefcase for another without saying a word. We are not going to find any of the truth of Mexico here. Madison Avenue seems to find ways to thrive whatever the climate.

For a different perspective we go to the train station to talk to señor Leonardo Rafael Aguilar, the manager of Passenger Services for FNM who has been so helpful to us during the past year. He is a tired, balding man with bags under his eyes and the look of one who is fatigued from plugging the holes in the dike. The passenger service limps along he tells us, though mixed passenger-freight trains have all been cut. Austerity measures are being taken while the talk of privatization continues and the railroads are not well taken care of. Rail employees are especially hurt by the economic crisis; they can't earn more with overtime and their wages cannot be raised. Anyone who makes less than thirty pesos a day has adopted the "forced diet"—beans and corn, just like in the old days. No rail workers have been laid off yet, but that is coming. Señor Aguilar's own job is not secure.

"Mexico is boiling with dissatisfaction," he says, and it's dangerous. The papers tell of bank robberies and muggings every day. "The more revolution there is, the less stable things will be and the worse it will become." In his opinion, those with good sense are stoic: "We have to wait—just wait."

The climate of diminished expectations has affected his own family. His oldest son, an engineer for Honeywell, believes there is no stability in marriage during these times, so he is not interested in starting a family. The two daughters, who work at a bank, do not want to bring children into this world when life is so hard. And these young people have decent jobs; how must it be for those who don't?

"We have to help them to do better than we have done," he says. "If we can't help materially, at least we can spiritually. We can offer love and stability in our families. But it's hard in a time of world-wide corruption and loss of values. It's not just Mexico."

His hope is that nothing is eternal. "Look at what happened to the communists of eastern Europe. We need that kind of renewal on this continent."

But there are voices that are not so restrained. Several times during our return to Mexico City we hear a rumor that Zedillo and his attempted reforms will have two years and then he will be "disappeared." In one scenario it is the PRI who will do away with him for threatening the status quo. In another, it will be the people, as retribution for his inevitable failure to effect change.

We go to a restaurant called L'Opera, known as a hangout for political types, hoping for a chance to talk to players in the current political world—and we get very lucky. After showing us the famous bullet hole in the ceiling, allegedly the result of a burst of Pancho Villa's revolutionary enthusiasm, and cataloguing the other heroes of revolution, sport, film, culture, and politics (all of the presidents but Zedillo) who have dined here, the maître d' gestures to a booth across the room where he says a pair of very important, very strange table mates dine regularly and are doing so right now. The suave-looking man in the brown suit is Pedro Peñaloza, head of the Human Rights Task Force of the PRD. The blue-suited man sitting with him is PRI deputy Rafael Luviano. They are well-known as friends, despite their political differences. We ask the maître d' if he might arrange for us to speak to them and he demurs, "They are very special, señor."

It doesn't take long for Lourdes to cross the room and strike up a conversation with Peñaloza, and soon she is gesturing for me to follow. They invite us to sit; we exchange smokes and order drinks. At first the conversation is mostly little teasing barbs between the two friends. Peñaloza: "Politics is a science where there are apparent friends and true enemies." Luviano: "Pedro looks so healthy, but the politician who isn't worn down is worn down."

They explain that their friendship has raised eyebrows; no, this is not a common thing in Mexico, where politics is personal and nasty. They endure jokes and innuendos; newspaper photographers love to snap them together at soccer matches. But they insist that besides their friendship, which goes back to childhood, they have a camaraderie based on their fight, in different forums, for the life of a city. Rafael sees his role as a voice of conscience within the PRI. Pedro sees his as a voice of civil moderation in the PRD. Ironically, though it is Pedro whose office and party affiliation are identified with the issue of human rights, it is Rafael, a young progressive in the PRI and former newspaper reporter, who has had personal experience with the jackboot.

One early morning in his former life as a reporter, he was returning from an all-night meeting, driving "a little over the speed limit" in the inner circle of the Mexico City freeway system. When the officer pulled him over, he leaned in the window and said, "Get out, because it will be worse for you if you don't." He then asked for documents and Rafael's license was expired. "It is common for people to drive around with expired licenses in Mexico City," he explains. "The bureaucracy for getting renewals is terrible." Still, the expired license combined with the speeding infraction were enough to put Rafael beyond the pale of a routine encounter with the law.

One cop got in Rafael's car and the other followed as they drove to a lonely factory yard. Once there, the officer asked, "What do you do?" When Rafael identified himself as a reporter, things turned ugly. "So you're a fucking reporter," the cop sneered, and he ordered Rafael out of the car. The cop in the cruiser stepped out with his pistol drawn. "Where are your drugs, your arms?" he demanded. When Rafael protested that he didn't have such things, they conducted an angry search of the car, confiscating his money, his watch, and his car stereo.

When Rafael resisted the taking of his money, the beating began in earnest, with the butt of the pistol, breaking Rafael's skull and his facial bones. Afterward, the police dumped him in the backseat and said, "If you even raise your hand, you die, you shitty newspaper man." And with that they left, laughing as they pulled away in the cruiser, taking his keys.

Rafael staggered bleeding through the early morning streets for an hour before he found a sympathetic cabby who would drive him to the hospital. There he waited eight hours for treatment, his condition suggesting that he was an unsavory character again outside the realm of normal consideration. During his long recovery, he suffered from ulcers, stress, and cranial problems. He is partially blind to this day.

But shortly after his ordeal he founded an organization called the Commission for Citizens' Defense and his case earned celebrity as a well-documented instance of something ordinary Mexicans knew happened all the time. Several years later he joined the PRI.

"There is no other party that both satisfies my views and allows access to the machinery that can promote change," he explains. "There are lots like me in the PRI these days."

We ask if that makes today's PRI a fractured party, and Pedro jumps in with an answer. Though he has spent twenty-six years of his life fighting against the PRI, he has a special place in his heart for Rafael and others like him who are trying to work within it. "What happens in the PRI is this. The PRI began when the generals of the revolution were still shooting. Their rifles were still smoking from bullets fired at each other as much as at the Díaz government. After defeating Carranza, Obregón and Calles created the PRI with two goals: to institutionalize and thus confirm the revolution, and to join the factions it created and thus to end it." Pedro believes that ambiguous birth has condemned the PRI to eternal schizophrenia ever since. It is a party of revolution born within the womb of the state. It is a platform for words about democracy and justice committed in its action to perpetuating the monolithic structure of society.

The crisis of the PRI, Pedro believes, is the crisis of the political model it follows. The killing of Colosio demonstrated all of its aspects. "Colosio proposed the elements of a truly modern, revolutionary party. One, he wanted to break with the logic of the imperial Mexican presidency, to end the vertical power with which the president could act within the PRI. Two, he called for a rupture between the PRI and the powerful Mexican corporations and the creation of truly free unions. Three, he committed to finally dealing honestly with social inequity." He would have been one hell of a PRI candidate for the PRD to try to campaign against. But the gerontocrats in the PRI made that unnecessary when they decided to kill him. He was simply too much of a challenge to an old system that was not yet ready to die.

What Colosio attempted was almost mythic in proportion. As Pedro explains, "He called for a break in the paternalism that has made the conscience of all Mexicans to wait for everything to come from the top down. It's the dark side of our Aztec inheritance, where everything that matters—life and death—happens in obscurity at the top of the pyramid."

Pedro says that while the current PRI does not seem to be openly fractured, it does have many currents and only a semblance of party solidarity. "The difference between the PRI and the PRD is that the PRD speaks the truth publicly, while the PRI kick each other under the table." He likens the situation in the PRI to that in Russia under Stalin. Stalin used to say, "If you speak evil of the Soviet regime, then you are playing into the hands of the imperialists." The PRI has similar unwritten laws. "He who moves will have a blurry picture in the photograph. He who moves too fast, like Trotsky or Colosio, will disappear from the photograph altogether."

Pedro pauses to drink and to light another cigarette, and Rafael now offers his critique of the PRD. He would like to see it have a lot more people like Pedro. "It has its own factions and big stigmas that prevent it from being the force that it could be." Namely, he says, the cults of personality that surround presidential candidate Cuauhtémoc Cárdenas and party president Muñoz Ledo. "It's almost like how Stalin became bigger than what his party stood for. And it has impeded the left from holding forth a true vision, an ideal for Mexico."

We ask what has happened since 1988, when Cárdenas and the PRD were so strong, and Pedro answers. "There were two contradictory moments. When Cárdenas broke with his former membership in the PRI and created the PRD, he embodied the possibility of real change, and the disastrous previous government made it all possible." At that time, Pedro believes, you could describe Cárdenas as a "pacific democrat." That's what people wanted, "The blood was already paid with the million who died in the revolution—people wanted change without instability. They wanted a new deal without inflammatory rhetoric." But after 1988, perhaps because the election had been stolen from him, Cárdenas moved further to the left to discourse that was incendiary. Personal hatred between Cárdenas and Salinas made it worse. Cárdenas distanced himself from the urban middle-class masses and focused on the poorest at the marginal sections of the society—the time-honored means for political gain. And so he came to be seen as "political" in the sense that Lourdes and I have heard so often. With that he lost the intellectuals and the middle class.

Rafael jumps in here. He liked Cárdenas himself at one time and thought he would change things. "But I saw the erosion of personality; everyone saw it [Pedro nods in agreement], and now he was just a politician who dragged along the ghost of his father."

Lourdes asks why all of this seems to be benefiting the right-wing PAN. Rafael answers that the PAN is inheriting the conservative tendency still left over from the last century. "People say, 'The PAN takes the water to the mill.' It's like the Nazis making the trains run on time; that's what people expect of the PAN." He and Pedro both agree that we shouldn't look at the PAN as a purely Mexican phenomenon. It is just this country's version of something that is happening in the United States and in many parts of the world. Rafael says, "The so-called center-right emerges because there is a crisis in the models of the traditional party system." He thinks that the fall of communism in eastern Europe has presented the rest of the world with this crisis, eliminating its point of reference for left and right, calling into question the terms "conservative," "liberal," and "revolutionary." The tension between Western democratic liberalism and revolutionary Marxism that was carved out during the cold war has evaporated. "What is left?" Rafael asks rhetorically. "Just the conservatives who have always been there knowing exactly what they stood for."

All of this discussion has taken place in a plush red velvet and hardwood booth, with mirrors on the walls and crystal chandeliers overhead. Waiters scurry about serving coffee and drinks while fashionably dressed men and women come and go. Lourdes and I point this out, and ask "What about the Zapatistas scrabbling around for survival and recognition down in the jungle of Chiapas?"

It is the only question of the entire conversation that seems to make the two friends uneasy. Pedro gives Rafael a look, fiddles with his cigarette, and answers that the Zapatistas are important. "They remind us this will all pass; the president's term is only six years, but the stars are forever. Only history will remember." But, despite the fact that the PRD openly supports the aims of the EZLN, he and Rafael are both mainstream party members, committed to stability and the renouncing of bloodshed. The Zapatistas are right, Pedro believes, but Mexico must not descend into civil war. Pedro reminds us of one of Colosio's most famous sayings: "We didn't inherit this world from our parents, and they didn't inherit it for us. Our children have lent it to us. Our children do not want war."

Not that it isn't difficult to remain committed to working within the peaceful political system, Rafael reminds us. Pedro agrees and adds that some people think the politician is a being sent down from some distant planet. "But we are like everyone else; we have jealousies; we are passionate and loving and have lived with a chain of defeats. But we are human beings who have made our own sacrifices."

Rafael says politics for the sincere is a personal sacrifice. He is always motivated by a saying—he does not know where it comes from—"The clarity you bring to the streets is the darkness you bring to your home."

Lourdes and I spend our last day in Mexico City in the company of Pedro Miguel, the leftist intellectual we met in Veracruz way back at the start of these journeys. As an editor at *La Jornada* and collaborator on a video documentary about the EZLN, he is well positioned to elucidate an alternative view for us. But first he insists on initiating us into his vision of Mexico. It begins with lunch at La Fonda don Chon, a restaurant serving exclusively pre-Hispanic food. The place is a hole-in-the-wall in the crowded streets of the barrio La Merced run by a very fat, very dark, and very slow-moving man who Pedro says is the last of the great Aztec chefs.

"This is how our true ancestors ate," he tells us as he orders a six-course meal consisting of fried worms with guacamole, fried grasshoppers with hot red sauce, a lizard fish *(pejelagarto)* paté on crackers, armadillo meatballs with mango sauce, tuna wrapped in mums with *guanábana* sauce, and boar sausage with hot green sauce. Lourdes likes it all, though I would have been happier without the first and last courses—the worms' insides tasted to me like soap, and the boar sausage was extremely gamy. Otherwise I found the lizard fish and the armadillo meatballs to be absolutely delicious.

During the meal, Lourdes and I summarize for Pedro Miguel the conversation with the two politicos, and he seizes on the comment about the parallel between today's regime and the dark side of the Aztec past as the truest of their words. Those who run things believe that the myth of monolithic, orderly power at the top of the pyramid must be perpetuated. But it's not there anymore. "The pyramid is cracked; there have been three political assassinations since we last talked in Veracruz. Everyone looks at the Colosio episode as some kind of aberration. It wasn't. It's the way things are now that the mantle of legitimacy as been peeled off the top of the pyramid."

Pedro Miguel believes that the government now cannot tell the truth about anything even if it wanted to. No one would believe them. He doubts even the "new candor" about Salinas's brother's involvement in the assassination of Colosio. It happened in Baja California, a state where the opposition was on the ascendancy and the local PRI leaders were furious with him. "It's quite possible that it was a local conspiracy with no connection to the top because there is no longer any control from the top. But because the PRI must perpetuate the Aztec myth of vertical control, and because people would probably have thought that placing the blame on local renegades was merely a whitewash by the people at the top, now the new people at the top say the old people at the top did it."

After lunch Pedro Miguel takes us for a walk to the *zócalo* and the Templo Mayor. Paved right over the ruins Cortés made of the central plazas of Tenochtitlán, this place remains what it has always been—the heart of the Mexican nation. Today there are three demonstrations in support of various indigenous groups struggling to gain title to their *ejido* lands. There is also a loud protest against human rights abuses with two men and two women speaking into bullhorns as children carry banners painted on bedsheets. In the corner of the *zócalo* that opens to the site of the Templo Mayor a block away, several groups perform spontaneous tribal dances, drums thrumming. Urban Mexicans pause to watch, and occasionally the free-spirited join right in with this celebration of their ancient roots.

At the Templo Mayor, we see how the ruins still reveal the key pattern of the pre-Hispanic world: The foundations show four concentric layers of temples, each built to enclose the previous structure. Crowds of Mexico City residents lean against the railings surrounding the site and just gaze. Those nearest us are happy to join in Pedro's description of how this or that layer represented a particular phase in Aztec history. Across the walkway from the Templo Mayor towers the National Cathedral, built by the Spanish to replace all that pagan culture. Pedro points out that the stones out of which the colonials built their edifices are the very fragments of the Aztec temples they tore down. In places the cathedral is tilted, the result of Mexico City's notorious earthquakes, but still it dominates as the colonials meant it to—a new layer, built out of the stuff of the old.

Back in the main *zócalo*, I ruminate that it would be something to dig up all of the Aztec ruins beneath our feet. Pedro Miguel is bemused by this blithe American who would rip up the *zócalo*.

"There is no need," he says. "We know everything that is under there and just where it is." The *zócalo* itself, with the history that has paraded across it and continues to work itself out this very day, is the central symbol of the nation. We stand for a few moments before the balcony of the Presidential Palace and imagine the leaders of Mexico's now institutionalized revolutions stirring the huge crowds that have jammed this vast space. "Will the new president, Zedillo, command that kind of power in his quest to change the fundamental nature of the system?" we ask.

"No way," says Pedro Miguel, shaking his head. Despite his noble pronouncements and possible noble intentions, Zedillo is a cipher in what will happen to Mexico now, Pedro believes. "The old rules that gave the president so much power in the past didn't exist anymore when Zedillo took office. There was no transfusion of power this time, not only because Salinas is a son of a bitch, but because there was such a crisis in Chiapas and internally in the PRI." With the exception of Echeverría, outgoing Mexican presidents have traditionally begun turning the reins over to their successors long before the day of inauguration. "That didn't happen this time because Salinas was so fearful of danger to himself."

Salinas broke the rules by holding on to power too long—for his own safety and for the sake of his global ambitions. Because he wanted to be president of the International Monetary Fund, he needed to keep his public image on the front page. So Zedillo was angry and paid him back with the unofficial exile in which Salinas now finds himself, and the charges of his family's involvement in the Colosio slaying.

Like others we have talked to, Pedro Miguel concedes that there has always been rancor between the incoming and outgoing president—that's part of the myth of the PRI being the party of institutional revolution. "But never has there been this public rupture. And never in the context of a time when the political system no longer is a representation of society."

I ask him to clarify what he means by that last statement; I have heard it and been puzzled by it before. He explains that the PRI was once an accurate model of Mexican history and social structure. Like the Aztec monarchies, there was absolute, almost deified power in the presidency at the top of the pyramid. But like the Aztec pyramids, the rest of the party beneath the president consisted of layers on layers that successfully co-opted all of the political alternatives. There was leftist socialism in the state-owned industries and official sympathy for revolutionary states such as Cuba. There was classic liberalism in the government programs for education and the open (if not honest) elections. There was a rightist element in the government's connections to the church, to Spain, to the big landowners and the corporate bosses. And there was ardent nationalism embracing all three elements. "Now all of that is blown away in cynicism, but real alternatives embodying those different politics have yet to emerge. And the PRI itself has only two wings—the dinosaurs and the democrats like Colosio and your friend Rafael."

Pedro Miguel holds little hope for the pacific democrats. "They believe Mexico can be somehow as orderly as say, Nebraska. They have a mentality that thinks Mexico's problem is its history and traditions. Salinas was once such a liberal. But to hold to his beliefs, he had to convince himself that the Indians do not exist anymore."

Eventually he believes the PRI will have to fall. The wars at the top have already doomed it—wars of political interest, wars over the future of the country, wars over ideology, wars over the economic crisis, and wars over the war in Chiapas. He thinks that one of the last two will be the decisive factor and hopes it is a crash of the economic system that will bring about change. That could make for a relatively peaceful revolution. But if the fall grows out of the war in Chiapas, it will mean war for the country.

We ask why the economic revolution is the best hope. "Because it involves global interests," he answers. "Mexico has been a laboratory for a great global experiment in economics; I mean NAFTA and all that. When it fails, as it already is doing, Mexicans may find solidarity in their traditional stance against foreign hegemony."

Why is Chiapas so dangerous? "Because the challenge of the Zapatistas is that the enemies are here at home—that the bad economics are the result of decisions by Mexican powers. And that those powers have trashed the fundamental values of the Mexican nation and the revolution—the communitarian society, the indigenous, spiritual identity, and the revolutionary promise of land for all."

Pedro Miguel is not optimistic about peace. He knows the Zapatistas well enough to know that they are the real revolutionary thing and that they are the only ones speaking the truth. Despite their differences, Zedillo and Salinas together have taken Mexico down a pathway that is alien to its very nature. Meanwhile no one has any faith in any remnant of the system. Like Mexicans in all walks of life that we have talked to, he fears revolutionary violence. "If we don't find a believable political solution true to our Mexican souls, things will be really bloody. The truth of Mexico is emerging and the real truth is dangerous," he says. "It makes the nightmares of the past seem like prophecies of the future."

In a country where the truth is dangerous and is so hidden behind masks and layers of myth and false history, it is a daunting task for visiting foreigners to draw conclusions. But Lourdes and I have talked long about Pedro Miguel's words as we have reviewed the history, our notes, and the letter of Marcos over and over again. And we have been moved to envision the struggle of Moctezuma as he wrestled to comprehend the coming of the bearded, white-faced ones under their spread wings, remembering the terrible prophecies of Nezahualpilli, which were soon to be fulfilled.

Under Moctezuma's predecessors, the Aztecs had engaged in an orgy of blood to hold together the myths of their sovereignty. Their practices had gone far beyond anything required by religious belief and had become, even to pre-Christian sensibilities, an inhumane and disproportionate mechanism for preserving the pyramid of power. Rebellions of subject tribes had broken out, and there were already signs that the empire was ready to crumble. Moctezuma was a sensitive man of thoughtfulness and imagination. Besides his oft-stated belief that Cortés was indeed Quetzalcóatl's descendant, come to reclaim his lands, there also might have been in his mind the thought of historic retribution for how the Aztecs had misappropriated their inheritance.

Though the Spanish would have come again and again, Moctezuma could have snuffed out that first expedition by Cortés, but myth and perhaps historical conscience stayed his hand. Likewise, the modern regime could have erased the Zapatistas from the headlines in the first few days of their ascendancy, but they chose to send emissaries and talk—just as did Moctezuma. Like Cortés, Marcos has brilliantly manipulated Mexican myth and history to make himself untouchable long enough that he has become the embodiment of a feared destiny to a Mexico that has to know it has squandered its revolutionary inheritance. And how perfectly unsettling that when the Zedillo government decided to strip away his mask in an attempt to expose this figure who spoke on behalf of the dark-faced indigenous, his face turned out to be white. Perhaps in the hearts of Mexicans lies a dream—a nightmare, a hope, a terror—that Quetzalcóatl has come again.

I have returned since the end of our working journeys—to Mexico City, to San Miguel de Allende, to Zihuatanejo, to Playa del Carmen and the Mayan ruins. I make long-distance telephone calls to my former wife who is today my friend, as she always was, and travel Mexico now as a father with his daughters and as a lover with the woman from Minnesota. I stop by a train station once in a while and watch the stoic campesinos wait so patiently for the train that always arrives so late. Whatever the impenetrable barriers to a foreigner's vision, I have learned to witness the things that are not changed by all of this historical challenge to the nation's soul: the fecundity of the land, the cacophony of market days where even under hard economic circumstances warm hands exchange real goods and produce in the open air, the release and the unbridled humanity of the festivals, the music and its transmutation of loss into an intensity of feeling, the earnest desire of every Mexican to make human contact even from behind a mask, the public conversation where even if everyone told the truth there would be kaleidoscopic variations on the nature of reality, and the renaissance of spirit that visiting this land provokes in the hearts of visitors like me from a world where humanity is too easily chartered and packaged into forms that can be marketed for profit.

The standoff between the past, the present, and the future continues, but the soul of this nation is true. It does not know what it wants to become in a changing world, but with instinct keen as the blade of an obsidian knife, it moves its own way and knows what it is not. This is not Nebraska. Its pathway is and ought to be inscrutable to us alien *norteamericanos.* The Spanish poet Antonio Machado, was speaking of the individual when he wrote, "Walker, there is no road. You make the road by walking it." He could have been speaking just as well for Mexico as a nation.

BIBLIOGRAPHY

Azuela, Mariano. *The Underdogs.* Translated by E. Munguia Jr. New York: Signet Classic, 1962.

Brandenburg, Frank. *The Making of Modern Mexico.* Englewood Cliffs: Prentice Hall, 1964.

Brenner, Anita. *Idols behind Altars: The Story of the Mexican Spirit.* Boston: Beacon Press, 1970.

Conrad, Jim, *Mexico: A Hiker's Guide to Natural History,* Seattle, Mountaineers, 1995.

Coy, Harold. *The Mexicans.* Boston: Little, Brown, 1970.

Creelman, James. *Díaz, Master of Mexico.* New York: Appleton, 1976.

Davies, Nigel. *The Ancient Kingdoms of Mexico.* London: Allen Lane, 1982.

De Fuentes, Patricia, ed. *The Conquistadores: First Person Accounts of the Conquest of Mexico.* New York: Orion, 1963.

del Castillo, Bernal Díaz, *The True History of the Conquest of Mexico.* New York: Grove Press, 1927.

Fuentes, Carlos. *The Buried Mirror.* New York: Farrar, Straus and Giroux, 1992.

Hellman, Judith Adler. *Mexico in Crisis.* New York: Holmes and Meyer, 1983.

Johnson, William Weber. *Heroic Mexico.* New York: Harcourt, Brace, Jovanovich, 1968.

Jones, Oakah L. Jr. *Santa Anna.* New York: Twayne, 1968.

Kandell, Jonathan. *La Capital.* New York: Henry Holt, 1988.

Marks, Richard Lee. *Cortés,* New York: Alfred A. Knopf, 1993.

Meyer, Michael C., and William L. Sherman. *The Course of Mexican History.* New York: Oxford University Press, 1979.

Paz, Octavio. *The Labyrinth of Solitude.* Translated by L. Kemp. New York: Grove Press, 1961.

————. *The Other Mexico: Critique of the Pyramid.* Translated by L. Kemp. New York: Grove Press, 1972.

Reed, John. *Insurgent Mexico.* New York: Simon and Schuster, 1969.

Reed, Nelson. *The Caste War of Yucatán.* Stanford: Stanford University Press, 1964.

Riding, Alan. *Distant Neighbors: A Portrait of the Mexicans.* New York: Alfred A. Knopf, 1985.

Ruiz, Ramón Eduardo. *Triumphs and Tragedy.* New York: W. W. Norton, 1992.

————. *The Great Rebellion: Mexico, 1905–1924.* New York: W. W. Norton, 1980.

Townshend, Richard. *The Aztecs.* London: Thames and Hudson, 1992.

Vaillant, George C. *Aztecs of Mexico.* Garden City: Doubleday, 1953.

INDEX

361

Index

Quetzalcóatl, 14, 16–17, 28, 41–42, 57, 246, 276, 356
  as opposed to human sacrifice, 26, 48

racism:
  American stereotypes of Mexicans, 2, 19, 300–301
  as cause of Chiapas rebellion, 333
  of *gachupines,* 78
  toward Guatemalans, 314, 315–316
  see also criollos; Indians; mestizos
railroads:
  foreign investment in, 135, 177–178
  land crisis exacerbated by building of, 178
  Mexican history and, 2–3, 177–179
  new centers of power and, 179
  revolution and, 177–178, 179
  see also trains, Mexican; *individual trains*
Ramírez, José, 100–102
Red Battalions, 214
Reforma, La:
  exploitation of *ejidos* in, 165
  as inspiration for Constitutional Congress of 1917, 214–215
  secularization of Mexico in, 164–165
Regio (café), 81
Regiomontano (train), 29–32, 90
Regional Confederation of Mexican Labor, 223
religion:
  of Aztecs, 23–24
  Catholic, *see* Catholics, Catholicism
repartimiento system, as wage peonage, 77
requerimiento, 40
revolution of Ayulta, 164
Reyes, Bernardo, 192
Riding, Alan, 1–2
Rincón Maya, 198
Rincón, Robelledo, 305, 313, 322, 334
Río Balsas canyon, 292
Río Bravo (Rio Grande), 125, 316
Río Chinipas Bridge, 139
Río Grande de Santiago Valley, 110
Río Nueces, 125
Río Septentrión Canyon, 139

Río Urique, 152
Rivera, Diego, 223
Robles, Rosa María, 20–21
Rogelio (philosopher of Patzcuaro), 271–272
Romancing the Stone (film), 44
Romano, Roberto, 259–260
Roosevelt, Franklin D., 249
rulers of Mexico, pre-Hispanic, 12–17
rurales, 167, 175, 191

Sahagún, Father, 79
Saint Patrick's Battalion, 126, 339–340
Salinas de Gortari, Carlos, 29, 31, 53, 102, 146, 325, 342
  economic policies of, 186–188
  rancor between Zedillo and, 353
Salinas de Gortari family, assassination of Colosio and, 329, 351
Saltillo, 29–30, 126
Salto de Aqua, 265
Salvatierra, Juan María de, 138
San Agustín, on Day of the Dead, 216–220, 227–228
  traditional performance in, 219–220
San Antonio, 116
San Cristóbal de las Casas, 102, 306
San Diego, Calif., 111
San José Mogote, 229–231
  archaeological site at, 230–231
San Juan de Ulúa, 40–41, 43
  fortress on, 44–46
San Juan Tuxco, 298
San Luis Potosí, 97, 211
San Miguel, 97, 159, 188, 269, 356
San Pedro, 95
Santa Anna, Antonio López de, 112
  exiles of, 117, 164
  Mexican War and, 126
  as president of Mexico, 114–115, 117, 126, 127
  Texan Army's confrontation of, 116
Santa Cruz, 297
Santa Fe, 108
Santa Fe Railroad, 138
Scott, Winfield, 126
Sea of Mexico, 9–10
Segura Dorante, Sostenes, 187–189